# PHYSICAL CONTROL OF THE MIND

## *Toward a Psychocivilized Society*

JOSÉ M. R. DELGADO, M.D.

HARPER COLOPHON BOOKS

Harper & Row, Publishers

New York, Evanston, San Francisco, London

This Colophon paperback edition reprints Volume XLI of the WORLD PERSPECTIVES series, which is planned and edited by RUTH NANDA ANSHEN. Dr. Anshen's Epilogue to this reprint appears on page 281.

First HARPER COLOPHON edition published 1971.

STANDARD BOOK NUMBER: 06-090208-6

# Contents

## PART III   EXPERIMENTAL CONTROL OF BRAIN FUNCTIONS IN BEHAVING SUBJECTS

# PART IV   EVALUATION OF ELECTRICAL CONTROL OF THE BRAIN

# PART V   TOWARD A PSYCHOCIVILIZED SOCIETY

# Acknowledgments

Since the beginning of my studies at the Madrid School of Medicine, I have been inspired by the memory of the Spanish histologist Santiago Ramon y Cajal and by his conception of the central nervous system, his penetrating advice about how to conduct scientific research, and his philosophical ideas about life and death. Sixty-five years ago, Cajal said that knowledge of the physicochemical basis of memory, feelings, and reason would make man the true master of creation, that his most transcendental accomplishment would be the conquering of his own brain.

My personal background is the usual rather specialized one of a biologist, but I have been compelled to venture beyond the limits of my science by the need to evaluate the experimental reality of motor behavior and mental phenomena directed by electrical and chemical stimulation of functioning brains. I have also felt the anxiety of our age, which requires a better understanding of the cosmological situation of man in order to give a rational and emotional purpose to human life; and I have been concerned by the urgent need to resolve archaic human antagonisms and to find a new conviviality based on biological reality rather than on wishful thinking. As T. M. Hesburg, president of Notre Dame University, has said, "Scientists cannot be neutral." We must understand the social responsibility attached to our research and the moral impact it has on the world of men, including ourselves. At least there is novelty in looking at behavioral manifestations not from outside the organism but from inside the spiking neurons where information is interpreted and responses are organized.

This book was begun during a sabbatical leave of absence from Yale University under a Guggenheim Fellowship. Part of its content was presented at the New York Academy of Sciences in December 1968 as Salmon Lectures. Dr. Paul Weiss' Rockefeller University evaluation of the preliminary manuscript was very helpful. Economic support for my research has been provided by grants from Foundations' Fund for Research in Psychiatry, United States Public Health Service, Office of Naval Research, United States Air Force 6571st Aeromedical Research Laboratory, NeuroResearch Foundation, and Spanish Council for Scientific Education. The experimental material originating in my laboratory has been the work of a group of investigators from different countries to whom I express my warm appreciation. Their names are mentioned in our published work. Our most recent collaborators included Dr. Lembit Allikmets (Estonia, USSR), Dr. Humberto Bracchitta (Chile), Dr. Ronald Bradley (United Kingdom), Dr. Francis DeFeudis (USA), Dr. Taiji Hanai (Japan), Dr. Victor Johnson (United Kingdom), Dr. Diego Mir (Spain), Dr. Rodney Plotnik (USA), Dr. Maria Luisa Rivera (Spain), Dr. Chico Vas (India) and Dr. Jan Wallace (USA).

Ideas and reciprocal influences exchanged with my brothers, Rafael and Alberto, through the years have been important to the structuring of my own mind; the many enjoyable hours of discussion with my wife, Caroline, who has been a close, sensitive, and intelligent collaborator, have been decisive in the creation of this book.

The Salmon Lectures of the New York Academy of Medicine were established in 1931 as a memorial to Thomas William Salmon, M.D., and for the advancement of the objectives to which his professional career had been wholly devoted.

Dr. Salmon died in 1927, at the age of fifty-one, after a career of extraordinary service in psychiatric practice and education, and in the development of a world-wide movement for the better treatment and prevention of mental disorders, and for the promotion of mental health.

This volume in *World Perspectives* had its original source in the invitation extended to me in 1963 by Dr. Ruth Nanda Anshen to write a volume for *World Perspectives* Series which she plans and edits. The Salmon Lectures I gave in 1968 were based on the text of a part of this volume.

José M. R. Delgado, M.D.

# PART I

# MENTAL EVOLUTION

# 1

# Natural Fate Versus Human Control: The Process of Ecological Liberation and Domination

Manifestations of life depend on a continuous interplay of natural forces. Worms and elephants, mosquitoes and eagles, plankton and whales display a variety of activities on the land, in the air, and in the sea with a purpose—or lack of it—which escapes human understanding, obeying sets of laws which antedate the appearance of human intelligence.

In the animal kingdom, existence of the genetic code represents a biological determination of anatomical and functional characteristics in the newborn. The growth and development of organisms after birth proceed according to a natural fate imposed by the correlations between individual structure and environmental circumstances. The fact that about 300 million years ago all the world's creatures lived in the sea did not depend on their own volition but on biological evolution and ecological factors. The appearance of dinosaurs 180 million years ago in the Triassic period, their supremacy on earth, and their peak in power 30 million years later were determined not by the will of these animals, which had disproportionately small brains and were probably rather stupid, but by a propitious warm and sticky climate which provided a soft slosh of water everywhere and land covered with a tangle of greenery, juicy palms, and huge fernlike trees extending almost to the North Pole.

The catastrophic end of the age of gigantic reptiles was simply the result of their inability to adapt themselves to a change in weather and lack of food. At the beginning of the Cenozoic era 70 million years ago, the air was drier and cooler than before. High plains emerged from shallow seas and ponds, and hardwood forests towered in place of ferns and palms. This changing ecology was unsuitable for dinosaurs and because they lacked the intelligence to understand their situation, to improve their food supply, or to modify their diet, natural fate forced these giants into extinction, and in their place small, warm-blooded, furry mammals slowly grew in size and number.

The appearance of man approximately one million years ago meant only the flourishing of one more kind of animal which shared with the others most biological laws and a complete dependence on natural forces. Men, like elephants and frogs, possessed lungs, bones, and brains; pumping of blood by the heart and other physiological phenomena were—and still are—very similar in all mammals, and proceeded according to pre-established mechanisms beyond awareness or voluntary control. Personal destiny was determined by a series of biological and environmental circumstances which could not be foreseen, understood, or modified. Natural fate meant that man, along with all animals, suffered the inclemencies of the weather, being decimated by cold temperatures, starvation, and all kinds of parasites and illnesses. He did not know how to make a fire or a wheel, and he was not yet able to influence the functions of his own body or to modify his environment.

A decisive step in the evolution of man and in the establishment of his superiority over other living creatures was his gradual achievement of *ecological liberation*. Why should man accept unnecessary hardships? Why should he be wet because the rain was falling, or cold because the sun was hidden, or be killed because predators were hungry? Why should he not cover his body with the soft skins of animals, construct tools and shelter, collect food and water? Slowly the first sparks of intelligence began to challenge natural fate. Herds of cattle were a more reliable source of food than hunting in the forest. Some fields were stripped of the vegetation which was growing according to capricious ecological destiny, and were placed under cultivation by man.

Attention was gradually directed toward the human body, and skills were learned for the treatment of injuries. Broken limbs no longer meant permanent disfunction but could be repaired by transitory application of branches tied with vegetable fibers. Personal experience was not lost, but could be transmitted from generation to generation; the accumulating culture preserved through a gradually elaborated spoken and written language represented a continuous advance of civilization. Men learned to work together, to exchange skills and knowledge, and to join their efforts to improve their circumstances. Curiosity grew continuously, and endless questions were formulated about the observed reality. Ecological liberation could progress not by hiding inside caves but by facing danger, and man challenged the immense power of natural forces, using a lever to lift weights heavier than muscular power could manage, tricking the wind to push sailing ships through the ocean, and taming the rivers to turn the grinding stones of the mills. Thus began the process of *man's ecological domination*, the victory of human intelligence over the fate of a mindless nature —a victory without precedent in the history of other animal species. Biological adaptation enabled man to survive under extreme climatic conditions including arctic areas, dry deserts, high altitudes, and hot tropics, but it was the intellectual and material development of civilization that really brought about the present degree of ecological liberation and domination. The winning of a considerable degree of independence from natural elements permitted human beings to direct their intelligence and energy toward endeavors more interesting than mere survival. The signs of man's power slowly extended throughout the world, transforming the earth's surface with cultivated fields, with cities, and with roads; joining oceans; tunneling through mountains; harnessing atomic power; and reaching for the stars. In spite of the problems associated with the development of civilization, the fact is that today the charting of our lives depends more on intelligent decisions than on ecological circumstances. The surrounding medium of modern societies is not nature, as in the past, but buildings, machines, and culture, which are man-made products. Modern medicine has created a healthier environment by reducing infant mortality, diminishing the number and gravity of illnesses, and considerably increasing the span of life. According to the biological law of only a few centuries ago, pestilence desolated mankind from time to time, insects spread infections, more than half of the newborn died before the age of three, old age began at thirty or forty, and only a minority survived to the age of fifty. Scientific knowledge has modified our own biology, providing better diet, hygienic practices, and pharmacological and surgical treatment.

Viewing evolution in terms of the opposition of human intelligence to natural fate has a dramatic appeal which emphasizes the relative importance of each factor in the determination of events. In reality, however, we should accept the fact that the existence of man, together with all of his attributes and creations, including his own ecological liberation and domination, is actually and inescapably the result of natural fate. Man did not invent man. No conscious efforts were ever made to design— or modify—the anatomical structure of his brain. Because the development of wings was a result of biological evolution, we cannot claim that birds have liberated themselves from the pull of gravity by flying in the air in defiance of natural laws. The fact that birds fly means that they have achieved one step of ecological liberation, escape from gravity by using the lifting support of the wind. Birds can live and play in the air above all other earthbound creatures. Their wings were a gracious gift of evolution which did not require knowledge of physics, mathematical calculations, or even the desire to own wings. Nature seems to be highly imaginative but excessively slow; many millions of years passed from the beginning of life on earth to the appearance of flying animals. The period from the emergence of the human mind to the invention of the airplane was much shorter. The tremendous acceleration in accomplishments was determined by the development of the unique powers of imagination and reason; and it may be expected that human inventions will have an increasing role in the control of activities on earth. Birds fly, and man thinks. Liberation from and domination of many natural elements have changed ecology, and are also influencing the needs, purpose, and general organization of human life, especially in the following aspects.

## Freedom of Choice

In contrast with the limitations felt by our ancestors and by members of still primitive societies, we enjoy nearly endless possibilities to pursue interests and activities of our own choice. Modern life is not bound by the physical restrictions of geography; our voices can be transmitted with the speed of light to anyone around the world; on television we can see events in any country as they actually occur; and we can travel to distant lands at supersonic speeds. We are not limited in food intake by our hunting skills. Instead, we may have available a variety of supermarkets which display the culinary products of many countries. In the acquisition of knowledge we are no longer limited to verbal contact, but have access to many centers of learning equipped with increasingly effective teaching aids, where the different aspects of man's recorded history are collected and preserved. We can select from a wide variety of entertainment, careers, ideas, and religions. Even parenthood can be planned, and the birth of children controlled, by the use of medical knowledge and contraceptive devices.

Today our activities are less determined by adaptation to nature than by the ingenuity and foresight of the human mind which recently has added another dimension to its spectrum of choices—the possibility of investigating its own physical and chemical substratum. Limitation and regimentation of our activities are imposed mainly by education, legislation, social pressure, and finances—which are creations of civilization—rather than by environmental determination, as was formerly the case. Civilized man has surrounded himself with a multitude of instruments which magnify his senses, skills, strengths, and the speed with which he can travel, without realizing, perhaps, that in his drive to be free from natural elements, he was creating a new kind of servitude dominated by levers, engines, currency, and computers. The concerns of earlier times for crops and predators were supplanted by economic worries, industrial problems, and the threat of atomic overkill. Despite the tremendous increase in possible courses of action, the freedom an individual enjoys is becoming more tied to mechanization which is replacing the natural environment as a determinant of behavior. Liberation from ecology is paralleled by a mechanized dependence which absorbs considerable manpower for the invention, construction, and maintenance of machines. The possibility of independent behavior is certainly contingent on the availability of different paths of conduct. But the element most essential to its achievement is awareness of the many factors influencing our actions in order to assure us that our responses will not be automatic, but deliberate and personal. As René Dubos has said, "The need to choose is perhaps the most constant aspect of conscious human life; it constitutes both its greatest asset and its heaviest burden" (69).*

### Awareness

The qualities which most distinctly separate man from other animals are the awareness of his own existence and the capacity to resist and even change what appears to be his natural fate. The degree of individual awareness differs according to per-

---

* Numbers in parentheses refer to sources listed in the Bibliography at the back of this book.

sonal circumstances. Consciousness is a rather expensive luxury in terms of time and effort, and we use it sparingly while performing many daily tasks based on complex series of automatic responses. Walking, for example, requires a tedious process of motor learning in early life, but once the necessary cerebral formulas for controlling movements have been established, we pay no attention to the onset, strength, speed, timing, and sequences of muscular performance; we simply stand up and walk while our minds are occupied with other thoughts. All these processes are automatic and, to a considerable extent, are characteristic of each individual. We can, however, refocus our attention on any motor aspect of walking and re-educate and modify the motor formulas to improve the elegance and gracefulness of movement, or to mimick the gait of sailors, tramps, or cowboys, as actors do.

Stopping at a red light does not require a decision because we are highly trained and conditioned to perform this action. If we pause to analyze our behavior, we may be aware of the motor activity involved in stepping on the brakes and of the reasons that we are stopping and obeying the traffic rules which only then may be questioned or even ignored. Choice is not involved in automatic responses, but if we appraise the reasons and circumstances surrounding our actions, new avenues of response are created. This applies to emotional reactions and social behavior as well as to motor activity.

Awareness is increased by knowledge of the mechanisms of the considered phenomenon. For instance, an expert is likely to notice any peculiar car engine noises, perceiving auditory signals which may not be detected by untrained drivers. Knowledge of the structure and mechanisms of the motor improves the probability of foreseeing and preventing possible breakdowns and also of correcting malfunctioning parts.

To a considerable degree, our behavior is composed of automatic responses to sensory inputs, but if we knew the genetic determinants, cultural elements, and intracerebral mechanisms involved in various kinds of behavioral performance, we could come closer to understanding the motivations underlying our actions. If we were cognizant of the factors influencing our behavior, we could accept or reject many of them and minimize their effects upon us. The result would be a decrease in automatism and an increase in the deliberate quality of our responses to the environment. Awareness introduces greater individual responsibility in behavioral activities.

## Responsibility

Primitive man did not have the choice of going to the movies, reading a book, or watching television. He was fully occupied searching for food and fighting for survival. Today's many behavioral alternatives require that we make a conscious effort to understand and evaluate the different possibilities, perhaps to modify or repress emotional reactions to them, and finally, to select a course of action. In many cases, these processes are performed at the subconscious level, and responses flow effortlessly; at other times we are aware of an impending act and its possible alternatives, and arriving at a decision may be difficult and tiring. The conscious selection of one path among many places greater responsibility on the individual because his activities are not determined by automatic mechanisms or external factors beyond his control. Intelligent judgment is based on an individual's personal qualities and especially on his ability to evaluate possible solutions. Individual choice entails assuming accountability for the direction of personal destiny, and the greater one's awareness and freedom, the greater the responsibility. In a small social group such as a tribe, the consequences of the leader's choice are rather limited, while in highly organized contemporary societies, the decisions of governmental elites will affect large numbers of people. The political actions of these powerful officials concerning foreign aid, cultural exchange, and peace and war will affect life in most parts of the world. We should remember that decision-making always involves the activity of intracerebral mechanisms which, as yet, are little known.

## Accumulation of Power

Industrial and technological developments have created unparalleled resources with immense constructive and destructive potentials. Already we have conquered the natural obstacles of rivers, seas, and mountains, and they are no longer insurmountable barriers to the activities of man. At the same time, we have accumulated megatons of atomic energy capable of obliterating all forms of life in the world.

Instruments have been invented to increase a millionfold the perceptivity of our senses, the power of our muscles, and our ability to process information. In addition to increasing our material power, we have greatly improved our capacity to organize and use available resources. Plans for the development of cities, industries, research, education, and the economy in general are carefully formulated by experts, and these plans are essential for the organization and evolution of our society. These developments again introduce the question of responsibility in the choice of objectives to be reached. Because of the magnitude of our material and intellectual powers, the directive resolutions made by elite groups may be decisive for the development of scientific and economic fields of endeavor, for the evolution of civilization in general, and for the very existence of man.

Major nations are constantly faced with the choice of how to use power, and conscious efforts are made to reach intelligent decisions which are expressed as national goals such as overcoming poverty, landing a man on the moon, or meeting timetables for industrial, agricultural, and scientific development. Because our resources are not unlimited, a major effort in one field, such as armaments or outer space exploration, restricts the development of other less-favored areas. The application of human energy to the control of natural forces is continually increasing, and perhaps it is time to ask if the present orientation of our civilization is desirable and sound, or whether we should re-examine the universal goals of mankind and pay more attention to the primary objective, which should not be the development of machines, but of man himself.

# 2

# The Imbalance Between
# Material and Mental Evolution

Originally, philosophy and science were unified in purpose, which was, in the words of Plato, "the vision of truth." They were also unified in their methodological exploration of reality, which consisted of observation and rational interpretation of what was observed. This happy marriage persisted for many centuries until ideological and technological revolutions introduced new methodologies and the need for greater specialization. Unable to resolve the developing differences in outlook and method, philosophy and science separated from one another, tearing apart what had been their common subject of inquiry. Philosophers and theologians carried with them the mind and soul; scientists kept matter and the body, and psychologists as newcomers lived for some time a schizokinetic existence between spirit and substance, without enough scientific recognition or philosophical support.

Mathematics, physics, and chemistry became increasingly important fields of study, and the application of experimental methods to biology was so fruitful that the interest of scholars was diverted from philosophy to science. Why should time be spent in semantic fencing and speculations when important questions could be asked directly of living organisms, rocks, and celestial bodies? Telescopes and microscopes explored opposite aspects of the natural world, and organic compounds were synthesized. The exploding sciences engaged most of the available intellectual and economic resources, directing them toward industry, biology, electronics, atomic energy, outer space exploration, and similar fields of endeavor. In contrast, only a minor effort was devoted to inquiry into the nature of mental faculties. This unbalanced situation was determined in part by methodological reasons. The mind was considered a metaphysical entity beyond experimental reach, and in spite of the obvious importance of understanding the psychological essence of man, it appeared more practical to invent combustion engines or to investigate the structure of cells than to speculate about emotions and thoughts. While it is true that the disciplines of psychology and psychiatry have greatly expanded in our century, a survey of the literature shows that a decade or two ago the brain was still treated as a "black box" which could be reached only through the senses. Psychological investigations analyzed correlations between sensory inputs and behavioral outputs but could not explore the intermediary processes which were hidden in the unknowns of brain physiology. Some authors doubted that the study of neurons could throw any light on understanding properties of the mind. Surprisingly enough, most investigators of the brain also contributed to this unbalanced situation because they studied heavily anesthetized subjects, and dealing with sleepy neurons, they failed to take into account the mental complexity of the waking brain.

The contrast between the fast pace of technological evolution and our limited advances in the understanding and control of human behavior is creating a growing danger. We are facing a situation in which vast amounts of accumulated destructive power are at the disposal of brains which have not yet learned to be wise enough to solve economic conflicts and ideological antagonisms intelligently. The "balance of terror" existing in the present world reflects the discrepancy between the awesome technology and the underdeveloped wisdom of man.

We may recall that many millenniums ago, during the Jurassic period, the gigantic brontosauri, weighing thirty tons and extending over seventy feet in length, reached their peak of power. With their long necks and tails they probably moved gracefully in the water, but on land they were clumsy and consumed large amounts of energy just in moving their weight around. Judged by fossil bones discovered in Colorado and Wyoming, their brute force was overwhelming, but this extraordinary physical power was directed by tiny brains weighing less than 0.5 kilograms. The organization of incoming signals and outgoing messages to keep these huge frames in working order must have occupied most of their brains, leaving little opportunity for more intelligent and adaptive behavior. The brontosauri became extinct because of their extremely limited mental powers; faced with an increasingly unfavorable climate and diminishing food supply, these animals were incapable of adaptation and could not survive in the changing environment.

The fate of these giants may have symbolic value for twentieth century civilization, which is also attempting to direct tremendous potential with disproportionately small brains. While our mental faculties are incomparably superior to those of the early land animals, we still lack adequate self-knowledge and control, and natural history teaches that when underdeveloped brains are in charge of great power, the result is extinction. Methods for the re-education and control of social antagonisms and undesirable emotional manifestations in man are urgently needed. While these processes are obviously related to environmental circumstances, they also depend on the activity of intracerebral mechanisms, which should be better known. When primitive man faced natural catastrophes like floods or pestilence, he was helpless and reacted with resignation, despair, or an appeal to supernatural powers. In contrast, modern man, being more perceptive, may decide to study his circumstances and apply his power and intelligence to the immediate problem; by constructing dikes or vaccinating the population, he may prevent or modify the forces of natural causality. It is reasonable to assume that just as more knowledge of natural mechanisms allows us to use and control natural forces, a clearer understanding of the central nervous system should enable us to educate and direct mental activity more intelligently. In a recent symposium concerning the "Education of Biologists for the Modern World," the distinguished investigator Beach (11) lucidly expressed the thoughts of many scientists by saying: ". . . man's greatest problem today is not to understand and exploit his physical environment, but to understand and govern his conduct. . . . If he is to survive he must proceed to explore himself and to control his own activities. . . . Science can and must provide the understanding necessary for prediction. . . . If science provides knowledge society will display wisdom."

# 3

# Mental Liberation and Domination

In the near future we can expect a rapid expansion in applications of atomic power, programed education, and production of machinery, along with higher standards of living and lengthening of human life. Even with this optimistic outlook, we may wonder where progress and technology are leading us.

The United States enjoys an economic level, educational system, and a technological development far superior to those of countries like Spain, Poland, or India, yet it is questionable whether its citizens experience greater happiness, family love, closer friendships, and less fear, anxiety, and psychological pressure than the people in less advanced countries. Neither East nor West has succeeded in resolving human conflicts, and the latest technology is being used to kill thousands of people around the world. If modern civilization with its many comforts does not provide greater individual and social happiness than less advanced societies do, the value of this type of civilization may well be challenged.

We should realize that in spite of our progress in other areas, psychic life and emotional reactions are little known. The solutions to present social conflicts proposed by sociologists, religious organizations, experimental institutes, and the United Nations have had only limited success. This is partly because the usual frames of reference for these solutions have been politics, economics, history, metaphysics, sociology, and psychology, while the basic cerebral mechanisms related to man's ideas, emotions, aggressions, desires, and pleasures have been ignored.

Individual reactions are determined by environmental factors acting through sensory inputs upon neurophysiological processes and are manifested through appropriate motor outputs as behavior. All of these intervening elements must be taken into consideration to understand the responses of individuals. To examine the problem only from outside of the organism, as is usually done, is as insufficient as if we were to ignore the environment and try to explain behavior solely in terms of neuronal activity.

At present, not only is there far greater emphasis on material environment than on the understanding of the mind, but what is even more dangerous, this lack of balance is self-perpetuating through education, economic incentives, and general orientation of civilized life (69). "The danger that the entire culture may become technological is obvious" (15), and the divorce of mind from life which is taking place catastrophically everywhere in the modern world (10) has evoked strong intellectual reactions and is one of the central themes of existential philosophy. Present civilization is geared to produce more and better machines and to increase physical power rather than to facilitate individual happiness. Most of our time is spent in performing technical skills, being transported by motorized vehicles, being entertained electronically, and in other occupations which reflect our increasingly mechanized environment.

The purpose of education is to further man's knowledge of himself and his surroundings through instruction in the arts and sciences. During the last few decades, technical fields of study have multiplied rapidly, overshadowing the humanities which until this century formed the basis of education. Although such information is increasingly available, scant effort is devoted specifically to providing an adequate foundation for self-knowledge or for the intelligent construction of individual personality. A curriculum may teach a student something about evolution and general physiology and may introduce him to various aspects of his cultural inheritance, but it usually explains very little about the most important organ, the brain, which alone is responsible for man's emergence as a unique anthropoid and on which every person must rely for immediate survival and future development. Study in the realms of philosophy and introspection is generally considered a nonessential diversion not directly related to the preparation of future members of the industrial society, and the inference that "man can succeed better in this world if he doesn't invest much time learning about his relation to it" further promotes the divergence between the technical world and the world of ideas. This pedagogic deficiency was understandable in the past, when psychophysiological knowledge was limited, but today science is providing the means to coordinate the diverse fields of philosophy and biology to form a new basis of inquiry into the nature of man. This is no longer a purely speculative endeavor but an exploration in a new direction already blazed with scientific landmarks. When present knowledge about the physical substratum of the human mind is disseminated in centers of learning, man will be better equipped to utilize his mental powers and to relate effectively to his environment, and the needed balance in orientation may be achieved.

This is our alternative: to accept, enjoy, and promote the increasing material progress without investing much hope or effort in an attempt to understand our power center, the brain, or to modify the present direction of civilization by shifting part of our available intellectual and economic resources toward an investigation of the mechanisms of mental activity. This redirection of goals could produce an evolution of the mental quest similar in significance to the processes of ecological liberation and domination which have already occurred.

The thesis of this book is that we now possess the necessary technology for the experimental investigation of mental activities, and that we have reached a critical turning point in the evolution of man at which the mind can be used to influence its own structure, functions, and purpose, thereby ensuring both the preservation and advance of civilization. The following pages contain a discussion of what the mind is, the technical problems involved in its possible control by physical means, and the outlook for development of a future psychocivilized society.

# PART II

# THE BRAIN AND MIND
# AS FUNCTIONAL ENTITIES

# 4

# What Is the Mind?

Throughout the centuries, the most powerful intellects have attempted to comprehend the mysteries of their own functioning. Long ago Socrates, leading his disciples through the colonnades of Athens, propounded eternal questions which have been repeated throughout history in endless variety: What is life? What is soul? What is mind? The essence of man evolves from the existence of mental functions which permit him to think and remember, to love and hate, to believe in myths and in science, to create and destroy civilizations. It is remarkable that after hundreds of years of philosophical inquiry, and despite the impressive intellectual advances of our present era, the concept of the mind remains elusive, controversial, and impossible to confine within linguistic limits. It is also surprising that in spite of the importance of the mind for individual survival and for the preservation of civilization, our generation is mainly interested in atoms, cells, and stars, and directs so little effort toward the exploration of the inner space of the psyche.

Before entering into a discussion of mental activities, it is important to clarify the meaning of certain words. Investigators often choose to avoid a definition of terms, utilizing operational descriptions instead. This procedure may be reasonable in some experimental work, but at other times it is inadequate because a particular function—for example, emotion—may be explored by different methods which lead to a diversity of operational definitions of the same term. The same holds true for metaphysical concepts, and the scientist cannot completely ignore them.

In spite of the difficulty involved, it is convenient to distinguish among the brain, mind, psyche, spirit, and soul, if only to avoid ambiguities. Unless each term is defined, the reader's conception may differ from the writer's. Classifications and definitions are only human agreements which try to capture the essence of a person, place, or event by describing several of its elements. They are like sketches, which may omit or distort details. Naturally, if there is no agreement on the subject under discussion, the meaning of related words and sketches will be useless. Definitions should be considered as working tools to guide us on confusing ideological battlefields. For example, the conventional distinction between static and dynamic processes used in this book may be understood as an artifact reflecting both our mental inability to capture the continuous flow of multiple events and our need to concentrate our attention on a selected moment. This procedure should not introduce excessive intellectual distortion provided we realize its existence and limitations. Theories, experimental tools, and descriptive language are all very different, depending on whether we are dealing with chemistry, action potentials, social relations, or ghosts. When the entity under consideration is very complex, as the mind is, it is necessary to employ different methods to analyze the various properties, and it may be difficult to integrate results obtained in a variety of ways which reveal diverse aspects of truth.

Few definitions are satisfactory; the multiplicity and variety of those describing the mind are evidence of the complexity of this subject as well as the lack of agreement among acknowledged experts. Dictionaries list words as they are popularly conceived, but current usage sometimes lacks scientific accuracy. Specialists employ terminology which often has a doctrinal bias. Conservative authors agree that the mind is indefinable at present and offer "raw material," "essays," "views," and "thoughts" leading toward a possible definition. This confusion has a venerable history. The concept of mind in the Western world was introduced into philosophy by Anaxagoras in the fifth century B.C. He called it *nous,* a substance which was infinite, self-ruled, mixed with nothing, forming part of all living things, being the source of motion, and having similar properties in animals and humans. The *nous* was considered an impersonal intellect regulating the movements of the cosmos. Aristotle and Plato noted that Anaxagoras himself found little use for this concept which was later elaborated by other philosophers. In *De anima,* Aristotle considered the mind different from and superior to the soul, saying, "We have no evidence as yet about the mind or the power to think; it seems to be a widely different kind of soul, differentiating what is eternal from what is perishable; it alone is capable of existence in isolation from all other psychical powers." Aristotle proposed that the fetus was endowed first with a vegetative soul which was exchanged later for a sensitive soul and finally replaced before birth, by God's donation, by a rational soul, which implied to Aristotle that he must once have possessed the other elemental functions, namely, the sensitive and the vegetative, which were both shared by animals.

Aristotelian thought has permeated most Occidental philosophical systems until modern times, and the classification of man's functions as vegetative, sensitive, and rational is still useful. In present popular usage, soul and mind are not clearly differentiated and some people, more or less consciously, still feel that the soul, and perhaps the mind, may enter or leave the body as independent entities.

Several attempts to define the mind follow:

1. ". . . an organized group of events in neural tissue occurring immediately in response to antecedent intrapsychic or extrapsychic events which it perceives, classifies, transforms, and coordinates prior to initiating action whose consequences are foreseeable to the extent of available information. The aspect of a biological organism that is not organic in nature . . . (in man it is experienced as emotions, imagination, or will)" (283).

2. The mind has been identified with "the faculty of memory," "thought," "purpose or intention," "the seat of consciousness, thoughts, volitions and feelings," "desire or wish," "the incorporeal subject of the psychical faculties," "the soul as distinct from the will and emotions" (169).

3. "The organized totality of psychical structures and processes, conscious, unconscious, and endopsychic" (67).

4. "The sum total of those activities of an organism, by means of which it responds as an integrated, dynamic system to external forces (usually) in some relation to its own past and future. The organized totality of conscious experience" (235).

5. ". . . restricted to 'conscious mind' in all its general operation field of perceiving, feeling, thinking, remembering, and willing. As such, mental phenomena are facts of experience . . ." (71).

6. "A highly developed neurological apparatus with which an animal interprets his inner and outer environmental stimuli. Attaining consciousness, mind initiates and carries through action or the delayed type of action called thought" (181).

7. "The group of events connected with the given event by memory-chains, backwards and forwards." "A mind and a piece of matter are, each of them, a group of events." "Some events may be neither mental nor material, and other events may be both" (193).

8. "Mind is thus synonymous with consciousness." "Consciousness can thus be defined as an orderly manifold of sensations and percepts. In an abbreviated enumeration, we may distinguish optic, tactile (in the wider sense), acoustic, olfactory, and gustatory percepts. In addition there are internal memory images, abstractions and thoughts, emotions and vague feelings" (134).

Despite variations in wording and in meaning, most concepts of the mind share several qualities which may be summarized and interpreted as follows:

1. The definitions express what the mind *does*, but not what it *is*, or when or how it is formed.

2. Mental functions are described as active processes, not as passive objects.

3. The principal functions of the mind are *interpretation, storage, and retrieval of both inner and outer stimuli* through processes of thinking, remembering, feeling, willing, and other phenomena which are not well identified.

In order to be more precise in our consideration of these phenomena, we may ask (1) if there is any mental function unrelated to inner or outer stimuli, (2) if there is any way the mind can manifest itself other than in behavior, and (3) if the mind could exist without a functioning brain. If these three questions have negative answers, then we may conclude that the mind is necessarily linked to stimuli, to behavior, and to the brain. In my opinion, *without stimuli (or without the brain), the mind cannot exist; without behavior, the mind cannot be recognized.* Because of its essential dependence on sensory inputs, both at birth and throughout adult life, the mind may be defined as the *intracerebral elaboration of extracerebral information.* The problem is then focused on the origins, reception, dynamics, storage, retrieval, and consequences of this information. The basis of the mind is cultural, not individual.

The term "psyche" constitutes the etymological root for the disciplines of psychology, psychiatry, and psychosomatic medicine. The words "mind" and "psyche" are usually considered interchangeable, and will be used here as such. But before we proceed with an analysis of the concept of the mind or psyche, we should clarify the metaphysical meanings that are often ascribed to these terms.

## Mind and Soul

The personal beliefs of scientists concerning the ultimate destiny of man are not usually related to their investigations. The study of carbohydrate metabolism, microwaves, or celestial bodies may not influence personal conceptions of immortality, free will, or God. Scientists are generally reluctant to combine experimental work with philosophy and usually reject consideration of possible theological implications of their studies even more vigorously. The domains of philosophy and science were clearly delimited by Bertrand Russell (192) who wrote: "Philosophy, as I shall understand the word, is something intermediate between theology and science. Like theology, it consists of speculations on matters as to which definite knowledge has, so far, been unascertainable; but like science, it appeals to human reason rather than to authority, whether that of tradition or that of revelation. All definite knowledge belongs to science; all *dogma* as to what surpasses definite knowledge, belongs to theology."

The possibility of a relationship between man and supernatural life is traditionally implied in the ordinary use of the words "soul," "anima," and "spirit." The Oxford Dictionary defines "soul" as "the principle of life; the principle of thought; the seat of emotions, feelings and sentiments"; and "the spiritual part of man considered in its moral aspect in relation to God" (169).

The first three descriptions, especially the third, could easily be attributed to the mind—which shows how confusing terminology is. In my opinion, it is preferable to consider the mind as a functional entity devoid of metaphysical or religious implications *per se* and related only to the existence of a brain and to the reception of sensory inputs. The words "soul" or "anima" will be used when reference is made to man's relationship with supernatural forces, life after death, or the existence of God.

The term "spirit" is sometimes equated with "soul," and it is disconcerting to realize that it is commonly applied to a wide range of disparate objects from an alcoholic beverage to a disembodied soul, as well as including the third person of the Christian Trinity. Another complication is that "Holy Ghost" is *Saint Spirit* in French and *Espiritu Santo* in Spanish, rendering the words "ghost" and "spirit" synonymous. Because the meanings of "spirit" are so varied, it seems wiser to use this term infrequently.

The soul is a metaphysical concept; it is incorporeal, immortal, and has possibilities for salvation or damnation. Acceptance or rejection of the existence of the soul depends on religious conviction, on faith, and on theological considerations which cannot be proved or disproved by present experimental methods. Science has conquered the mind as a subject of experimental investigation, but the soul remains outside the realm of scientific inquiry. The scientist may regard the soul as a myth created by psychological needs; he may consider the soul as a religious interpretation of the mind, carrying responsibility for a future life; or he may accept its existence as a religious truth. In any case, the soul exists in the human mind as a concept which should not be ignored. While the intellectual polemic over its existence and the definition of its qualities and manifestations belong to theologians and philosophers, the emotional and rational elements leading to acceptance or rejection of the concept of the soul are manifestations of the mind. As such they are dependent on cerebral physiology and thus become part of the scientist's domain subject to experimental research. Here we find a good example of philosophical and religious questions which may face neurophysiologists in the future.

Thoughts and beliefs are necessarily dependent on neurophysiological activity of the brain. We cannot believe in eternal life or in any of the religious concepts if we do not have a functioning brain, if all cerebral excitability has been blocked by anesthesia, or if the thinking process has been inhibited by electrical stimulation of the septal area of the brain. Under these conditions, beliefs and desires disappear, but this fact cannot be interpreted operationally by saying that religious faith is a function of the septum or of any other part of the brain. A natural question would be whether or not the soul could be modified by experimentation, because thoughts, remorse, responsibility, vices, and virtues are revealed precisely through behavior, and behavior is determined by cerebral activity. Perhaps it is too soon to pursue these questions, but it is necessary for scientists to clarify the terms in which such problems are stated. Theologians, also, certainly need to redefine what they have settled upon as the characteristics or manifestations of the soul because, for example, the properties of the anima as stated by Catholic doctrine, namely memory, understanding, and will, are now known to be activities subject to experimental investigation and related to the chemistry of ribonucleic acids, electrical activity of the hippocampus, and anatomical integrity of the frontal lobes.

The dilemma of the soul is this: If we accept mental activities as manifestations of the soul, then the modifications of these functions by physical means, such as electrical stimulation of the brain, would signify the manipulation of the soul by electricity —which is illogical because the soul is incorporeal by definition. If, on the other hand, we deprive the soul of all mental functions which can be demonstrated to be dependent on brain physiology, then the soul is reduced to an abstraction, not only incorporeal, but also with a minor symbolic relation to reality.

The alternative would be to consider the mind and the soul as different aspects of the same reality, in much the same way as corpuscular and undulatory theories of light are complementary interpretations of reality with relatively independent sets of properties. This is a solution based neither on logic nor on experimental theory; it is a speculation which may serve as a working hypothesis to be proved or disproved.

In this book the soul, or anima, will be considered a theological concept beyond the limits of our discussions, while the mind will be understood as an entity, devoid of theological implications, which can be investigated experimentally regardless of positive or negative religious bias.

### The Brain Defined

In contrast with the difficulties and controversial issues encountered in the attempt to characterize soul and mind, definition of the brain is relatively easy. The brain, or cerebrum, is a material entity located inside the skull which may be inspected, touched, weighed, and measured. It is composed of chemicals, enzymes, and humors which may be analyzed. Its structure is characterized by neurons, pathways, and synapses which may be examined directly when they are properly magnified.

To function, the brain must be alive, meaning that the neurons are consuming oxygen, exchanging chemicals through their limiting surfaces, and maintaining states of electrical polarization interrupted by brief periods of depolarization; but even when it is dead—meaning that chemical and electrical phenomena are absent—the brain can still be recognized, preserved in formaline, and dissected for examination of its anatomical structures. The brain is essentially a chemical and physical entity with many complex functions related to genetic and environmental influences. It functions as a part of the body, but it can survive independently for a limited period when appropriate circulation is provided.

Some of the brain's functions are recognized as mental activities, but other of its chemical, thermal, and electrical phenomena subserve physiological needs unrelated to the mind. One quality of the brain is that it may be considered in *static and material* terms, at least with respect to morphological, cytological, and chemical characteristics which are self-contained. In contrast, the mind is a *functional* entity which cannot be preserved in formaline or analyzed under the microscope. It is not autonomous but depends on the cerebral reception of a temporal sequence of phenomena and a continuous exchange of information with the environment in order to function properly, as will be discussed later. The term "mind" is an abbreviation for the ill-defined group of mental activities. The existence of mind depends on the existence of a functioning brain, and without brain there is no mind. The contrary, however, is not true, and in the absence of mental manifestations, for example during deep anesthesia, several brain functions, such as maintainance of respiration, may still continue at physiological levels. The common usage of the terms "brain" and "mind" as equivalent may be acceptable provided we are aware of the points of contact and divergence of their respective meanings.

## The Mind as a Functional Entity

The dynamic concept of the mind as a group of functions rather than as an object introduces a linguistic and grammatical dilemma which has been recognized by several authors (195). In languages with European roots, nouns are generally used to designate things which have a passive character (book, chair, table). Actions, movements, and dynamic processes are usually expressed by verbs (reading, running, eating). The fact that mind is considered as a noun and that its functions are expressed by verbs (thinking, willing, feeling), indicates a conceptual dichotomy which distorts general understanding. The mind should not be identified with other nouns like brain or heart: functions depend on, but should not be classified as, organs.

The mind or psyche, however, has been regarded as an organ comparable to other organs or systems such as the liver or kidney. A psychiatric dictionary (110) states that "there is the organ called the psyche, which, like other organs, possesses its own form and function, its embryology, growth, and microscopic anatomy, physiology, and pathology. . . . The mind, like all other organs of the body, has its own local functions, and also those functions that are intimately associated with adjacent and distant organs. It is like the cardiovascular system in that it reaches all parts of the body." While most laymen as well as psychologists and philosophers would reject the concept that the mind is an organ, it is convenient to analyze the controversy briefly in order to clarify the ideas involved.

Organs such as the heart, the stomach, or the brain are tangible objects with a shape, structure, and chemical composition which can be identified even after the death of the host organism, when all normal functions have ceased. Mental functions do not form part of brain anatomy; they are related to cerebral physiology. The mind cannot be inspected visually; only its dynamic expression as behavioral performance is observable.

The functions of organs such as the heart are genetically

determined. They are ready to start at the moment of birth, do not depend on environmental stimuli, and do not require learning. Mental activities have exactly contrary characteristics, and the development of their functional substratum within the brain depends essentially on extragenetic factors. This will be discussed later.

In biology, the physiology of structures cannot be completely ascertained from examination of the anatomy. For example, the circulation of the blood should be differentiated from the supporting organs such as the heart, arteries, and other parts of the cardiovascular system because blood pressure, flow, and circulation are dynamic concepts related to spatial and temporal changes in the blood as it moves through the vessels. The blood itself can be analyzed in order to discover its chemical and morphological properties, and this information will facilitate the understanding of its possible functions. It will not, however, explain the dynamics of circulation, which depends on the summation of systolic volume, heart rate, arterial elasticity, vasomotility, blood volume, blood viscosity, and many other factors, none of which are synonymous with circulation. In like manner, the mind should not be considered identical with its supporting organ, the brain. Information about the anatomy, physiology, and biochemistry of neurons will facilitate the understanding of mental manifestations because these activities depend upon cerebral functions. This information, however, will not fully explain mental dynamics because the mind is related not only to the structure of neurons but also to their spatial-temporal relations and to important extracerebral factors.

## Heterogeneous Qualities of the Mind

On previous pages, the mind has been referred to as a single entity, and it is very common in layman's language as well as in philosophical and scientific discussions to find that the mind is considered as a unit. In reality, however, mental activities such as talking, understanding, or problem solving not only have different sensory inputs and behavioral manifestations but depend on different cerebral structures and mechanisms. Even within a particular mental function there may be considerable anatomical and physiological specificity, as demonstrated by disturbances in speech recognition which may affect the written or the spoken word exclusively.

One of the main difficulties in attempts to define the mind is that we try to supply a common denominator for all mental manifestations, insisting upon similarities among entities which are basically unlike. Cats, monkeys, and men are homogeneous as mammals but heterogeneous as species, and many of the morphological and functional characteristics present in one group cannot be attributed to the others. Man, for example, does not enjoy catching and eating mice, nor are monkeys able to play chess. Unfortunately, some discussions about the mind concern elements as dissimilar as cats, monkeys, and men. It is only natural that agreement will be difficult if authors think that they are referring to the same subject—the mind—when one is considering free will, another consciousness, and still another creative writing. When consulting the literature we should not assume that different phenomena are equivalent merely because authors use the same words to identify them. We should remember that mental functions include a variety of heterogeneous phenomena.

One additional problem involves the dynamic quality of the mind. The heart can be taken out of an organism and stopped in order to study its valves, the thickness of its walls, or the shape of its cells, but we cannot remove the brain to study the mind because it vanishes; we cannot preserve intelligence in formalin. The dynamic and temporal elements of mental activity are crucial and reflect the elusive and everchanging qualities of the phenomenon.

The mind is so complex and heterogeneous that it is difficult to answer the classical questions, "What is the mind?" and "Where is the mind?" In my opinion, these questions are incorrectly stated. Present knowledge requires us to approach the problems in a new way and to rephrase them if we wish to progress in understanding. We should seek neither general nor total answers, but information about specific problems or fractions of problems. Today we are in an intellectual and technical position to ask, for example, which parts of the brain do—or do not—play a role in memory, problem solving, or visual recognition. Experiments may be designed and performed to investigate these subjects.

In my discussion of the physical exploration of the mind, I propose to examine the problem not in general, but in some detail, asking questions and presenting experimental data about modifications of pleasure, sensations, behavioral responses, and other manifestations of mental activities obtained by direct manipulation of the brain.

# 5

# Extracerebral Elements of the Mind: When and How the Mind Is Formed

In Plato's works, Socrates is presented as a kind of intellectual midwife who extracted knowledge already existent in the person he questioned. According to the doctrine of recollection, learning is only the remembering of knowledge possessed in a former life. In *Phaedo,* the second argument for the survival of the soul is that knowledge is recollection, and therefore the soul must have existed before birth.

Aristotle rejected the theory of inborn ideas and proposed the metaphorical *tabula rasa,* which was subsequently accepted in the seventeenth and eighteenth centuries by empirical physiologists, including Locke and Helvétius. The newborn mind was considered a blank tablet on which experience would write messages, and the dissmilarities between individuals were attributed solely to differences in education.

The Aristotelian principle, "Nihil est in intellectu quod no prius suent in sensu" (St. Thomas, *De Veritatis,* II, 3), repeated among others by Leonardo da Vinci ("Ogni nostra cognizioni principia dai sentimenti"), expressed the idea still prevalent in present times that "nothing is in the intellect which was not first in the senses." Some authors, including Epicurus and the sensualists, stressed the importance of sensory inputs to its limit, proposing that the intellect is only *what* is in our senses.

Between the extremes of considering the mind either sophisticated or naive at birth, contemporary opinion holds that both genetic and experiential components are essential, although their functions and relative importance remain controversial. According to several child psychiatrists, heredity and experience are equipotent (156, 225). Piaget (178) has emphasized that while the human brain is an almost entirely hereditary regulatory organ, it has practically "no hereditary programming of these regulations, quite unlike the case of so many instincts in birds or fishes. . . ." Intelligence combines two cognitive systems: experience and endogenous regulations. The last system is a source of intellectual operations; by prolonging the feedbacks and correcting the mistakes, it transforms them into instruments of precognition.

The genetic determination of mental functions has been supported by Rainer (181), who believes that the fertilized ovum contains "the primordia of what we later call mind," and that "the newborn infant is already as much of an individual 'mentally' as he is physiognomically." According to the evolutionary theories of William James (119), "the new forms of being that make their appearance are really nothing more than results of the redistribution of the original and unchanging materials . . . the evolution of the brains, if understood, would be simply the account of how the atoms came to be so caught and jammed. In this story no new *natures* [James's emphasis], no factors not present at the beginning are introduced at any later stage."

In agreement with these ideas, Sherrington (206) writes: "Mind as attaching to any unicellular life would seem to me unrecognizable to observation; but I would not feel that permits me to affirm it is not there. Indeed, I would think that since mind appears in the developing soma, that amounts to showing that it is potential in the ovum (and sperm) from which the soma sprang. The appearance of recognizable mind in the soma would then be not a creation *de novo* but a development of mind from unrecognizable into recognizable."

The importance of the prenatal period as a determinant of future behavior crystallized in the concept of "ontogenetic zero"

(88) has been accepted by most child psychologists (30). At the moment of fertilization, the life of a unique individual is initiated (at birth, a child is already nine months old); and some experts have suggested that its beginning should be traced back through evolution of the parental reproductive cells or even through previous generations.

These theories have the merit of stressing the role of genetics in the formation of the mind, but they give the false impression that genetic factors alone are able to create a mind, or that in some mysterious way, a minute, undeveloped mind already exists in the cells. At the core of this discussion is the meaning of "potentiality," which is a convenient concept provided that we understand its limitations. If we say "a block of marble is potentially a piece of sculpture," we mean that marble is an element which can be shaped into a symbolic pattern by using chisels and hammers with appropriate skills. We may say that all shapes and artistic creations potentially exist in the marble, but the reality is that in the absence of a sculptor, the piece of stone lacks, per se, the essential elements to become a work of art. It would be incorrect to think that tools or skills are hidden within the block of marble, or that if we waited long enough, a statue would emerge spontaneously from the block. This type of incorrect reasoning has been called the "error of potentiality" (137). It has infiltrated the field of embryology and has influenced analyses of the origin and evolution of mental functions by assuming, at a certain stage of development, the existence of properties which are present only at a later stage and which depend on a series of essential conditions neither present in nor determined by the stage under consideration.

If we say that the mind is in the sperm, we can also say that each man has one million children, that a newborn baby will be the inventor of spaceships, or that a worm may evolve into a monkey. These statements may be potentially valid, but their fulfillment is contingent upon a constellation of factors which are not present in the original material. In spite of his genes and his potentials, a man cannot create a single child without the collaboration of a woman; and a baby will not invent rockets unless he is exposed to a highly sophisticated level of physics. We believe that worms have evolved into more complex forms of life, and that potentially they may produce dinosaurs, supermen, or inhabitants of the moon, but before we allow our imagination to wander among the limitless possibilities of nature, it is preferable to identify the factors responsible for the observed reality among an infinite number of theoretical potentials.

According to early theories of preformism, the germinal cell—the ovum—held a miniature organism with microscopic eyes, arms, legs, and other parts of the body which eventually would grow. The ovaries of Eve had potentially the bodies—and minds—of all mankind. As soon as scientific embryology began, it was evident that the germinal cell did not contain a compressed homunculus, but only a plan which required the interaction of other elements in order to develop into a human being.

A relatively small group of organization centers (the genes), with the collaboration of molecules supplied from the outside (the mother), produce another series of organizers (enzymes, hormones, and other active substances) which will arrange patterns of molecules for the construction of cells, tissues, and organs and will also produce a new series of organizers to direct the interaction of these new elements. The organizers are not completely stereotyped in performance but are influenced by their medium. A particular gene may have different phenotypic effects in different environments, and "genes control the 'reaction norm' of the organism to environmental conditions" (31). Blood vessels, muscles, and the various organs are differentiated; neurons appear, their interconnections are established, and the brain evolves. Chromosomes have neither heart nor brain—only a set of architectonic plans which under suitable conditions will evolve into a complete organism. These plans are unfulfilled for millions of sexual cells and for countless embryos that are casualties in spontaneous abortions. The possibilities of evolution are far from accomplished realities.

If we accept these ideas, we may also state that the fecundated germinal cell does not talk, understand, or think, and that the resulting embryo has no mental functions before the medullary plate rolls up to form the neural tube. When can we detect the first signs of a functioning mind? How are they correlated with the anatomical development of the central nervous system? The study of these questions may be simplified if we first examine the initial signs of a functioning brain as revealed by behavioral expression in lower animals. Before the development of muscles, motor neurons are already growing out to establish neural contacts with them. The order of growth is a "progressive individualism within a totally integrated matrix, and not a progressive integration of primarily individuated units" (34). Motions, therefore, are basically a part of a total pattern, and their relative individualization is only a secondary acquisition. Some efferent motor pathways appear before any afferent fiber enters the cerebrum. Initially, the cerebral association system develops toward the motor system and the peripheral sensory fibers grow toward the receptor field. Significant conclusions from these facts are that "the individual acts on its environment before it reacts to its environment" (35), that efferent nerves must be stimulated by products of the organism's metabolism, and that "behavior in response to such stimulation is spontaneous in the sense that it is the expression of the intrinsic dynamics of the organism as a whole" (37). Total behavior is not made up of reflexes; rather, "the mechanism of the total pattern is an essential component of the performance of the part, i.e., the reflex," and behavior therefore "cannot be fully expressed in terms of S-R (Stimulus-Response)" (37). It is significant that in man vestibular connections develop before vestibular sense organs, because this reveals that "the cerebral growth determines the attitude of the individual to its environment before that individual is able to receive any sensory impression of its environment. Hence, the initiative is within the organism" (36).

Some of these findings have been confirmed in the toadfish and the cunner (228). On the first day that the cunner larva swim around freely, they do not respond to external stimuli. Thus under natural conditions, this species moves about without an effective exteroceptive mechanism, evidently propelled by a "mechanism of motility activated from within." The afferent sensory system grows gradually until it finally "captures" the primitive motor system. The conclusion is that behavior has two components: "endogenous activity, the fundamental motility conditioned by the inner physiological adjustments of the organism; and exogenous activity, the oriented activity by which endogenous activity is so modified as to render response to external stimuli possible" (70).

This information emphasizes the importance of genetic determination and indicates that some mechanisms for behavorial performance are organized in the absence of environmental inputs. It is generally accepted that development of the nervous system is basic for the onset and elaboration of mammalian behavior, but it is not clear whether any factor can be singled out as decisive. Without synaptic conduction, impulses obviously cannot be transmitted: thus the functional maturity of synapsis must be essential (104, 144, 205, 241). Objections have been raised about the acceptance of synaptic permeability as the main reason for onset of behavior (140), and other factors may be equally important. Activity of peripheral nerve fibers is considered essential for the differentiation and specificity of behavioral performance (72, 78), and the anatomical development of neurofibrillae may be specifically related to the onset of behavior (136). These and other studies have provided important information, but its interpretation has often been biased by methodological distortions.

It is a common error in behavioral embryology, and in science generally, to try to simplify the observed phenomena and to reduce causality to a single factor, excluding all other variables. This is the *fallacy of the single cause* (121), or failure to understand that a biological phenomena is always the product of a complex situation, not of a single determinant. With this pitfall in mind, we must face the task of identifying the several

elements essential for the development of any given phenomenon, and both conduction and synaptic mechanisms are certainly basic for the onset of behavior.

Myelin is a substance with insulating properties covering the
nerves, and its appearance in neuronal sheaths has often been associated with the onset and differentiation of behavior by neuro-
anatomists. A correlation perhaps exists for some specific
behavior patterns in the cat and the opossum (138, 226), but
most authors today agree that the myelogenetic law cannot be
generalized. In the newborn rat, myelination does not take place
for several days although the fetus starts moving many days
before birth, and some discrete reflexes and inhibitory activity
in higher centers can be observed in a rat fetus nineteen days
after conception (5). Myelination, therefore, cannot be interpreted as necessary for the conduction of impulses or for functional insulation.

Differences in anatomical and behavioral evolution certainly
exist between mammals and lower life forms. In the guinea
pig, for example, limbs are well formed in the embryo before
appearance of the first behavioral response, while in the sala-
mander motor behavior is initiated before morphological
differentiation of the limbs. Evidently embryologic studies of
man cannot be as extensive and as well controlled as those of
amphibia, but valuable information on this subject already
exists (30). Inside the uterus, the human embryo has a comfortable and sheltered life without facing responsibilities or making
choices. Cells multiply automatically and organs take shape
while the growing fetus floats weightless in the silent night of
amniotic fluid. Food and oxygen are provided and wastes are
removed continuously and effortlessly by the maternal placenta.
As the fetus grows, many organs perform something like a dress
rehearsal before their functions are really required. This is
usually referred to as the principle of anticipatory morphological maturation. The heart starts to beat when there is no blood
to pump; the gastrointestinal tract shows peristaltic movements
and begins to secrete juices in the absence of food; the eyelids

open and close in the eternal darkness of the uterus; the arms and legs move, giving the mother the indescribable joy of feeling a new life inside herself; even breathing movements appear several weeks before birth when there is no air to breathe (1).

Some extensive information about human fetal behavior has been obtained by indirect methods in pregnant women, while other findings were obtained directly from fetuses surgically removed for medical reasons (112, 155, 176). The first movement observed in a four-millimeter-long, three-week-old fetus is the heart beat, which has intrinsic determinants because it starts before the organ has received any nervous connections. The neural elements needed for a reflex act can be demonstrated in the spinal cord at the second month of embryonic life, and at that time, cutaneous stimulation may induce motor responses. A fourteen-week fetus shows most of the responses which can be observed in the neonate with the exception of vocalization, the tonic grasping reflex, and respiration. With fetal growth, spontaneous motility increases inside the mother's womb and it is well known that responses from the fetus may be elicited by tapping the mother's abdominal wall.

Sensory perception of the fetus has been investigated in detail by several scientists (27, 30, 240). Cutaneous reception is well developed long before birth, and mechanical or thermal stimulation of the skin elicits appropriate motor activity related to the stimulated area. The existence of pain perception is doubtful. Proprioceptors of the muscles (the spindles) develop at the fourth month of fetal life, and the labyrinth is evident even earlier. Both organs are active during fetal life; they are capable of postural adjustments and may be partially responsible for fetal motility in the uterus.

The possibility of fetal perception of gastrointestinal movements, hunger, thirst, suffocation, and other types of organic experience has been debated, and it is generally accepted that internal stimuli may activate skeletal musculature. Distinction of sweet from other tastes and of unpleasant odors such as asafetida has been demonstrated in premature babies, showing that these receptor mechanisms are already developed. It is doubtful, however, that with the nose and mouth immersed in amniotic fluid, the fetus could have gustatory or olfactory experiences before birth.

The auditory apparatus is well developed at birth, but the general consensus (180) is that the infant is deaf until the liquid of the fetal middle ear is drained through the Eustachian tube by breathing, crying, and perhaps yawning. Loud noises, however, might be perceived, and some cases of presumed fetal hearing have been reported (79).

The optic apparatus is sufficiently developed in the newborn infant to permit perception of light and darkness, but the optic nerve is not yet fully developed, and its evolution continues after birth and is probably influenced by sensory perception (180). It is highly improbable that the fetus has any visual experience during its uterine life.

In summary, it is unlikely that before the moment of birth the baby has had any significant visual, auditory, olfactory, or gustatory experience, and it is probable that it has received only a very limited amount of tactile, organic, and proprioceptive information. The newborn has an elaborated system of reflexes; and coughing, sneezing, sucking, swallowing, grasping, and other actions may be evoked by the appropriate sensory stimulation. In an experimental study of seventeen behavioral responses, their intercorrelations proved to be zero, indicating that "there is no mental integration in the newborn child" (82). This integration usually takes place during the first postnatal month.

Whether or not the fetus was capable of conscious experience was a classical philosophical and psychological problem debated at length with a flourish of words and speculations but with little factual support (39, 86, 135, 147, 175). It is difficult to understand the basis of this controversy since there is no evidence that the fetus has visual, auditory, olfactory, or gustatory stimulation. The possibility of fetal awareness is therefore reduced to a limited input of organic sensations of proprioception and touch in the absence of the main sensory faculties. Whether or not these phenomena can by themselves create consciousness is mainly a question of definition and arbitrary agreement, but it may be stated that they cannot produce manifestations comparable to those of consciousness in children or adults, which are mainly based on visual and auditory perception and experience. The mystery is perhaps insoluable due to the impossibility of establishing verbal communication with the newborn.

Anticipatory morphological maturation is present in various mechanisms which remain quiescent in the fetus, ready to perform with physiological efficiency as soon as they are needed. Their necessary links are established before birth and are triggered by appropriate stimulation. These functions, which include oral suction, respiration, kidney secretion, and gastrointestinal activity, are able to act several weeks before an expected delivery, in case the baby is born prematurely.

No comparable provisions exist for mental functions. The newborn brain is not capable of speech, symbolic understanding, or of directing skillful motility. It has no ideas, words, or concepts, no tools for communication, no significant sensory experience, no culture. The newborn baby never smiles. He is unable to comprehend the loving phrases of his mother or to be aware of the environment. We must conclude that there are no detectable signs of mental activity at birth and *that human beings are born without minds.* This statement may seem startling, but it should not be rejected by saying, "Well, you don't see mental functions during the first few days, but everything is ready for action; wait a few weeks, or perhaps a few months; it is just a slight lack of maturity, but the baby's mind is there." Potentiality should not be confused with reality. A project is not an accomplished fact, especially when essential elements are lacking in the original design. Naturally a baby lacks experience, but by recognizing this fact, we are accepting the essentiality of extracerebral elements which originate in the outside world and are independent of both the organism and its genetic endowment. As Cantril and Livingston (29) have said, organisms are in a constant "transaction," in a "process of becoming," constantly changing into something different from what they were before. Early in life, an infant is attracted to sources of comfort and repelled by sources of distress. These experiences lead to the "intelligent" recognition of objects and persons associated with positive or negative reinforcement, and they will determine selective patterns of behavioral response. "It is at this point, we think, that 'mind' is born" (29).

The concept of the mindless newborn brain is a useful hypothesis because it clarifies our search for the origin of the mind. If this origin depended on genetic endowment, then mental functions should appear in the absence of other external elements (as respiratory functions do). If genetic determination alone is not sufficient, then we must investigate the source and characteristics of the extracerebral elements responsible for the appearance of the mind as the baby matures.

# 6

# The Mindless, Newborn Brain

Psychoanalytical interpretations of fetal life are not in accord with the concept of a mindless, newborn brain which I propose, and some authors (183, 193) present a different viewpoint in approximately the following terms. In the intimate cloister of the mother, a growing being lives a peaceful, sheltered existence. In this uterine paradise, without fears or anxieties, the embryo must have a mother libido, and it experiences pleasure and pain, as demonstrated by impulsive movements and by the sucking responses which are expressions of pleasurable sexual sensations related to mental states of the fetus. Thinking and willing are perhaps present to only a limited extent, but feeling exists in the embryo with hypertrophic sensitivity.

One day, something terrible happens. The carefree, parasitic existence is terminated, and there is a brutal separation of the child from the libido object—the mother—causing a psychic trauma, the primal or original anxiety state. Later on, the child will try to return symbolically to its mother's womb, and subconsciously he may remember forever the states of embryonic life and the anxiety of birth. The child's neurosis is a natural result of his traumatic arrival. He is usually able to overcome it, although occasionally it persists during adult life. Sadger (193) reported that when he could not relate some patients' neuroses to their embryonic periods, he induced them to recall what happened to their original spermatozoa and ova, or even to remember possible parental attitudes which could have produced a trauma in the delicate germinal cells before conception. Sadger maintained that these cells have a psychic life of their own with the capacity to learn and to remember.

It is difficult to accept the introspective statement of a neurotic patient who claims to possess a spermatozoic memory, since experimental studies show that the reactions of newborn babies are so elemental that they can hardly be considered signs of a functioning mind. It is doubtful, if not indeed illogical, to attribute a higher degree of mental activity to a fetus at an even earlier stage of embryonic development.

The possible existence of psychic functions in the newborn has been repeatedly debated. Some authorities accept the presence in the infant of three primary emotions, fear, rage, and love, and believe that all other emotions result from the conditioning of these innate patterns by environmental stimuli (237). The theory of differential emotional patterns in the neonate suffered a serious blow when it was demonstrated that competent observers of infant behavior could not agree on their interpretations of emotional patterns recorded by moving pictures unless they knew the type of stimuli applied (204). The term "emotion" should not be ascribed to infant behavior because it lacks differentiated responses, and the existence of a "mind" in the neonate is really a matter of definition (116, 222).

The mind is characterized by many heterogeneous functions, some of which exist at birth, if only in elemental form. Symbolic processes as determined by correlation procedures (82) do not exist in the neonate, but temporary learning of simple conditioned responses has been demonstrated (213). Four conditions have been proposed as prerequisite to acceptance of the existence of intelligent behavior in any organism: (1) a functional cerebral cortex; (2) functional distance receptors; (3) an upright posture; and (4) the achievement of substitutive or symbolic behavior. According to these criteria, the neonate does not qualify for intelligent behavior, and its activities should not be considered signs of mental life (117).

Careful studies of infants demonstrate that their eyes will

follow small moving spots of light as early as two weeks after birth (32). Auditory sensitivity is controversial, and pitch discrimination and differential responses related to the patterning of sound seem to be absent (219). Auditory conditioning has been unsuccessful until the second month of life (125). The existence of olfactory perception and even gustatory discrimination is rather doubtful, but sour and bitter solutions influence sucking and may evoke facial responses. The newborn baby's ability to orient toward the nipple of the mother's breast is the most important response in his repertoire (172).

Human beings are born with such cerebral immaturity that their very survival depends completely on exterior help, and their behavior is similar to that of a purely spinal being, or at most, of a brain stem or midbrain preparation (44, 45, 139, 173). Most neurologists agree that the neonate is a noncortical being. After birth, there is a transitional period during which the cerebral cortex starts to function, and then its activities progressively increase until a reciprocal functional correlation is established with the rest of the brain.

It had been generally assumed that mammals were born with most of their cerebral neurons present and that further development was limited to some synaptic elaboration of the already existing neuronal network. Recent studies performed with radio tracers have revealed, however, that at least in the hippocampus, olfactory bulb, and cerebellar cortex of mammals, *as many as 80 to 90 per cent of the neurons form only after the animal is born* (3). Experience provided by sensory inputs from the environment influences the number as well as the structual connections of these postnatal cells. Moreover, as Cajal (25) suggested long ago, the microneurons of the cerebellum, which serve as association elements, develop after birth under the influence of the infant's behavioral activities. Therefore it can be said that the environment is absorbed as a structural part of the neurons in the developing brain.

The conclusive proof that performance of neonate behavior does not require a mind—or even a brain—derives from the study of several anencephalic beings in whom reflexes and behavioral manifestations were similar to those of normal babies. Some of these infants, born without cerebrums, lived for only one or two days, but others survived for two or more months and could be studied in great detail. One of the most famous cases was the mesencephalic child which had only midbrain, pons, and cerebellum, lacked pallidum, striatum, and cortex, and had only a few traces of diencephalon (84). This abnormal being had reduced motor performance, but the startle reaction and grasping reflexes were well preserved. He was able to assume a sitting position spontaneously when both lower legs were pressed, and occasionally he yawned and stretched his arms. He had periodic alternating states of quietude and activity resembling sleep and wakefulness. His feeding behavior was nearly normal and he could follow a moving finger with his eyes and head. He cried and was observed to suck his thumb spontaneously. The main difference between anencephalic and normal infants is that in a child lacking cortex and other parts of the brain, responses and activities remain stationary while a normal infant quickly develops new behavior patterns.

Having seen that mental functions in man cannot be demonstrated at birth, we may ask which elements are essential for their appearance and development, and we may wonder why the newborn baby is mindless. Why isn't the mind detectable at birth? Because it is hidden or dormant inside the neurons, or because it doesn't yet exist within the brain? These questions correspond to the following differing hypotheses: (1) Human beings, in comparison with other animals, are less developed at birth, being anatomically and physiologically immature and requiring a postnatal growing period in order to reach their expected potential. In this case, *the essential elements for the appearance of the mind, which are determined genetically, are already present at birth,* and only need time to develop and demonstrate their existence. The mind is there even if it cannot be detected. (2) A different point of view is that *the brain is not sufficient* to produce mental phenomena. The brain is only a reactive organizer of transactions of elements located in the environment and transmitted to the individual by sensory receptors and pathways. According to this hypothesis, the reception of *extracerebral factors*—the experience of living—is essential for the appearance of the mind and is the basic element upon which mental development is conditional. While instinctive behavior may appear even in the absence of experience, mental activity cannot.

Confronting these two theories, we face again the basic questions of the origin of mind and whether mental functions could appear simply by process of anatomical maturation. To find answers, we must be acquainted with some experimental facts. It is known that cerebral maturity in animals is of only relative value for behavioral performance. With merely 20 per cent of their neurons myelinated, 24-day-old white rats are trainable and can learn associations as well as adult rats (236). Early visual experience is important for the normal development of higher animals but is not essential in lower species. Rats raised in darkness since birth have no visual deficits when exposed to light for the first time (101). Birds also manage quite well, although ringdoves which have worn translucent goggles to block visual patterns but not light show a moderate decrease in the speed of learning pattern discrimination when their goggles are removed (207).

Studies of early visual deprivation in higher animals tell a different story. In one investigation, four baby chimpanzees were separated from their mothers shortly after birth and each was kept in a darkened room and given only ninety minutes' daily exposure to a limited, diffuse light (184). Seven months later, testing of the animals showed normal pupillary reactions to light, but lack of eye blink, visual fixation, and pursuit of moving objects. Unlike the control animals, these chimpanzees did not appear upset if they were fed by strangers, nor did they recognize their feeding bottles. In visual discrimination and conditioning tests, the animals reared in darkness required more than twice as many trials as did the control animals and committed over twice as many errors. After living for $3\frac{1}{2}$ months outside the darkened room, only one of the chimpanzees began to converge his eyes on an object brought into contact with his lips. In this animal, discrimination of vertical versus horizontal strips was soon acquired, while recognition of faces took much longer.

Biochemical studies have confirmed the importance of sensory stimulation for normal cerebral development. In animals deprived of sight or hearing, the corresponding neurons of the system do not develop biochemically. Their structure appears normal, but inside they are like "empty bags, impoverished in both RNA and proteins" (115). The importance of adequate sensory stimulation for postnatal neurochemical maturation has also been demonstrated by Brattgärd in his studies of retinal ganglion cells (22). During the early postnatal period, animals receiving normal light stimulation showed 100 per cent increase in cellular mass, as measured by the total amount of organic substance, while animals deprived of light did not show this change. Moderate sensory stimulation of the vestibular system caused by rotation of the body resulted in a 40 per cent increase in the RNA concentration in the vestibular ganglion cells and also an increase in amino acid absorption (91).

During the last fifteen years, researchers at Berkeley (13, 132, 190) have performed chemical-behavioral studies demonstrating that individual experience can lead to measurable alterations of the chemistry and anatomy of the brain. They started with the search for relations between naturally occurring differences in brain chemistry and differences in learning ability and then analyzed the effects of experience on brain chemistry. It was known that enriched early sensory inputs benefit subsequent learning, and the investigations were oriented to find the biochemical link between early environment and later effects. Experimental studies in rats proved that exposing litter mates to either enriched or impoverished environments for eight days produced in the enriched group significant increases in (1) the weight of cerebral cortex, (2) total activity of the enzyme acetylcholine esterase throughout the brain, (3) total activity of cholinesterase in the cortex, (4) thickness and vascularization of the cerebral cortex. Because acetylcholine is a possible transmitter substance, changes in the enzymes which regulate its appearance and breakdown have important functional significance. Increase in the number and connections of neurons should also have obvious consequences. Many years ago, the great Spanish histologist Cajal (25) suggested that cerebral activity could be correlated with the ramifications of cerebral neurons, and he drew attention to the small cells rich in synaptic connections. The total brain mass should be less important than its internal organization and wealth of connections for the exchange of information. Cajal knew that a talented person or even a genius did not necessarily have a large brain. Quality rather than total volume is crucial.

It is generally accepted that the brain of a newborn human baby is incomplete to a remarkable degree (41, 76, 118). In the primary sensory areas and the motor cortex, many characteristics including myelination, cortical width, and the number and size of cells are in an embryonic state. While anatomical maturation must influence brain functions, it is doubtful whether it is the decisive factor in mental activity. The limited role of maturation is illustrated by the behavior of premature babies, born after seven months of intrauterine life. Two months after birth, their reactions are more similar to those of a normal, full-term two-month-old baby than to a newborn. It is also true that although the pyramidal tract does not mature for two years, children are able to coordinate, walk, and perform voluntary movements many months before.

If a human being could grow physically for several years under complete sensory deprivation, it could be ascertained whether the appearance of mental activity is dependent upon extragenetic, extracerebral elements. My prediction is that such a being *would not have mental functions*. His brain would be empty and void of ideas; he would be without memory and incapable of understanding his surroundings. Such a person, although maturing physically, would remain as mentally naive as on the day of his birth. This experiment is, of course, unfeasible. It would be unacceptable ethically, and it is technically impossible because even if sight, sound, taste, and olfaction could be blocked, touch and visceral proprioception extend throughout most of the body and could not be completely suppressed. Although the final proof of this extreme experiment will never be forthcoming, we have partial medical proof of the adverse effects of sensory deprivation on physiological development of children.

It is known that people who have lived for several years without a sensory receptor lack the mental functions related to the receptor that must transduce, bias, and pass on the incoming information. Some babies have been born with congenital cataracts in both eyes but have not suffered atrophy of the optic nerve. They grow up without any visual experience of shapes, objects, or patterns, being able to perceive only diffused light. During childhood, they learn to recognize surroundings by touch and by ear. They can identify a book, glass, or chair, and know people by their footsteps or voices. When some of these blind children were twelve to fourteen years old, their cataracts were removed, and for the first time they could see the physical world. During the first days, this visible world had no significance, and familiar objects such as a walking stick or favorite chair were recognized only when explored manually. A tedious learning process was necessary before these children could learn to evaluate lights and shades and interpret the barrage of optic sensations which were initially so confusing. After a long training period their visual recognition improved considerably, but it remained permanently impaired. For example, the distinction between a square and a hexagon required laborious and often erroneous manual counting of the corners, and a rooster was confused with a horse because both have tails (202). A very intelligent blind boy, whose sight was restored when he was eleven, identified a fish as a camel because he confused its dorsal fin with a camel's hump (239). Although this clinical data is based on a small number of patients some of whom may have had brain lesions as well as cataracts (243), the results indicate that the *ability to perceive patterns does not pre-exist in cerebral organization, but is learned through experience,* and that in man the early postnatal period is of decisive importance in the acquisition of cerebral mechanisms for the perception and symbolization of sensory stimuli.

In agreement with the results of visual deprivation in patients is the very poor performance of native African children in the form board intelligence test (162). The natives were far superior to white men in detecting hunting tracks in the forest but were completely unfamiliar with and unable to discriminate between the geometrical patterns used in the test. These findings illustrate that visual discrimination is one mental activity which must be learned, and that in the human brain, cerebral development and organization are not sufficient for the performance of mental functions. Genetic factors are not enough; experience is essential. "At conception individuals are quite alike in intellectual endowment. . . . It is the life experience and the sociocultural milieu influencing biological and psychological function which . . . makes human beings significantly different from each other" (170).

The decisive role of infantile experiences in the development of individual personality and its disorders was the main theme of Freud's historic investigations (80), which have shaped the thinking of psychologists, psychiatrists, psychoanalysts, and laymen to the present time. The central experience of the period of childhood is the infant relation to his mother, and the events of the first years leave a much greater mark on physiological and behavioral characteristics than those which occur later in life. Piaget also has stressed that the first eighteen months of life are crucial for the establishment of sensory motor intelligence and for the formation of the ego (177).

Perhaps the most dramatic evidence that the capacity to love is not inherited but may appear "at first sight" is the process of imprinting. As Lorenz (149) has shown, the young of some bird species become attached to the first moving object they perceive. Normally this object is their mother, but in his work with ducks, Lorenz presented himself at the moment of hatching as the mother substitute. The little ducklings were imprinted with the image of Dr. Lorenz and followed him obediently with apparent filial affection. The strength of bonds established in the young depend on the qualities of the stimulus (shape, sounds, odors) and on the timing of the reception. In the duck, the most effective imprinting takes place soon after hatching, while beyond a certain age it cannot take place at all.

The studies of the Harlows (92, 94) in rhesus monkeys confirmed the decisive importance of early sensory inputs as determinants of behavior and also the existence of a critical period early after birth for establishment of the capacity for affection. Deprivation incurred by isolating baby monkeys from their mothers or peers irreversibly blighted the animals' capacity for social adjustments. The period between the third and sixth months was found to be most critical for their development. Animals deprived of contact during this phase exhibited aberrant behavior which persisted throughout their adulthood even when they were placed within control groups. The behavioral abnormalities included staring fixedly into space, stereotyped motility, clasping their heads in their hands, rocking for long periods of time, development of compulsive habits, self-aggressive tendencies with self-inflicted body damage, and abnormal sexuality with unsuccessful mating. In monkeys the ability to love is not inherited and if it is not learned during early life, the deprived individual forever loses the capacity to establish bonds of affection and remains socially and sexually aberrant.

In another series of experiments, it was demonstrated that "the ability to solve problems without fumbling is not inborn but is acquired gradually" (93). When monkeys faced a simple discrimination test such as selection of an object according to its color or shape for the reward of raisins or peanuts, learning was initially haphazard. After the animals had learned to solve several similar problems, their behavior changed dramatically and they showed increasing insight until eventually, when faced with a new problem, they could solve it in a single trial. Parallel studies have been performed with children showing that in man, as in monkeys, there is no evidence of any innate endowment that enables them to solve instrumental problems. The conclusions of these findings are that "animals, human and subhuman, must learn to think. Thinking does not develop spontaneously as an expression of innate abilities; it is the end result of a long learning process," and that "the brain is essential to thought, but the untutored brain is not enough, no matter how good a brain it may be" (93).

The classical controversy about the nature-nurture dichotomy has lost its original simplicity. The problem is not to separate innate from learned behavioral patterns, because in most cases there is a reciprocal influence between pre-existing and acquired factors. The problem is to identify the specific roles and mechanisms in the collaborative effort between heredity and environment (102, 227). To be specific, let us consider language as the most outstanding manifestation of human mental qualities. The *potentiality* to talk depends on *genetic factors* which exist in man at the moment of birth, while they are lacking in the rest of the zoological scale, including the big apes. It is known that after the most patient training, some chimpanzees living with human foster parents have been able to pronounce a few simple words such as "papa" and "mama" and "cup," but they have never learned to converse or to say complex phrases. Language potentiality in the human baby signifies the existence of a functioning brain that *can be trained* to store information and also to combine, modify, and use it for performance of the specific function of talking. Potentiality is like a beautiful highway, able to accommodate traffic and facilitate the exchange of visitors among many cities. The highway, however, cannot create cars, trucks, merchandise, businessmen, workers, and all the life which circulates along it. The road makes functions possible, but by itself it is a useless stretch of pavement. The potential of verbal communication is not enough to learn to talk, and it is necessary to be repeatedly exposed to sensory inputs from an environment which includes family and friends. The baby brain does not invent language nor can it choose to learn either English or Chinese: It is entirely dependent on information which must *come from the outside*. The genetic structure of the individual establishes the mechanisms for receiving and handling the inputs, and in the case of language it may also be responsible for the modulation of accessory elements of speech, such as tone and inflexion of voice, and for the facilitation of some tendencies related to learning of words and formation of concepts, but if a baby is not exposed to language, then there are no materials to be received, modulated or facilitated, and his potentialities will remain dormant.

This is true for many other mental functions which will not appear in the absence of appropriate sensory inputs. An important point is that the choice of the necessary information cannot be made by the baby himself because at the beginning he is completely helpless and dependent. The decisive responsibilities of providing information to structure the initial organization of the baby's mind is assumed by those in charge of the infant. As stated by Geertz (85), "there is no such thing as a human nature independent of culture. Men without culture would not be the clever savages of Golding's *Lord of the Flies*. They would not be, . . . as classical anthropological theory would imply, intrinsically talented apes who had somehow failed to find themselves. Instead, they would be monstrosities with few useful instincts, fewer recognizable sentiments, and no intellect."

# 7

# Sensory Dependence of the Adult Mind

Even if reception of sensory information is accepted as totally essential for the onset and development of mental functions, it is more or less explicitly assumed that an adult has a well-established mental capacity which functions with relative independence of the environment. Individuality, initiative, and free will are expressed in the ability to accept or reject ideas and select behavioral responses. A man can isolate himself, meditate, and explore the depths of his own thoughts. To a great extent education, especially in Occidental cultures, is based on the belief that individual personality is a self-contained and relatively independent entity with its own destiny, well differentiated from the surroundings, and able to function by itself even when isolated from earth and traveling in an orbiting capsule.

A more detailed analysis of reality, however, shows that cerebral activity is essentially dependent on sensory inputs from the environment not only at birth but also throughout life. Normal mental functions cannot be preserved in the absence of a stream of information coming from the outside world. The mature brain, with all its wealth of past experience and acquired skills, is not capable of maintaining the thinking process or even normal awareness and reactivity in a vacuum of sensory deprivation: *The individual mind is not self-sufficient.*

Support for this statement derives from neurophysiological and psychological experimentation. In mammals, the central organization of motor activity is localized in special regions of the cerebral cortex where muscles and ideokinetic formulas are represented. The motor pathways descend through the spinal cord and emerge through the ventral roots to form plexus and motor nerves. As should be expected, experimental destruction in animals or pathological damage in man of the ventral roots produces complete motor paralysis because the cerebral impulses cannot reach the muscle target. Considering the input side, we know that all sensory information from the periphery, including proprioceptive impulses from the muscles, is carried by the dorsal roots of the spinal cord. As anticipated, *destruction of all dorsal roots* produces a loss of sensation, but in addition, there is also a *paralysis* of the musculature as pronounced as when the motor roots are interrupted. These experiments show that in the absence of sensory information, motor activity is totally disrupted. The brain and motor pathways are not sufficient in themselves, and for proper motor behavior, sensory inputs are absolutely necessary.

The studies of Sprague et al. (217) in the cat confirmed the importance of incoming information for normal functioning of the brain. These authors destroyed the lateral portion of the upper midbrain, including the main sensory pathways, and they observed that, in addition to the expected marked sensory deficit, the cats exhibited a lack of affect, aggression, and pleasurable responses, and did not solicit petting. The animals remained mute, expressionless, and showed minimal autonomic responses but in spite of this passivity, they showed hyperexploratory activity with incessant stereotyped wandering, sniffing, and searching as if hallucinating. "Without a patterned afferent input to the forebrain via the lemnisci, the remaining portions of the central nervous system . . . seem incapable of elaborating a large part of the animal's repertoire of adaptive behavior" (217).

Psychological data also confirm the essential importance of continuous reception of inputs. Experiments on sensory deprivation in animals and man have shown that maintenance of normal mental activity is difficult or impossible when sensory information is reduced and, moreover, that monotonous sensation is aversive. Animals and humans require novelty and continual and varied stimulation from their surroundings.

Perception of the environment has positive reinforcing properties, and when monkeys were confined in a cage, they would press levers and perform other instrumental responses for the reward of opening a little window and looking at the outside world. Curiosity derives from expectancy of novel sensory stimulation and motivates exploratory behavior in both animals and man, while boredom has negative reinforcing properties and is related to the absence of novel sensory inputs (16, 95). To be entertained means to be provided with new and changing sensations, mainly visual and auditory. Primitive man probably derived pleasure from looking at the changing beauty of nature, which retains its fascination to the present day. Civilization has provided the technical means for a far greater choice of inputs, and a major portion of our time, effort, mental activity, and economic resources are now devoted to entertainment through books, theaters, radio, television, museums, and other cultural media.

Symbolically we may speak about "psychic energy" as the level of intracerebral activity which could perhaps be identified in neurophysiological terms by electrical and chemical processes located at specific neuronal fields. This psychic energy may be considered a main determinant of the quantity of intellectual and behavioral manifestations. While this energy obviously depends on cerebral physiology (and indirectly on the health of the whole body), its actual source is extracerebral because mental activity is not a property of neurons, but is contingent on the received information which activates stored information and past experiences, creating emotions and ideas.

To be alone with our own mind is not enough. Even if all past experiences are included, the exclusion of new perceptions creates serious functional difficulties. This has been shown for instance in the studies of Hebb and his group (18, 103) in which college students were asked to lie comfortably on beds in sound-proof, lighted cubicles, wearing translucent goggles to minimize optic sensation and gloves with cardboard cuffs to limit tactual perception. The purpose of this isolation experiment was not to cut out all sensory stimulation, but only to remove patterns and symbolic information. Most of the subjects expected to spend their idle time alone reviewing their studies, planning term papers, or organizing ideas for lectures. The surprising result—for the investigators as well as for the participants—was that the students "were unable to think clearly about anything for any length of time, and their thought process seemed to be affected in other ways." After several hours of isolation, many of them began to see images, such as "a rock shaded by a tree," "a procession of squirrels," or "prehistoric animals walking about in a jungle." Initially the subjects were surprised and amused but after a while their hallucinations became disturbing and vivid enough to interfere with sleep. The students had little control over these phenomena which, in some cases, included acoustic as well as optic perceptions such as people talking, a music box playing, or a choir singing in full stereophonic sound. Some subjects reported sensations of movement or touch, or feelings of "otherness," or that another body was lying beside them on the bed. Isolation also tended to increase the belief in supernatural phenomena and several of the students reported that for a few days after their isolation experiment, they were afraid that they were going to see ghosts. The conclusion was that "a changing sensory environment seems essential for human beings. Without it, the brain ceases to function in an adequate way and abnormalities of behavior develop" (103).

In patients with long-term hospital confinement in bed or in an iron lung or body cast, psychotic-like symptoms have appeared including anxiety, delusions, and hallucinations which did not respond to standard medical or psychiatric treatment but were easily alleviated by social contact or by sensory stimulation from a radio or television set (141).

In our century the classic punishment of solitary confinement has been combined with sleep deprivation and used in psychological warfare. Exhaustion and decreased sensory inputs are known to cause mental disturbances and reduce defense mechanisms, and they have been effectively manipulated during "brainwashing" or "thought reform" procedures to indoctrinate prisoners (143, 244).

The literature on sensory deprivation is voluminous (197) and shows conclusively that the cerebral cortex requires a stream of stimulation for the preservation of behavioral and mental normality. We should realize, therefore, that our cerebral and mental functions rely on the umbilical cord of sensory inputs and become disrupted if isolated from the environment. This fact has been recognized by philosophers and is reflected in the words of Ortega y Gasset (167) who wrote: "Man has no nature; what he has is a history," and "I am I and my circumstance." The recognition of environmental inputs as a part of personal identity is one of the important contributions of Ortega, and this idea is presented in *Meditations on Quixote* (166), when one of the characters states that "circumstantial reality forms the other half of my person," and "reabsorption of circumstances is the specific destiny of man." A similar thought is expressed in Tennyson's poem "Ulysses" when Ulysses says, "I am a part of all that I have met."

Ortega's position is important to philosophical thinking, but we should probably go further and question the existence of that half of personal identity thought not to originate in the environment. If we could erase all individual history, all circumstances and experiences, would there be anything left of our personality? The brain would remain and neuronal nets would perhaps continue their spiking activity, but devoid of history— of past experiences and knowledge—there could be no mental activity and the mind would, in fact, be an Aristotelian *tabula rasa*. Let us remember with Dobzhansky (64) that "genes determine not 'characters' or 'traits' but reactions or response." The frame of reference and the building blocks of our personality are the materials received from the outside. The role of cerebral mechanisms, which to a great extent are also determined by previous experience, is to receive, bias, combine, and store the received information, but *not to create it*. Originality is the discovery of novel associations between previously received information. We must realize that the anatomical structure of the brain has not evolved perceptibly in the past several millenniums of man's history; what has changed is the amount of information received by the brain and the training to deal with it. The major differences between a cave man and a modern scientist are not genetic but environmental and cultural.

For centuries philosophical tradition has accepted the existence of the "I," "soul," or "ego" as an entity, more or less metaphysical, relatively independent of the environment (and perhaps even of the genes), which is the "essence" that endows individual man with his unique personal identity and characteristics, and may later be threatened or disallowed by the social medium.

The concept of this mythical "I" is so strong that it has permeated the thinking of authors as original and revolutionary as Marcuse. In *One-dimensional Man* (151), he distinguishes between true and false needs, declaring:

False are those which are superimposed upon the individual by particular social interest in his repression. . . . Most of the prevailing needs to relax, to have fun, to behave and consume in accordance with the advertisements, to love and hate what others love and hate, belong to the category of false needs . . . which are determined by external forces over which the individual has no control. . . . The only needs that have an unqualified claim for satisfaction are the vital ones—nourishment, clothing, lodging.

According to Marcuse, inner freedom "designates the private space in which man may become and remain 'himself.' . . . Today the private space has been invaded and whittled down by technological reality."

The basic questions are obviously, Who is this "himself," and what is the origin of its structural elements? Is there any way to provide the experience which will form a baby's mind except by means of the "external powers" of parents, teachers, and culture over which the baby has no control? Are we then going to classify a child's needs as false because they were inculcated? Where is the inner man?

Marcuse's pleas for "intellectual freedom" and his criticism of "material and intellectual needs that perpetuate obsolete forms of the struggle for existence" are certainly valid, but the state of unqualified liberty cannot be supposed to exist for the infant who is totally dependent physically and psychologically on his surroundings. Freedom must be taught and created.

The mutual dependence of the individual and the "psychic environment" or "noosphere" has been elaborated by Teilhard de Chardin (223), who wrote that the Universal and Personal "grow in the same direction and culminate simultaneously in each other, . . ." the "Hyper-Personal" consciousness at the "Omega point." While it is true that each of us personally receives, interprets, and feels the world around us, why should our individual half be opposed to the noospheric half? Teilhard de Chardin, like Ortega y Gasset and most other philosophers, accepts the existence of the quasi-mystical, inviolable self, an entity somehow identified with the individual mind, ego, or personality, which is related to the environment but has a relatively independent existence.

Recent neurophysiological and psychological studies discussed here reveal that this is not the case. The origin of memories, emotional reactivity, motor skills, words, ideas, and behavioral patterns which constitute our personal self can be traced to outside of the individual. Each person is a transitory composite of materials borrowed from the environment, and his mind is the intracerebral elaboration of extracerebral information. The "personal half" is a regrouping of elements of the environment. For the final result, which is manifested as individual reactivity and behavioral responses, the building blocks from culture are more decisive than the individual substratum within which the regrouping is performed.

It is impressive that this is actually the philosophy, as described by Lévi-Strauss (142), of the Bororo Indians, a very primitive tribe living by the Vermelho River in the Amazon jungles of Brazil. For the Bororo, a man is not an individual but a part of a sociological universe. Their villages exist "for all eternity," forming part of the physical universe along with other animate beings, celestial bodies, and meteorological phenomena. Human shape is transitory, midway between that of the fish and the arara. Human life is merely a department of culture. Death is both natural and anticultural, and whenever a native dies, damage is inflicted not only on his relatives but on society as a whole. Nature is blamed and Nature must pay the debt; therefore, a collective hunt is organized to kill some sizable animal, if possible a jaguar, in order to bring home its skin, teeth, and nails which will constitute the dead man's *mori*, his everlasting personal value.

The conclusion that human beings are part of culture does not deny the fact that "individuals" have "individual" reactions and that their brains are unique combinations of elements, but simply points to the source and quality of the factors of personal identity. The cerebral mechanisms which allow us to receive, interpret, feel, and react, as well as the extracerebral sources of stimuli, can and should be investigated experimentally. Then we shall gain a new awareness of the structure of the individual and its relations with the surrounding noosphere.

# 8

# Working Hypothesis for the Experimental Study of the Mind

One of the most important consequences of recent scientific discoveries is the new attitude toward the course of human life. This attitude has modified our traditional acceptance of fatalistic determination by unknown factors related to heredity, body functions, and environment, and has intensified the search for knowledge and technology to direct our lives more intelligently. The genetic code is being unraveled, introducing the possibility that some time in the future, we may be able to influence heredity in order to avoid illnesses like Mongolism or in order to promote transmission of specific anatomical and functional characteristics. Neurophysiological investigation has established correlations between mental phenomena and physicochemical changes in the central nervous system, and specific electrical responses of different areas of the brain can be identified following sensory stimulation of the eye with patterns, shapes, or movements. Advances in other scientific areas have proved that mental functions and human behavior can be modified by surgery (frontal lobotomy), by electronics (brain stimulation), and by chemistry (drug administration), thus placing the mind within experimental reach.

The ability to influence mental activity by direct manipulation of cerebral structures is certainly novel in the history of man, and present objectives are not only to increase our understanding of the neurophysiological basis of mind but also to influence cerebral mechanisms by means of instrumental manipulation.

The working hypotheses may be summarized as follows: (1) There are basic mechanisms in the brain responsible for all mental activities, including perceptions, emotions, abstract thought, social relations, and the most refined artistic creations. (2) These mechanisms may be detected, analyzed, influenced, and sometimes substituted for by means of physical and chemical technology. This approach does not claim that love or thoughts are exclusively neurophysiological phenomena, but accepts the obvious fact that the central nervous system is absolutely necessary for any behavioral manifestation. It plans to study the mechanisms involved. (3) Predictable behavioral and mental responses may be induced by direct manipulation of the brain. (4) We can substitute intelligent and purposeful determination of neuronal functions for blind, automatic responses.

In any evaluation of experimental results, we should remember that there is always a congruence between the methodological approach and findings obtained, in the sense that if we study the brain with an oscilloscope, we can expect information about spike potentials and other electrical data but not about the chemical composition of the neurons. Psychological reactions and behavioral performance often escape neurophysiological methodology, and a coordinated interdisciplinary approach is needed. Music does not exist in a single note but is the product of a spatiotemporal sequence of many sounds. Mental activity does not emanate from the activity of single neurons but from the interaction of many neuronal fields. Rage, for example, is characterized by changes in electrochemical, autonomic, sensory, and motor functions which are overtly expressed in social relations. Some electrical manifestations of rage have been recorded as discharges at the single neuronal level, but the phenomenon involves multilevel responses, and for its proper investigation the whole organism should be observed in a social setting.

The development of new methodology to explore and communicate with the depth of the brain while the experimental subject engages in spontaneous or evoked activities now enables the scientist to analyze and control basic neurological mechanisms of the mind and represents a unique means of understanding the material and functional bases of individual structure. The future should see collaboration between those investigators who formerly studied neuronal physiology while disregarding behavior and other scientists who have been interested in behavior while ignoring the brain.

# 9

# Historical Evolution of Physical Control of the Brain

| EXPERIMENTAL FACTS | IMPLICATIONS |
|---|---|
| Frog muscle contracted when stimuated by electricity. Volta, 1800; Galvani, 1791; DuBois-Reymond, 1848. | "Vital spirits" are not essential for biological activities. Electrical stimuli under man's control can initiate and modify vital processes. |
| Electrical stimulation of the brain in anesthetized dog evoked localized body and limb movements. Fritsch and Hitzig, 1870. | The brain is excitable. Electrical stimulation of the cerebral cortex can produce movements. |
| Stimulation of the diencephalon in unanesthetized cats evoked well-organized motor effects and emotional reactions. Hess, 1932. | Motor and emotional manifestations may be evoked by electrical stimulation of the brain in awake animals. |
| In single animals, learning, conditioning, instrumental responses, pain, and pleasure have been evoked or inhibited by electrical stimulation of the brain in rats, cats, and monkeys. Delgado et al. 1954; Olds | Psychological phenomena may be controlled by electrical stimulation of specific areas of the brain. |

and Milner, 1954; see bibliography in Sheer, 1961.

In colonies of cats and monkeys, aggression, dominance, mounting, and other social interactions have been evoked, modified, or inhibited by radio stimulation of specific cerebral areas. Delgado, 1955, 1964.

Social behavior may be controlled by radio stimulation of specific areas of the brain.

In patients, brain stimulation during surgical interventions or with electrodes implanted for days or months has blocked the thinking process, inhibited speech and movement, or in other cases has evoked pleasure, laughter, friendliness, verbal output, hostility, fear, hallucinations, and memories. Delgado et al. 1952, 1968; Penfield and Jasper, 1954; see bibliography in Ramey and O'Doherty, 1960.

Human mental functions may be influenced by electrical stimulation of specific areas of the brain.

## Summary

Autonomic and somatic functions, individual and social behavior, emotional and mental reactions may be evoked, maintained, modified, or inhibited, both in animals and in man, by electrical stimulation of specific cerebral structures. Physical control of many brain functions is a demonstrated fact, but the possibilities and limits of this control are still little known.

Part III

# EXPERIMENTAL CONTROL OF BRAIN FUNCTIONS IN BEHAVING SUBJECTS

In our present technological environment, we are used to the idea that machines can be controlled from a distance by means of radio signals. The doors of a garage can be opened or closed by pushing a button in our car; the channels and volume of a television set can be adjusted by pressing the corresponding knobs of a small telecommand instrument without moving from a comfortable armchair; and even orbiting capsules can now be directed from tracking stations on earth. These accomplishments should familiarize us with the idea that we may also control the biological functions of living organisms from a distance. Cats, monkeys, or human beings can be induced to flex a limb, to reject food, or to feel emotional excitement under the influence of electrical impulses reaching the depths of their brains through radio waves purposefully sent by an investigator.

This reality has introduced a variety of scientific and philosophical questions, and to understand the significance, potentials, and limitations of brain control, it is convenient to review briefly the basis for normal behavioral activity and the methodology for its possible artificial modification, and then to consider some representative examples of electrical control of behavior in both animals and man.

# 10

# Physicochemical Bases of Behavioral Activity

In the vegetable as well as in the animal kingdom, the dynamics of biological processes are related to ionic movements and electrical changes across the membranes which separate cells from the surrounding medium. For example, during the process of photosynthesis, the leaf of a tree captures energy from the sun and a negative potential is created on its receptive surface. In a similar manner, activation of a squid axon, a frog muscle, or the human brain is accompanied by a negative wave which invades cellular membranes and then disappears. This transmembrane change of potential induces a flow of electrical currents into the cellular cytoplasm and surrounding conducting fluids. Cellular activity may therefore be investigated by recording the electrical potentials appearing across the membranes or by detecting differences in potential which appear in the extracellular fluid, even if the recording electrodes are placed at a considerable distance from the electromotive source. This is the basic principle of recording electrical activity of the heart (electrocardiogram = EKG) through electrodes placed on the extremities, or of studying electrical potentials of the brain (electroencephalogram = EEG) by means of leads attached to the scalp. If electrodes are placed closer to the source of negativity, for example in the depth of the brain, recordings will be more accurate and may reveal the location of generators of electrical activity. Conversely, by using an external potential, an electrical field may be established through the extracellular fluid, and some of this current flows through the cellular membranes, modifying their charge and permeability and producing the self-propagating process called "stimulation."

In order to stimulate, it is necessary to reduce quickly the positive charge which normally exists on the surface of a resting cell until it reaches a critical point of local depolarization. Then the ionic permeability of the membrane is modified, triggering a pre-established sequence of electrical and chemical phenomena. Excitation takes place in the vicinity of the negative electrode (cathode) because the application of negative charges will neutralize the normally existing positivity at the external part of the cellular membrane. When stimulation is over, the positive polarity is re-established on the membrane surface with the aid of energy provided by specific chemical reactions, and the cell is ready for a new stimulation. The relatively simple processes of depolarization and repolarization of cell membranes are the essential elements of neuronal excitation, and they are responsible for the extraordinary complexity of all behavioral performance.

Our knowledge gap between understanding electrical events at the cellular level and deciphering the chain of phenomena taking place during the response of a whole organism is certainly formidable. How can we explain activities such as walking, problem solving, or ideation in terms of polarization and repolarization of membranes? Behavior certainly cannot occur without concomitant spike potentials and ionic exchanges, but the same statement holds true for oxygen and sugar consumption, and we must differentiate the mechanisms supporting basic nonspecific cellular activities, such as metabolic requirements, from the mechanisms more specifically related to behavioral responses. Electrical activity of the neurons seems to have the dual role of indicating nonspecific activity and transmitting coded information. This ability to transmit coded information is the most important and least understood property of the nerve cell, and it represents the functional unit for nervous communication. In architecture, given a number of brick units an infinite number of different houses can be constructed. We need to know both the properties of the individual bricks and the pattern of their organization in order to ascertain the properties and qualities of the final building. The characteristics of behavioral responses are determined by the combination of many depolarization phenomena, organized in space and repeated sequentially in time. Their arrangement is often so complex that it defies experimental analysis, and we must begin by examining very simple phenomena. The squid axon was for years a popular object of investigation in neurophysiology. Great caution should be observed, however, when applying experimental results with that preparation to the understanding of motor responses or mental activity. We should remember that knowledge of the letters of the alphabet will not explain the meaning of a phrase or reveal the beauty of a poem.

In addition to investigating the spontaneous changes in membrane potentials, we can artificially depolarize membranes by electrical stimulation of cerebral neuronal pools in order to investigate their functional organization and behavioral consequences for the whole organism. Both of these experimental approaches should be used simultaneously in order to correlate cellular functions with behavioral results. Our present knowledge of the physicochemical bases of biological activity, which has an extensive bibliography (23, 182, 203), permits statement of the following principles: (1) All behavioral manifestations including their mental aspects require the existence of waves of negativity accompanied by electrical and chemical changes at the cellular level. (2) Membrane depolarization, artificially induced by electrical or chemical means, may be followed by observable behavioral manifestations. (3) While the complexity of these responses is extraordinary and many of their aspects are unknown, explanations of motor behavior and psychic activity do not require "vital spirits" or any other metaphysical principle because they are related to physical and chemical laws which can be investigated experimentally.

The classical experiments of Galvani, showing that the legs of a decapitated frog contract in response to electrical stimulation, are repeated many times every year in high school and college laboratories. These simple experiments demonstrate that a process of life, muscle contraction, can be elicited at the will of the investigator as many times as electricity is applied to the tissue. In the absence of stimulation, the legs do not contract. If the cells of the muscle are dead, excitability and contractability are lost and the preparation does not respond. The contraction of the frog's legs is similar regardless of whether the muscle is stimulated directly through its motor nerve or through the brain, and this muscle action is also comparable to its activation during voluntary movements of the intact frog. The applied electricity does not create the limb movement but acts only as a depolarizing agent, starting a chain of events which depends on the properties of the stimulated organ.

The reliability and apparent simplicity of the muscle contraction may be misleading because in reality the contraction depends on tremendously complex processes which include: depolarization of the resting membrane, changes in its permeability, precipitous exchange of potassium, sodium, and other ions, creation of electrical fields, reorientation of proteic molecules within the muscle fiber with a shortening in the length of its chain, decomposition and synthesis of adenosin triphosphate, exchange of phosphoric acids, degradation of hexosaphosphate into lactic acid, and many other enzymatic and biochemical reactions which follow each other according to a genetically determined plan within the muscle fiber and independent from the agent which initiates them. The *mechanisms for contraction and relaxation of the muscle fiber are pre-established in the biological structure of the cells. Electricity, like the nervous system itself, acts as a trigger for these processes.* This principle is fundamental for an understanding of the electrical control of biological functions. Organisms are composed of a large number of biological sequences, some of them inherited and others learned through experience. When a chain reaction has started, it proceeds according to an intrinsic plan which can be modified by feedback or by the arrival of new stimulations. In some cases the trigger may be nonspecific and, for example, muscular contraction can be initiated by mechanical, thermal, osmotic, chemical, electrical, or neuronal stimulation. In investigations of the brain as well as the muscle, electrical activation is preferable because it is not harmful for the cells and permits repeated studies of the same biological processes. By applying electricity we can activate pre-established functional mechanisms of a structure and discover its possible role in spontaneous behavior. By means of ESB (electrical stimulation of the brain) it is possible to control a variety of functions—a movement, a glandular secretion, or a specific mental manifestation, depending on the chosen target. Necessary methodology and examples of selected results are discussed in the following chapters.

# 11

# Methodology for Direct Communication with the Brain

The depth of the central nervous system can be reached very easily through the natural windows of sensory receptors. Stimuli such as patterns of light travel fast from the eye's retina through optic pathways to the visual cortex located in the occipital lobe. Would it be possible to explore the local activity of cortical neurons during the process of symbolic perception? Could we evoke similar sensations by direct stimulation of specific neurons? Can we reach the mind of an individual without using the normal ports of sensory entry? Can we direct the functions of the brain artificially? These and similar problems have attracted the interest of many investigators, but the brain is well protected by layers of membranes, spinal fluid, bone, and teguments, a formidable shield which for a long time has kept the secrets of mental functions away from scientific curiosity.

## Implantation of Electrodes in Animals

Starting in the last century, many investigators have explored the brain, first in animals and recently in human patients as part of diagnosis and therapy. In these studies it was necessary to open both skin and skull, and because the procedure was painful it was mandatory to use anesthesia. It blocked pain perception, but it also inhibited some of the most important functions of the nervous system. Emotions, consciousness, and free behavior were certainly absent under heavy sedation, and for many years scientists directed their attention to sleeping subjects and overlooked the complexity of awake brains. Textbooks of cerebral physiology were concerned with pathways, connections, reflexes, posture, and movement; mental functions and behavior were considered to belong to a different discipline.

The methodological breakthrough which made it possible to study the brain of behaving animals came in the 1930s when W. R. Hess (106) devised a procedure to implant very fine wires within the brain of anesthetized cats. After the effects of anesthesia had disappeared, the relatively free and normal animal could be electrically stimulated by connecting long leads to the terminals of the implanted electrodes. This procedure was refined in the early 1950s (47, 49) by reducing the size of the electrodes while increasing the number of intracerebral contacts and using aseptic precautions during implantation. Surgical accuracy in reaching chosen cerebral targets was also improved by means of micromanipulators and a precise system of anatomical coordinates which made it possible to reach similar structures in different subjects. Using biologically inert materials such as gold, platinum, or stainless steel wires insulated with teflon allows the electrodes to be left inside of the brain indefinitely. A diagram of the cerebral implantation of one assembly of seven contacts is shown in Figure 1 and the X ray of the head of a monkey after implantation is seen in Figure 2. Through a small opening in the skull, the shaft is introduced down to a predetermined depth and is secured with dental cement at the point where it passes through the skull. Then the upper portion of the shaft is bent over the bone surface and secured again a short distance away, and the terminal socket is exteriorized on the head. Each contact of the socket corresponds to a determined point in the depth of the brain which is accessible merely by plugging in a connector, a procedure as simple as connecting any electrical appliance to a wall outlet. This technique has been used for ESB in thousands of animals in

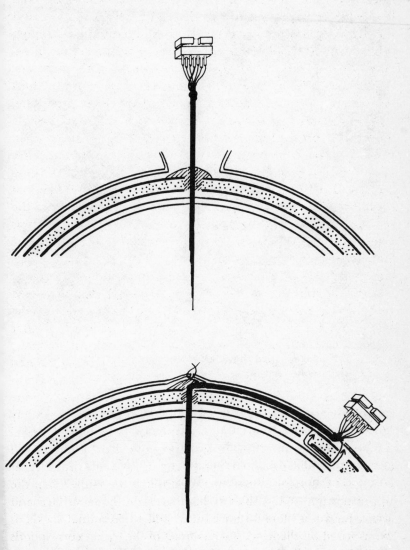

*Figure 1*

Diagramatic representation of an electrode assembly implanted within the brain and anchored to the skull. The depth of the brain is thus accessible simply by plugging in a connector (52).

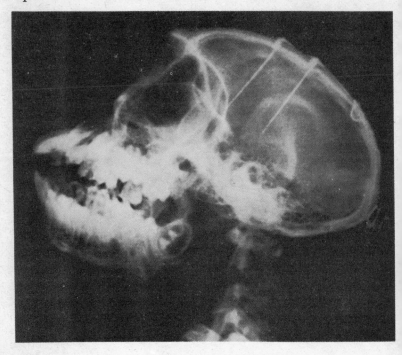

*Figure 2*
X rays of a monkey's head showing two assemblies of electrodes implanted in the frontal lobes and in the thalamus (49).

many laboratories around the world, and there is ample experience of its efficiency, accuracy, and safety, resolving the initial skepticism that introduction of wires into the brain would be technically difficult, dangerous for the subject, and grossly disruptive of normal functions. It is true that implantation of electrodes destroys neurons along the path of penetration, breaking capillary vessels and later producing a local reaction involving the formation of a thin fibrotic capsule along the implantation tract. It has been proven, however, that local hemorrhage is neglible and that because of the well-known functional redundancy of neural tissue with abundance of duplication in its circuits, the destruction of a relatively small group of neurons

*Figure 3*
Chimpanzees Paddy (left) and Carlos, each with 100 intracerebral electrodes and boxes for instrumentation. In spite of this massive implantation, no detectable behavioral deficits have been found, and the animals are still alive and in excellent health two years after surgery.

does not produce any detectable deficit. The thin reactive encapsulation is electrically conductive and is not an obstacle to stimulation or recording. Beyond this 0.1–0.2 millimeter capsule, the brain appears histologically normal. Judged by the absence of abnormal electrical activity, the reliability of effects evoked by ESB, and the consistency of thresholds of excitability through months of experimentation, the electrodes seem to be well tolerated. Some of our monkeys have had electrodes in their heads for more than four years. The anchorage is very solid, and after some initial pulling and scratching of the terminal sockets, the monkeys seem to ignore their presence.

As shown in Figure 3, as many as 100 contacts have been implanted in the brain of some chimpanzees without any noticeable neurophysiological or behavioral disturbance, and in several monkeys, contacts have been placed in areas as critical and delicate as the respiratory centers of the medulla without any surgical problems. Electrodes have been used in laboratory animals such as rats, cats, and monkeys, and also in less frequently studied species including crickets, roosters, dolphins, and brave bulls.

## Electrodes in the Human Brain

Our present knowledge of the central nervous system is based principally on investigations in animals. Experience has shown that many questions about implantation in humans, such as biological tolerance of electrodes by the neural tissue, can be successfully answered in cats or in lower species. Some of the electrochemical events of neural conduction can be analyzed just as adequately in squids as in mammals, and for certain studies of memory, the octopus has proven an excellent subject. The rat has been—and still is—the animal preferred by experimental psychologists because it is a small and inexpensive mammal which can be used in large quantities to provide behavioral results suitable for statistical evaluation. The limited behavioral repertory of lower animals, however, cannot be compared with the complex activities of monkeys and apes. These species, being closer relatives of man, are more appropriate subjects for the neurophysiological study of intelligent behavior, and when we want to investigate the highest psychological functions of the brain which involve verbal communication, there is no possible substitute for man himself.

The human brain, like any other part of the body, may suffer traumatic accidents, tumors, or illnesses, and it has often been necessary to explore the affected areas in order to identify structures, assess abnormality of the tissues, test excitability, and learn the location of important functions which should not be disrupted during surgical procedures. Conscious participation of the patient was required in some of these explorations, for example, to ascertain whether the aura of epileptic attacks could be triggered by electrical stimulation of a specific cortical point, thus providing information about the possible source of epileptic discharges which could be removed by surgery. For this kind of investigation the brain was exposed under local anesthesia, presenting an exceptional opportunity to study behavioral and psychological responses evoked by ESB in fully awake subjects. The most extensive work in this area has been carried out by Penfield and his associates in Montreal (174), and a considerable number of similar studies have been performed by other neurosurgeons as well (2, 8, 97, 124, 163, 215).

Exploration of the exposed brain has, however, some obvious limitations. It has to be brief to avoid prolongation of surgery; electrodes are usually held in place by hand, causing variability in the applied mechanical pressure; the exposed brain is subject to possible thermal, mechanical, and chemical trauma; the cortical areas are identified only by visual inspection; and the physical and psychological stress of the patient undergoing operation introduces factors difficult to control. Most of these handicaps can be avoided with the use of implanted electrodes, and given the experience of animal experimentation it was natural that some investigators should contemplate the application of this methodology to patients for diagnostic and therapeutic purposes (19, 59, 98). Neurosurgeons had already proved that the central nervous system is not as delicate as most people believe, and during therapeutic surgery parts of the cerebral tissue have been cut, frozen, cauterized, or ablated with negligible adverse effects on the patients. Exploratory introduction of needles into the cerebral ventricles is a well-known and relatively safe clinical procedure, and since electrodes are smaller in diameter than these needles, their introduction into the brain should be even less traumatic. Experience has confirmed the safety and usefulness of long-term implantation of electrodes in man, and the procedure has been used in specialized medical centers around the world to help thousands of patients suffering from epilepsy, involuntary movements, intractable pain, anxiety neurosis, and other cerebral disturbances. In general several assemblies of fine electrodes with a total of twenty to forty contacts are placed on the surface and/or in the depth of the brain, with the terminal connectors exteriorized through the scalp and protected by a small head bandage (see Figure 4). In some cases the electrodes have remained for nearly two years with excellent tolerance.

Leaving wires inside of a thinking brain may appear unpleasant or dangerous, but actually the many patients who have undergone this experience have not been concerned about the fact of being wired, nor have they felt any discomfort due to the presence of conductors in their heads. Some women have shown their feminine adaptability to circumstances by wearing attractive hats or wigs to conceal their electrical headgear, and many people have been able to enjoy a normal life as outpatients, returning to the clinic periodically for examination and stimulation. In a few cases in which contacts were located in pleasurable areas, patients have had the opportunity to stimulate their own brains by pressing the button of a portable instrument, and this procedure is reported to have therapeutic benefits.

Chronically implanted electrodes enable careful diagnostic explorations to be performed without time limit, and repeated electrical excitations or well-controlled coagulations can be graded according to the reactions of the patient. As a bonus, important information about psychophysiological correlations, providing direct knowledge about the cerebral basis of human behavior, is being acquired. In our studies (60, 109, 150), an interview situation was selected as the method most likely to offer a continuous supply of verbal and behavioral data. While the electrical activity of eight pairs of cerebral points was being recorded, we taped about one hour of conversation between therapist and patient. Notes of the observable behavior were also taken. During the interview, electrical stimulations of the brain were applied for 5 seconds with intervals of three or more minutes, and each significant point was explored several times.

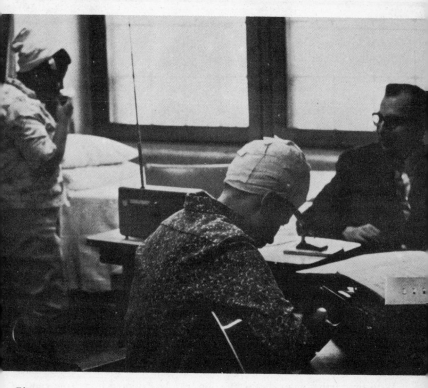

*Figure 4*

Two girls who were suffering from epileptic seizures and behavioral disturbances requiring implantation of electrodes in the brain for diagnostic and therapeutic purposes. Under the cap, each patient wears a "stimoceiver," used to stimulate the brain by radio and to send electrical signals of brain activity by telemetry while the patients are completely free within the hospital ward (60). One example of electrical recordings is shown in Figure 17.

## Two-way Radio Communication with the Brain

Electronic technology has reached a high level of sophistication, and two-way radio communication with automobiles, airplanes, and outer space vehicles is commonplace today. The notable lag in development of similar instrumentation for

*Figure 5*
A monkey instrumented with 28 implanted electrodes, a two-channel telemetric unit on top of the head, and a three-channel radio stimulator around the neck. The animal has learned to press a lever to obtain food. With this methodology, brain functions can be explored by remote control without disturbing the behavior under observation.

communciation with the depth of the brain reflects the already mentioned unbalanced evolution of our technological civilization, which seems more interested in accumulating power than in understanding and influencing the basic mechanisms of the human mind.

This gap is now being filled, and as Figures 4 and 5 show, it is already possible to equip animals or human beings with minute instruments called "stimoceivers" for radio transmission and reception of electrical messages to and from the brain in completely unrestrained subjects. Microminiaturization of the instrument's electronic components permits control of all parameters of excitation for radio stimulation of three different points within the brain and also telemetric recording of three channels of intracerebral electrical activity. In animals, the stimoceiver may be anchored to the skull, and different members of a colony can be studied without disturbing their spontaneous relations within a group. Behavior such as aggression can be evoked or inhibited. In patients, the stimoceiver may be strapped to the head bandage, permitting electrical stimulation and monitoring of intracerebral activity without disturbing spontaneous activities.

Stimoceivers offer great promise in the investigation, diagnosis, and therapy of cerebral disturbances in man. Preliminary information about use in patients with temporal lobe seizurees (see Figure 4) has demonstrated the following advantages over other methods of intracerebral exploration (60): (1) The patient is instrumented simply by plugging the stimoceiver to the head sockets. (2) There is no disturbance of the spontaneous individual or social behavior of the patient. (3) The subject is under continuous medical supervision, and stimulations and recordings may be made day and night. (4) Studies are carried out during spontaneous social interactions in the hospital environment without introducing factors of anxiety or stress. (5) The brain in severely disturbed patients may be explored without confinement to a recording room. (6) As connecting wires are not necessary there is no risk of dislodgment of electrodes during abnormal behavior. (7) Therapeutic programed stimulation of the brain can be prolonged for any necessary amount of time.

It is reasonable to speculate that in the near future the stimoceiver may provide the essential link from man to computer to man, with a reciprocal feedback between neurons and instruments which represents a new orientation for the medical control of neurophysiological functions. For example, it is conceivable that the localized abnormal electrical activity which announces the imminence of an epileptic attack could be picked up by implanted electrodes, telemetered to a distant instrument room, tape-recorded, and analyzed by a computer capable of recognizing abnormal electrical patterns. Identification of the specific electrical disturbance could trigger the emission of radio signals to activate the patient's stimoceiver and apply an electrical stimulation to a determined inhibitory area of the brain, thus blocking the onset of the convulsive episode.

This speculation is supported by the following experiments completed in June, 1969, in collaboration with Drs. Johnston, Wallace, and Bradley. Chimpanzee Paddy (Figure 3), while free in her cage, was equipped with a stimoceiver to telemeter the brain activity of her right and left amygdaloid nuclei to an adjacent room, where these waves were received, tape-recorded, and automatically analyzed by an on-line analog computer. This instrument was instructed to recognize a specific pattern of waves, a burst of spindles, which was normally present in both amygdaloid nuclei for about one second several times per minute. The computer was also instructed to activate a stimulator, and each time the spindles appeared, radio signals were sent back to Paddy's brain to stimulate a point in her reticular formation known to have negative reinforcing properties. In this way electrical stimulation of one cerebral structure was contingent on the production of a specific EEG pattern by another area of the brain, and the whole process of identification of information and command of action was decided by the on-line computer.

Results showed that about two hours after the brain-to-computer-to brain feedback was established, spindling activity of the amygdaloid nucleus was reduced to 50 per cent; and six days later, with daily two-hour periods of feedback, spindles were drastically reduced to only 1 per cent of normal occurrence, and the chimpanzee was quieter, less attentive, and less motivated during behavioral testing, although able to perform olfactory and visual tasks without errors.

The computer was then disconnected, and two weeks later the EEG and Paddy's behavior returned to normal. The experiment was repeated several times with similar results, supporting the conclusions that direct communication can be established between brain and computer, circumventing normal sensory organs, and also that automatic learning is possible by feeding signals directly into specific neuronal structures without conscious participation.

One of the limiting factors in these studies was the existence of wires leading from the brain to the stimoceiver outside of the scalp. The wires represented a possible portal of entry for infection and could be a hindrance to hair grooming in spite of their small size. It would obviously be far more desirable to employ minute instruments which could be implanted completely beneath the skin. For this purpose we have developed in our laboratory a small three-channel stimulator which can be placed subcutaneously and which has terminal leads to be implanted within the brain (Figure 6). The instrument is solid state, has no batteries, and can work indefinitely. Necessary electrical energy, remote control of parameters of stimulation, and choice of channels are provided by transdermal coupling, using a small coil which is activated by frequency-modulated radio signals. In February, 1969, an experiment was begun in monkey Nona and in chimpanzee Suzi who were equipped with subcutaneous stimulators to activate their brains from time to time for the rest of their lives. Terminal contacts were located in motor pathways in order to evoke flexion of the contralateral leg, an effect simple enough to be observed and quantified without difficulty. Study of Nona and Suzi and preliminary investigations in other animals have demonstrated that subcutaneous instrumentation is efficient, reliable, and well tolerated. Behavioral responses were consistent, and local motor excitability was not modified by repeated experimentation. Thus the technical problems of stimulating any desired area of the brain for as long as necessary in the absence of conductors passing through the skin have been solved, therapeutic and scientific possibilities have been multiplied, and the comfort of subjects has been considerably increased.

The next technical step will be to combine transdermal

*Figure 6*
Both sides of a three-channel transdermal stimulator. This instrument has no batteries, is activated by radio, and can be used for life, so that the brain can be stimulated indefinitely. Chimpanzee Suzi (right) has two units (six channels) implanted on her back underneath the skin.

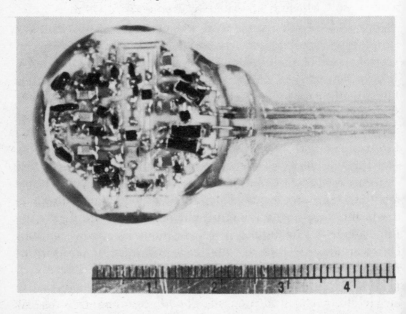

stimulation of the brain with transdermal telemetry of EEG. In this case the stimoceiver will not be outside the skin as it was in Paddy (Figure 3), nor will it be limited to only transdermal stimulation (Figure 6) as in Nona and Suzi: the whole instrument will be totally subcutaneous. The technology for nonsensory communication between brains and computers through the intact skin is already at our fingertips, and its consequences are difficult to predict. In the past the progress of civilization has tremendously magnified the power of our senses, muscles, and skills. Now we are adding a new dimension: the direct interface between brains and machines. Although true, this statement is perhaps too spectacular and it requires cautious clarification. Our present knowledge regarding the coding of information, mechanisms of perception, and neuronal bases of behavior is so elemental that it is highly improbable that electrical correlates of thoughts or emotions could be picked up, transmitted, and electrically applied to the suitable structure of a different subject in order to be recognized and to trigger related thoughts or emotions. It is, however, already possible to induce a large variety of responses, from motor effects to emotional reactions and intellectual manifestations, by direct electrical stimulation of the brain. Also, several investigators have learned to identify patterns of electrical activity (which a computer could also recognize) localized in specific areas of the brain and related to determined phenomena such as perception of smells or visual perception of edges and movements. We are advancing rapidly in the pattern recognition of electrical correlates of behavior and in the methodology for two-way radio communication between brain and computers.

Fears have been expressed that this new technology brings with it the threat of possible unwanted and unethical remote control of the cerebral activities of man by other men, but as will be discussed later, this danger is quite improbable and is outweighed by the expected clinical and scientific benefits. Electronic knowledge and microminiaturization have progressed so much that the limits appear biological rather than technological. Our greatest need is for more experimental information about the neuronal mechanisms related to behavioral and mental processes, and research in unrestricted subjects promises to reveal new understanding of normal minds and more efficient therapy of disturbed brains.

# Electrical Stimulation of the Brain (ESB)

The master control for the whole body resides in the brain, and the new methodology of implanted electrodes has provided direct access to the centers which regulate most of the body's activities. The brain also constitutes the material substratum of mental functions, and by exploring its working neurons we have the possibility of investigating experimentally some of the classical problems of mind-brain correlations. In addition to new answers, implantation of electrodes has introduced new problems: Is it feasible to induce a robotlike performance in animals and men by pushing the buttons of a cerebral radio stimulator? Could drives, desires, and thoughts be placed under the artificial command of electronics? Can personality be influenced by ESB? Can the mind be physically controlled?

In scientific literature there is already a substantial amount of information demonstrating the remarkable effects induced by ESB. The heart, for instance, can be stopped for a few beats, slowed down, or accelerated by suitable stimulation of determined cortical and subcortical structures, illustrating the physiological reality that it is the brain which controls the heart, and not vice versa. Respiratory rate and amplitude have been driven by ESB; gastric secretion and motility have also been modified by brain stimulation; the diameter of the pupil can be adjusted at will (Figure 7) from maximum constriction to maximum dilatation, as if it were a photographic camera, simply by changing the intensity knob of an electric stimulator

*Figure 7*
The diameter of the pupil can be electrically controlled as if it were the diaphragm of a photographic camera. Above, the normal eyes, and below, constriction of the right pupil evoked by stimulation of the hypothalamus. Some effects of ESB such as this are indefatigable and can be maintained for days as long as stimulation is applied (61).

connected with the hypothalamic region of the brain (61). Most visceral functions have been influenced by ESB, as have sensory perceptions, motor activities, and mental functions. Rather than examine each type of finding in detail, we have selected a few typical examples to illustrate the main aspects of electrical control of the brain and its behavioral consequences.

# 13

# Motor Responses

Behavior is the result of motor activities which range from a simple muscular twitch to the creation of a work of art. If we consider the skill involved in nest building, the strategies of fighting animals, or the precision of piano playing, it is obvious that these activities are not solely the result of physical and chemical processes of muscular contraction but depend on conscious direction—on the refined complexity of their cerebral command.

Very little is known about the automatic aspects of voluntary acts, how purpose is related to performance, or how contractions are organized in time and space. Present methodology, however, has placed some of these questions within experimental reach. The fact that ESB can induce simple movements was discovered in the nineteenth century, and today we know that the cerebral organization of motility is located mainly in the cortex of the parietal lobe. Stimulation of this area induces movements on the opposite side of the body, while its destruction results in paralysis. These findings have been expressed in attractive diagrams showing the motor areas of the brain as an "homunculus" lying upside down in the parietal cortex, with a big face and a big thumb, like a caricature of a little man in charge of motility. This image was partly responsible for consideration of the cortex as the supreme and intelligent organizer of behavior.

However, further research demonstrated that motor responses obtained from this cortex are rather crude and that other areas in the depth of the brain have a decisive role in the organization of skilled motility. Modern concepts suggest that the cortex should not be considered the highest hierarchical structure of the motor system or even the starting point of motor impulses, but rather a way station, one more link in the loops of sensory-motor correlations. The multiplicity and complexity of motor representation is logical when we consider the tremendous variety of behavioral manifestations which constitute the only means of communication between the individual and his surroundings. This relation requires a motor performance with precise temporal and spatial coordination among many functional units and the processing of a great deal of information for the adjustment and guidance of movements and for instantaneous adaptation to changes in circumstances. Because of the complexity of these mechanisms, it has been assumed that the artificial ESB could never induce refined and purposeful motor performance. The surprising fact is that, depending on its location, electrical stimulation of the brain is able to evoke not only simple responses but also complex and well-organized behavior which may be indistinguishable from spontaneous activity.

## Motor Activation in Animals

A classical experiment for medical students is to anesthetize a rabbit or other small mammal and to expose its brain in order to stimulate the motor cortex. In this way simple responses, such as contraction or extension of the limbs, may be demonstrated. These responses usually involve a small group of muscles, are stereotyped, and lack adaptability, but in spite of these limitations students are generally impressed by seeing the movements of an animal placed under the command of a human being. The demonstration is far more elegant if the experimental animal is completely awake and equipped with electrodes implanted in the brain. Then the responses appear more physiological, and we can investigate the mutual influence of spontaneous and evoked motility.

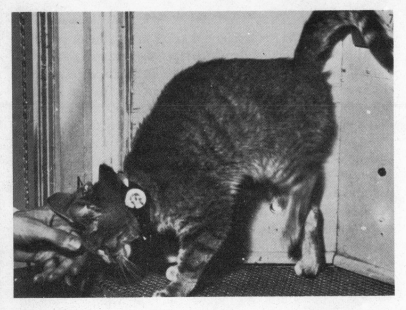

*Figure 8*
Electrical stimulation of the right-side motor cortex produced flexion of the left hind limb proportional in amplitude to the electrical intensity used. Observe the animal's harmonious postural adaptation to the evoked movement and lack of emotional disturbance. During these experiments cats were alert and friendly as usual, purring and seeking to be petted.

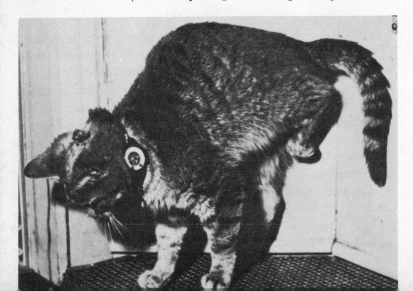

Electrical stimulation of the right-side motor cortex of a cat may produce flexion of the left hind leg with an amplitude of movement proportional to the applied intensity. For example, in one experiment when the animal was standing on all fours, the intensity of 1.2 milliamperes evoked flexion of the leg barely off the ground. At 1.5 milliamperes, the hind leg rose about 4 centimeters, and when 1.8 milliamperes were applied, leg flexion was complete (Figure 8). The evoked movement began slowly, developed smoothly, reached its peak in about two seconds, and lasted until the end of the stimulation. This motor performance could be repeated as many times as desired, and it was accompanied by a postural adjustment of the whole body which included lowering of the head, raising of the pelvis, and a slight weight shift to the left in order to maintain equilibrium on only three legs. The electrical stimulation did not produce any emotional disturbance, and the cat was as alert and friendly as usual, rubbing its head against the experimenter, seeking to be petted, and purring.

If, however, we tried to prevent the evoked effect by holding the left hind leg with our hands, the cat stopped purring, struggled to get free, and shook its leg. Apparently the evoked motility was not unpleasant, but attempts to prevent it were disturbing for the animal, suggesting that stimulation produced not a blind motor movement but also a desire to move, and the cat cooperated spontaneously with the electrical command, adjusting its posture before performing the leg flexion. It was evident that the animal was not in a hurry and took its time in preparing for the induced movement. Preliminary adjustments were not seen if the cat's posture was already adequate for the leg flexion. In cases of conflict between the spontaneous movements of the animal and those elicited by the experimenter, the final result depended on the relative strength of the opposing signals. For example, if the cat was walking, threshold stimulations of 1.2 milliamperes for slight leg flexion were ineffective. If the cat was stimulated while jumping off a table to reach food, stronger intensities of up to 1.5 milliamperes, which usually evoked a clear motor response, were also ineffective; physiological activity seemed to override the artificial excitation and the cat landed with perfectly coordinated movements. If the intensity was increased to 2 milliamperes, stimulation effects were prepotent over voluntary activities; leg flexion started during the jump, coordination was disrupted, and the cat landed badly. A similar experiment is described on page 186.

In monkeys, electrical stimulation of motor areas has evoked contralateral movements similar to those described for the cat. The stimulated animal showed no signs of fear or hostility (Figure 9), nor did he interrupt his spontaneous behavior, such as walking, climbing, or eating. Evoked and spontaneous movements influenced each other, and the final response was a combination of both.

Simultaneous stimulation of two cerebral points with opposite effects could establish a dynamic balance without any visible effect. For example, if excitation of one point produced turning of the head to the right and another one produced turning to the

*Figure 9*
Stimulation of the temporal lobe (rhinal fissure) induced opening of the mouth and movement of the arm without signs of fear or hostility (49).

left, the monkey did not move his head at all when both points were stimulated. This equilibrium could be maintained at different intensity levels of simultaneous stimulation.

Brain stimulation of different areas has elicited most of the simple movements observed in spontaneous behavior, including frowning, opening and closing the eyes, opening, closing, and deviation of the mouth, movements of the tongue, chewing, contraction of the face, movements of the ears, turns, twists, flexions, and extensions of the head and body, and movements of the arms, legs, and fingers. We must conclude that most if not all of the possible simple movements can be evoked by electrical stimulation of the brain. Abnormal responses, disorganized movements, loss of equilibrium (as shown in Figure 10), and epileptiform convulsions have also been produced, depending on the cerebral area and parameters of stimulation investigated.

Turning now to more complex responses, we must realize that normal activities in animals and man involve a succession of different acts well coordinated in space and in time. Walking, for example, is a displacement of the body with alternate flexion and extension of the extremities requiring refined control of strength, amplitude, and speed for the contraction of different groups of muscles with precise timing and mutual correlation aimed toward a common goal. In addition, postural adaptation and corrective movements of the head and body are necessary. To induce walking in an animal by programed electrical stimulation of individual muscles would be a formidable task requiring the wiring of perhaps 100 muscles, the use of a complex computer, sophisticated timing mechanisms, large numbers of stimulators with instantaneously adjustable intensities, many sensors, and the help of a team of scientists and technicians, in addition to a cooperative animal and a measure of good luck. The surprising fact is that electrical pulses applied directly to the brain activate cerebral structures which possess the necessary functional complexity to induce walking with apparently normal characteristics.

In one of our experiments, monkey Kuru was sitting in the colony cage picking some food when radio stimulation of his thalamus, located in the center of the brain, began. The animal slowly got up and started walking around the cage on all fours at a speed of about 1 meter per second, without bumping against the walls or against other animals, in a normal manner without any signs of anxiety, fear, or discomfort. At the end of 5 to 10 seconds of stimulation, the monkey calmly sat down and resumed picking food. As soon as stimulation was reapplied, Kuru resumed walking around the cage. In some studies this effect was repeated as often as sixty times in one hour.

The speed and pattern of a motor response vary according to the cerebral structure stimulated. The effect most often observed

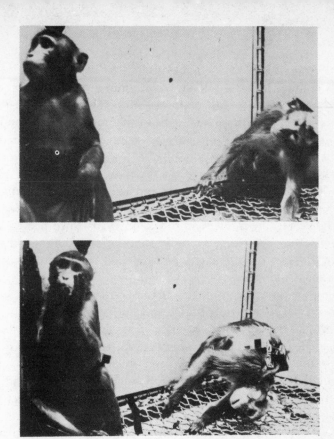

*Figure 10*
Progressive clockwise rotation of the body along the longitudinal axis with complete loss of equilibrium produced by radio stimulation of specific areas of the brain (in this case, the tectum).

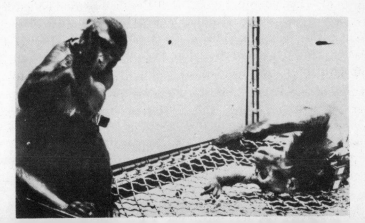

in cats and monkeys, obtained by stimulation of limbic structures and extrapyramidal pathways, is walking in circles. Usually the response begins with slow head turning, followed by body turning, getting up, and walking around the cage. In other studies, during stimulation of the fimbria of the fornix, a monkey ran around the cage at a speed of 2.4 meters per second, showing excellent coordination and orientation, avoiding obstacles or other animals in its path. In this experiment, as shown in Figure 11, one monkey in the colony learned to press a lever in the cage which triggered radio stimulation of the test animal. Repetition of these excitations produced conditioning in the stimulated monkey.

Another type of complex motor response induced by ESB has been described as sequential behavior (54) in which different patterns of behavior follow each other in a precise order, as indicated in the following typical example. Monkey Ludy had one contact implanted in the red nucleus, and when it was stimulated for 5 seconds, the following effects appeared (see Figure 12): (1) immediate interruption of spontaneous activity; (2) change in facial expression; (3) turning of the head to the right; (4) standing on two feet; (5) circling to the right; (6) walking on two feet with perfect balance, using both arms to maintain equilibrium during bipedestation; (7) climbing a pole; (8) descending to the floor; (9) uttering a growl; (10) threatening and often attacking and biting a subordinate monkey; (11) changing aggressive attitude and approaching the rest of the group in a friendly manner; (12) resuming peaceful spontaneous behavior. This complex sequence of events took place during ten to fourteen seconds always in the same order but with considerable flexibility in the details of performance. Ludy avoided obstacles in her path, walked with excellent coordination, and used normal strategies in her fights. The sequential response was so reliable that it persisted after 20,000 stimulations repeated once every minute. Demonstrating the specificity of evoked effects, Figure 13 shows Ludy's very different response evoked by radio stimulation of another red nucleus point located three millimeters away.

## Figure 11

The monkey at left has learned to press the lever inside the cage which triggers radio stimulation of another monkey in the fimbria of the fornix, inducing fast running with excellent coordination. After repetition of these excitations, conditioning is established in the stimulated animal who shows restlessness and stands in a cage corner ready to start the running response as soon as another monkey approaches the lever.

*Figure 12*

Stimulation of the red nucleus in monkey Ludy produced a response which included turning of the head, walking on two feet, turning around, and other sequential effects. The experiment was repeated more than 20,000 times with reliable performance (54).

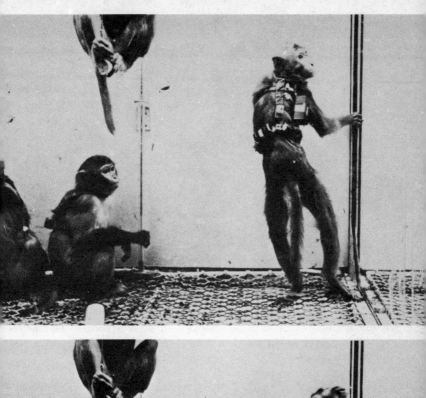

*Figure 13*
Radio stimulation of Ludy in another red nucleus point 3 millimeters away produces only the simple response of yawning. If the monkey was sleeping, brain stimulation was less effective.

Many questions were aroused by these experiments. Why was Ludy walking on two feet? Why the chain of behavioral events? Why was she aggressive a few seconds after the end of stimulation? More studies are needed in order to understand these problems, but the fact that similar sequences have been evoked in other monkeys indicates that we are dealing with rather specific mechanisms of intracerebral organization.

When reviewing the motor responses that can be induced by electrical stimulation several important limitations should be considered: (1) *Lack of predictability*: When a point of the brain is stimulated for the first time, we cannot predict the effects which may be evoked. When the upper part of the motor cortex is stimulated, it is highly probable that the contralateral hind-limb will contract, but we cannot foresee the quality of this movement or the participation of other body muscles, or know whether this response will affect the whole leg or only the foot. Once the evoked effect is known, repeated stimulations give predictable results provided that the experimental situation is constant. (2) *Lack of purpose*: In some cases the evoked response is directed by the animal in a purposeful way, but the movements and sequential responses are usually out of context, and there is no reason or purpose for yawning, flexing a hand, or walking around, apart from ESB. It is important to differentiate these aimless motor responses from other types of behavior described later in which the aim is of primary importance and the motor performance secondary. (3) *No robot performance*: Brain stimulation activates cerebral mechanisms which are organized for motor performance, but it cannot replace them. With the present state of the art, it is very unlikely that we could electrically direct an animal to carry out predetermined activities such as opening a gate or performing an instrumental response. We can induce pleasure or punishment and therefore the motivation to press a lever, but we cannot control the sequence of movements necessary for this act in the absence of the animal's own desire to do so. As will be discussed later, we can evoke emotional states which may motivate an animal to attack another or to escape, but we cannot electrically synthetize the complex motor performance of these acts.

## Motor Effects in Man

The most common effect obtained by electrical stimulation of the human brain is a simple motor response such as the contraction of an extremity. This effect is often accompanied by lack of voluntary control of the muscles involved, and occasionally it is limited to a local paralysis without any other observable symptoms. In general, the evoked contractions are simple in performance, artificial in character, lacking purpose, and without the elegance of spontaneous motility. For example, in one of our patients, stimulation of the left parietal cortex through implanted electrodes evoked a flexion of the right hand starting with contraction of the first two fingers and continuing with flexion of the other fingers. The closed fist was then maintained for the rest of the 5-second stimulation. This effect was not unpleasant or disturbing, and it developed without interrupting ongoing behavior or spontaneous conversation. The patient was aware that his hand had moved involuntarily but he was not afraid and only under questioning did he comment that his arm felt "weak and dizzy." When the patient was warned of the oncoming stimulation and was asked to try to keep his fingers extended, he could not prevent the evoked movement and commented, "I guess, Doctor, that your electricity is stronger than my will." If this stimulation was applied while the subject was voluntarily using his hand, for instance to turn the pages of a magazine, this action was not blocked but the induced hand flexion distorted voluntary performance and resulted in crumpling and tearing of pages. In our experience and in reports by other investigators, electrical stimulation of the motor cortex has not induced precise or skillful movements, and in all cases the evoked responses have been clumsy and abnormal.

Excitation of the supplementary motor area, located near the main motor cortex, may induce three types of effects (174): (1)

There can be postural changes, in which the movement starts slowly and attains a determined end point with more or less general involvement of the body. (2) The movements can have a phasic character such as pawing with the hand, stepping with the foot, or flexing and extending the fingers or wrist. (3) The response can consist of uncoordinated movements. Of special interest is the possibility of activating paralyzed limbs by means of ESB. For example, one patient was suffering from sudden paralysis of the left arm and leg probably caused by an embolus, and after four years he had begun to experience burning pain in the left side of his body which was exacerbated by touching his left thorax or arm. After other treatments failed, two surgical interventions were performed to ablate parts of the sensorimotor cortex, and it was observed that electrical stimulation in the supplementary motor area produced vocalization, raising of the paralyzed arm, and other motor responses. These effects were similar to those evoked in other patients without paralysis. Thus it is clear that the supplementary cortex has pathways independent from the classical motor pathways and that evoked movements may be independent from the integrity of the main motor representation in the cortex.

ESB apparently produces similar results whether applied to the motor area of a child or an adult, of a manual laborer or of an accomplished artist. Skills and refined movements do not seem to be represented in the cortex, or at least they have not been aroused by its electrical stimulation. The motor cortex is probably like a large keyboard located on the efferent side, dealing with the output of activity, able to play the strings of muscular contraction and to produce movements, but requiring the direction of other cerebral structures which as yet are little known.

In contrast to these effects, ESB may evoke more elaborate responses. For example, in one of our patients, electrical stimulation of the rostral part of the internal capsule produced head turning and slow displacement of the body to either side with a well-oriented and apparently normal sequence, as if the patient were looking for something. This stimulation was repeated six times on two different days with comparable results. The interesting fact was that the patient considered the evoked activity spontaneous and always offered a reasonable explanation for it. When asked "What are you doing?" the answers were, "I am looking for my slippers," "I heard a noise," "I am restless," and "I was looking under the bed." In this case it was difficult to ascertain whether the stimulation had evoked a movement which the patient tried to justify, or if an hallucination had been elicited which subsequently induced the patient to move and to explore the surroundings.

There are very few clinical reports of complex movements evoked by ESB which are comparable to the sequential responses observed in monkeys, and this may indicate that cerebral organization is less stereotyped in man than in animals. Temporal lobe stimulation in man has induced automatisms, including fumbling with surgical drapes or with the patient's own hands, and well-organized movements aimed at getting off the operating table. Usually these evoked automatisms have not been remembered. Vocalizations and more or less intelligible speech may also be included among complex motor responses, although they represent the activation of motor and ideational mechanisms. Vocalizations have been obtained by stimulation of the motor area in the precentral gyrus and also of the supplementary motor area in both hemispheres. The response usually consists of a sustained or interrupted cry with a vowel sound which occasionally has a consonant component (174).

# 14

# Hell and Heaven Within the Brain:
# The Systems for Punishment and Reward

When man evolved above other powerful animals, the size and complexity of his brain increased, giving him superior intelligence along with more anguish, deeper sorrow, and greater sensitivity than any other living creature. Man also learned to enjoy beauty, to dream and to create, to love and to hate. In the education of children as well as in the training of animals, punishment and reward constitute the most powerful motivations for learning. In our hedonistic orientation of life to minimize pain and seek pleasure, we often attribute these qualities to the environment without realizing that sensations depend on a chain of events which culminates in the activation of determined intracerebral mechanisms. Physical damage, the loss of a beloved child, or apocalyptic disaster cannot make us suffer if some of our cerebral structures have been blocked by anesthesia. Pleasure is not in the skin being caressed or in a full stomach, but somewhere inside the cranial vault.

At the same time pain and pleasure have important psychic and cultural components related to individual history. Men inhibited by some extraordinary tribal or religious training to endure discomfort have been tortured to death without showing signs of suffering. It is also known that in the absence of physical injury, mental elaboration of information may produce the worst kind of suffering. Social rejection, guilt feelings, and other personal tragedies may produce greater autonomic, somatic, and psychological manifestations than actual physical pain.

There is strong reluctance to accept that such personal and refined interpretations of reality as being afraid and being in love are contingent on the membrane depolarization of determined clusters of neurons, but this is one aspect of emotional phenomena which should not be ignored. After frontal lobotomy, cancer patients have reported that the pain persisted undiminished, but that their subjective suffering was radically reduced, and they did not complain or request as much medication as before surgery. Lobotomized patients reacted to noxious stimuli as much, if not more, than before their operations, jumping at pinpricks and responding quickly to objective tests of excessive heat, but they showed decreased concern. It seems that in the frontal lobes there is a potentiating mechanism for the evaluation of personal suffering, and after lobotomy the initial sensation of pain is unmodified, while the reactive component to that feeling is greatly diminished. This mechanism is rather specific of the frontal lobes; bilateral destruction of the temporal lobes fails to modify personal suffering.

Important questions to resolve are: Do some cerebral structures have the specific role of analyzing determined types of sensations? Is the coding of information at the receptor level essential for the activation of these structures? Not too long ago, many scientists would have dismissed as naive the already demonstrated fact that punishment and reward can be induced at will by manipulating the controls of an electrical instrument connected to the brain.

## Perception of Suffering

In textbooks and scientific papers, terms such as "pain receptors," "pain fibers," and "pain pathways" are frequently used, but it should be clarified that peripheral nerves do not carry sensations. Neuronal pathways transmit only patterns of electrical activity with a message that must be deciphered by the central nervous system, and in the absence of brain there is no pain, even if some reflex motor reactions may still be present. A decapitated frog cannot feel but will jump away with fairly good motor coordination when pinched in the hind legs. During competitive sports or on the battlefield, emotion and stress may temporarily block the feeling of pain in man, and often injuries are not immediately noticed. The cerebral interpretation of sensory signals is so decisive that the same stimulus may be considered pleasant or unpleasant depending on circumstances. A strong electrical shock on the feet scares a dog and inhibits its secretion of saliva. If, however, the same "painful" excitation is followed for several days by administration of food, the animal accepts the shock, wagging its tail happily and salivating in anticipation of the food reward. Some of these dogs have been trained to press a lever to trigger the electric shock which preceded food. During sexual relations in man, bites, scratches, and other potentially painful sensations are often interpreted as enjoyable, and some sexual deviates seek physical punishment as a source of pleasure.

The paradox is that while skin and viscera have plentiful nerve endings for sensory reception, the brain does not possess this type of innervation. In patients under local anesthesia, the cerebral tissue may be cut, burned, pulled apart, or frozen without causing any discomfort. This organ so insensitive to its own destruction is, however, the exquisite sensor of information received from the periphery. In higher animal species there is sensory differentiation involving specialized peripheral receptors which code external information into electrical impulses and internal analyzers which decode the circulating inputs in order to give rise to the perception of sensations.

Most sensory messages travel through peripheral nerves, dorsal roots, spinal cord, and medulla to the thalamic nuclei in the brain, but from there we lose their trail and do not know where the information is interpreted as painful or pleasurable, or how affective components are attributed to a sensation (212, 220).

Although anatomical investigations indicate that thalamic fibers project to the parietal "sensory" cortex, stimulation of this area does not produce pain in animals or man. No discomfort has been reported following electrical excitation of the surface or depth of the motor areas, frontal lobes, occipital lobes, cingulate gyrus, and many other structures, while pain, rage, and fear have been evoked by excitation of the central gray tegmentum, and a few other regions.

Animals share with man the expressive aspect of emotional manifestations. When a dog wags its tail, we suppose it is happy, and when a cat hisses and spits we assume that it is enraged, but these interpretations are anthropomorphic and in reality we do not know the feelings of any animal. Several authors have tried to correlate objective manifestations with sensations; for example, stimulation of the cornea of the eye provokes struggling, pupillary dilatation, and rise of blood pressure (87), but these responses are not necessarily related to awareness of feelings, as is clearly demonstrated by the defensive agility of the decapitated frog. Experimental investigation of the mechanisms of pain and pleasure is handicapped in animals by their lack of verbal communication, but fortunately we can investigate whether an animal likes or dislikes the perceived sensations by analyzing its instrumental responses. Rats, monkeys, and other species can learn to press a lever in order to receive a reward such as a food pellet or to avoid something unpleasant such as an electric shock to the skin. By the voluntary act of instrumental manipulation, an animal expresses whether or not the food, shock, or brain stimulation is desirable, allowing for the objective qualification of the sensation. In this way, many cerebral structures have been explored to identify their positive or negative reinforcing properties.

At present it is generally accepted that specific areas of the brain participate in the integration of pain sensations, but the mechanism is far from clear, and in our animal experiments we do not know if we are stimulating pathways or higher centers of integration. The concept of a straight conduction of pain messages from the periphery up to the central nervous system was too elemental. Incoming messages are probably processed at many levels with feedbacks which modify the sensitivity and the filtering of information at many stages including the peripheral receptor level. Brain excitation, therefore, may affect transmission as well as the elaboration of inputs and feedback modulation. Electrical stimuli do not carry any specific message because they are a monotonous repetition of similar pulses, and the fact that they constitute a suitable trigger for central perception of pain means that the reception of a patterned code is not required, but only the nonspecific activation of neuronal pools which are accessible to investigation. In addition to the importance of these studies for finding better therapies for the alleviation of pain, there is another aspect which has great social interest: the possible relations between pain perception and violence.

## Violence Within the Brain

The chronicle of human civilization is the story of a cooperative venture consistently marred by self-destruction, and every advance has been accompanied by increased efficiency of violent behavior. Early man needed considerable physical strength and skill to defend himself or attack other men or beasts with stones, arrows, or swords, but the invention of explosives and subsequent development of firearms have made unskilled individuals more powerful than mythical warriors of the past. The technology for destruction has now placed at the disposal of man a vast arsenal of ingenious weapons which facilitate all forms of violence including crimes against property, assassinations, riots, and wars, threatening not only individual life and national stability but the very existence of civilization.

Ours is a tragically imbalanced industrial society which devotes most of its resources to the acquisition of destructive power and invests insignificant effort in the search which could provide the true weapons of self-defense: knowledge of the

mechanisms responsible for violent behavior. They are necessarily related with intracerebral processes of neuronal activity,
even if the triggering causality may reside in environmental
circumstances. Violence is a product of cultural environment
and is an extreme form of aggression, distinct from modes of
self-expression required for survival and development under
normal conditions. Man may react to unpleasant or painful
stimuli with violence—he may retaliate even more vigorously
than he is attacked—but only if he has been taught by his
culture to react in this manner. A major role of education is
to "build internal controls in human beings so that they can
withstand external pressures and maintain internal equilibrium" (157). We should remember that it is normal for an
animal to urinate when the bladder is full and to mount any
available female during the mating season, but that these be-
haviors may be controlled in man through training. The distinctly human quality of cerebralization of behavior is possible
through education.

Human aggression may be considered a behavioral response
characterized by the exercise of force with the intent to inflict
damage on persons or objects. The phenomenon may be
analyzed in three components: *inputs,* determined by environmental circumstances perceived through sensory receptors and
acting upon the individual; *throughputs,* which are the personal
processing of these circumstances through the intracerebral
mechanisms established by genetic endowment and previous
experiences; and *outputs,* represented by the expressions of
individual and social behavior which constitute the observable
manifestations of aggression. Increasing awareness of the need
to investigate these subjects has already resulted in the creation
of specialized institutes, but surprisingly enough the most
essential element in the whole process of violence is usually
neglected. Attention is directed to economic, ideological, social,
and political factors and to their consequences, which are expressed as individual and mass behavior, while the essential link
in the central nervous system is often forgotten. It is, however.

an incontrovertible fact that the environment is only the provider of sensory inputs which must be interpreted by the brain,
and that any kind of behavior is the result of intracerebral
activity.

It would be naive to investigate the reasons for a riot by
recording the intracerebral electrical activity of the participants,
but it would be equally wrong to ignore the fact that each participant has a brain and that determined neuronal groups are
reacting to sensory inputs and are subsequently producing the
behavioral expression of violence. Both neurophysiological and
environmental factors must be evaluated, and today methodology is available for their combined study. Humanity behaves
in general no more intelligently than animals would under the
same circumstances, and this alarming reality is due largely to
"that spiritual pride which prevents men from regarding themselves and their behavior as parts of nature and as subject to its
universal laws" (148). Experimental investigation of the cerebral
structures responsible for aggressive behavior is an essential
counterpart of social studies, and this should be recognized by
sociologists as well as biologists.

In animals, the first demonstration that offensive activity
could be evoked by ESB was provided by Hess (105), and it has
subsequently been confirmed by numerous investigators. Cats
under electrical stimulation of the periventricular gray matter
acted "as if threatened by a dog," responding with unsheathed
claws and well-aimed blows. "The animal spits, snorts or growls.
At the same time the hair on its back stands on end, and its tail
becomes bushy. Its pupils widen sometimes to their maximum,
and its ears lie back or move back and forth to frighten the nonexisting enemy" (106). In these experiments it is important to
know how the cat really feels. Is it aware of its own responses?
Is the hostility purposefully oriented to do harm? Or is the entire
phenomenon a pseudoaffective reaction, a false or sham rage
containing the motor components of offensive display without
actual emotional participation? These issues have been debated
over the years, but today it is clear that both sham and true rage

*Figure 14*
At upper left, the control, two friendly cats. At lower left, electrical stimulation of the anterior hypothalamus evoked an aggressive expression not directed against the other cat which, however, reacts with a defensive attitude. Above, the normal cat attacks the stimulated animal which lowers its head, flattens its ears, and does not retaliate. This experiment is an example of false rage (53).

can be elicited by ESB depending on the location of stimulation. Excitation of the anterior hypothalamus may induce a threatening display with hissing and growling which should be interpreted as false rage because, as shown in Figure 14, the display was not directed against other animals. When other cats reacted by hissing and attacking the stimulated animal, it did not retaliate or escape and simply lowered its head and flattened its ears, and these brain stimulations could not be conditioned to sensory cues.

In contrast, true rage has been demonstrated in other experiments. As shown in Figure 15, stimulation of the lateral hypothalamus produced an aggressive display clearly directed toward

*Figure 15*

Electrical stimulation of the lateral hypothalamus evoked true rage which is characterized by aggressive display oriented toward another cat (above); attack with well-oriented claws directed against other cats (below);

attack against investigators with whom relations had previously been
friendly (above); learning of instrumental responses, such as rotating
a paddle wheel, in order to stop the brain stimulation (below). In this
way the cat expresses its dislike of being stimulated in a particular area (53).

a control animal which reacted properly in facing the threat. The stimulated animal started prowling around looking for fights with other subordinate animals, but avoided the most powerful cat in the group. It was evident that brain stimulation had created a state of increased aggressiveness, but it was also clear that the cat directed its hostility intelligently, choosing the enemy and the moment of attack, changing tactics, and adapting its movements to the motor reaction of its opponent. Brain stimulation determined the affective state of hostility, but behavioral performance depended on the individual characteristics of the stimulated animal, including learned skills and previous experiences. Stimulations were usually tested for 5 to 10 seconds, but since it was important to know the fatigability of the effect, a longer experiment was performed, reducing the applied intensity to a level which did not evoke overt rage. The experimental subject was an affectionate cat which usually sought petting and purred while it was held in the experimenter's arms. Then it was introduced into the colony with five other cats and was radio stimulated continuously for two hours. During this period the animal sat motionless in a corner of the cage, uttering barely audible growls from time to time. If any other cat approached, the stimulated animal started hissing and threatening, and if the experimenter tried to pet it, the growls increased in intensity and the animal often spat and hissed. This hostile attitude disappeared as soon as the stimulation was over, and the cat became as friendly as before. These experiments demonstrated that brain excitation could modify reactions toward normal sensory stimuli and could modulate the quality of the responses in a way similar to modulation during spontaneous emotional states.

Monkeys are more interesting subjects than cats for the study of social interactions because of their more numerous and skillful spontaneous activities. It is well known that monkey colonies constitute autocratic societies in which one animal establishes itself as boss of the group, claiming a large portion of the territory, feeding first, and being avoided by the others, who usually express their submissiveness by grimacing, crouching, and offering sexual play. In several colonies we have observed that radio stimulation of specific points in the thalamus or central gray in the boss monkey increased his aggressiveness and induced well-directed attacks against other members of the group, whom he chased around and occasionally bit, as shown in Figure 16 (56). It was evident that his hostility was oriented purposefully and according to his previous experience because he usually attacked the other male who represented a challenge to his authority, and he always spared the little female who was his favorite partner.

A high-ranking monkey expresses rage by attacking submissive members of the colony, but what would be the consequences of stimulating the brain of lower-ranking animals? Could they be induced to challenge the authority of other monkeys, including perhaps even the boss, or would their social inhibitions block the electrically induced hostility? These questions were investigated in one colony by changing its composition to increase progressively the social rank of one member, a female named Lina, who in the first grouping of four animals ranked lowest, progressing to third rank in the second group and to second rank in the third group. Social dominance was evaluated during extended control periods using the criteria of number of spontaneous agonistic and sexual interactions, priority in food getting, and territoriality. On two successive mornings in each colony Lina was radio stimulated for 5 seconds once a minute for one hour in the nucleus posterolateralis of the thalamus. In all three colonies, these stimulations induced Lina to run across the cage, climb to the ceiling, lick, vocalize, and according to her social status, to attack other animals. In group 1, where Lina was submissive, she tried to attack another monkey only once, and she was threatened or attacked 24 times. In group 2 she became more aggressive (24 occurrences) and was attacked only 3 times, while in group 3 Lina attacked other monkeys 79 times and was not threatened at all. No changes in the number of agonistic acts were observed in any group before or after the stimulation

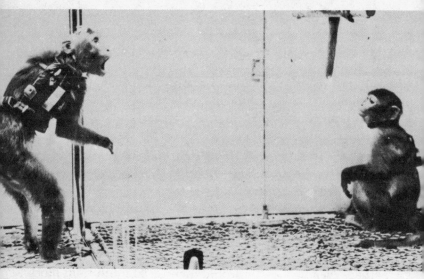

*Figure 16*
Examples of threatening attitude and aggressive behavior produced by brain stimulation. Observe that the stimulated monkey chooses another

one as a specific target, and this animal usually expresses submissiveness by grimacing, crouching, or escaping. A toy tiger is also a suitable target for aggressive display.

hour, showing that alterations in Lina's aggressive behavior were determined by ESB.

In summary, intraspecies aggression has been evoked in cats and monkeys by electrical stimulation of several cerebral structures, and its expression is dependent on the social setting. Unlike purely motor effects including complex sequences which have no social significance, an artificially evoked aggressive act may be directed against a specific group member or may be entirely suppressed, according to the stimulated subject's social rank.

Many questions remain to be answered. Which cerebral areas are responsible for spontaneous aggressive behavior? By what mechanisms are environmental inputs interpreted as undesirable? How does cultural training influence the reactivity of specific cerebral areas? Can neurophysiological mechanisms of violence be re-educated, or are individual responses set for life after early imprinting? It is interesting that application of ESB modified the interpretation of the environment, changing the peaceful relations of a group of animals into sudden overt hostility. The same sensory inputs provided by the presence of other animals, which were neutral during control periods, were under ESB the cue for a ferocious and well-directed attack. Apparently brain stimulation introduced an emotional bias which altered interpretation of the surroundings.

While neurophysiological activity may be influenced or perhaps even set by genetic factors and past experience, the brain is the direct interpreter of environmental inputs and the determinant of behavioral responses. To understand the causes and plan remedies for intraspecific aggression in animals and man require knowledge of both sociology and neurophysiology. Electricity cannot determine the target for hostility or direct the sequences of aggressive behavior, which are both related to the past history of the stimulated subject and to his immediate adaptation to changing circumstances. Artificially triggered and spontaneously provoked aggression have many elements in common, suggesting that in both cases similar areas of the brain have been activated.

While individual and collective acts of violence may seem rather distant from the electrical discharges of neurons, we should remember that personality is not in the environment but in the nervous tissue. Possible solutions to undesirable aggression obviously will not be found in the use of ESB. This is only a methodology for investigation of the problem and acquisition of necessary information about the brain mechanisms involved. It is well known that medical treatment of cardiac patients is based on anatomical and physiological studies of the heart, and that without this information it would not have been possible to discover new drugs or to give effective medical advice. Similarly, without knowledge of the brain it will be difficult to correlate social causality with individual reactivity.

### Anxiety, Fear, and Violence Evoked by ESB in Man

Anxiety has been considered the alpha and omega of psychiatry. It is one of the central themes of existential philosophy, and it shades the normal—and abnormal—life of most human beings. Several emotional states may be classified under the heading of anxiety, including fear, fright, panic, and terror, which are variations of the same basic experience. One of the most complex mental disturbances, unreasonable or excessive anxiety, including phobias and compulsive obsessions, often does not respond to standard therapies, and in some instances it has been improved by electrocoagulation of discrete areas of the frontal pole. Grey Walter (234) has claimed an 85 per cent total social recovery in a group of sixty patients with anxiety and obsessions treated with carefully dosified coagulations made through electrodes implanted in the frontal lobes.

Without entering into semantic discussions, we may consider anxiety an emotional state of conscious or subconscious tension related to real or imaginary threats to psychological or physical individual integrity. A mild degree of anxiety may mobilize, while excessive degrees may paralyze somatic and mental activity. Beyond a certain limit, anxiety has unpleasant characteristics. In normal circumstances, it is produced, as is any other emotion, by sensory inputs from the environment and by recollections, both of which require mental elaboration of messages which may be influenced by humoral and neuronal factors. In addition, there is abundant evidence that anxiety and fear may be induced as either a primary or a secondary category of response by direct electrical stimulation of the brain. The perception or expectancy of pain can be frightening, and in some cases when ESB produced localized or generalized discomfort, patients have expressed concern about continuation of the exploratory procedures. In addition to the natural fear of possible further discomfort, there may have been a component of primary anxiety which would be difficult to evaluate.

Destruction of discrete parts of the thalamus produces relief from anxiety neurosis and obsessive-compulsive neurosis which is probably related to the interruption of tonic pathways to the frontal lobes. Stimulation of the thalamic nucleus, however, very seldom produces anxiety, and the reports of patients are limited to feelings of weakness, being different, dizziness, floating, and something like alcoholic intoxication (214).

Clearer demonstrations of direct induction of fear without any other accompanying sensations have been reported by several investigators. Lesions in the medial thalamus give effective pain relief with a minimal amount of sensory loss, and for this reason this area has often been explored electrically in cancer patients. In some cases it has produced acute anxiety attacks, which one patient vividly described as: "It's rather like the feeling of having just been missed by a car and leaped back to the curb and went B-r-r-r." Something in his guts felt very unpleasant, very unusual, and he certainly did not want to feel like that again (73). The surprising fact is that the unpleasant sensation of fear was felt in one side of the body, contralateral to the brain stimulation. Sweet (221) has reported the case of a very intelligent patient, the dean of a graduate school, who after a unilateral sympathectomy to treat his upper limb hyperhydrosis, found that his previous and customary sensation of shivering while listening to a stirring passage of music occurred in only one side and he could not be thrilled in the sympathectomized half of his body. These cases were interesting because emotions are usually experienced in a rather diffuse and bilateral fashion unless innervation has been specifically interrupted.

The role of the thalamus in the integration of fear is also suggested by the study of a female patient whose spontaneous crippling attacks of anxiety of overwhelming intensity had led to several suicide attempts and a chronic state of depression and agitation quite refractory to drugs and psychotherapy. Stimulation of the dorsolateral nucleus of the thalamus evoked precisely the same type of attack at a level of symptomatology directly proportional to the applied intensity. It was possible to find the electrical threshold for a mild anxiety or to increase it to higher levels simply by turning the dial of the stimulator. "One could sit with one's hand on the knob and control the level of her anxiety" (73).

In one of our female patients, stimulation of a similar area in the thalamus induced a typical fearful expression and she turned to either side, visually exploring the room behind her. When asked what she was doing, she replied that she felt a threat and thought that something horrible was going to happen. This fearful sensation was perceived as real, and she had a premonition of imminent disaster of unknown cause. The effect was reliable on different days and was not altered by the use of lights and a movie camera to document the finding. Her motor activity and choice of words varied according to the environmental setting, but her facial expression and acute sensation of nonspecific, unexplainable, but real fear were similar following different stimulations. The response started with a delay of less than one second, lasted for as long as the stimulation, and did not leave observable aftereffects. The patient remembered her fear but was not upset by the memory.

Some patients have displayed anxiety and restlessness when the pallidum was stimulated at frequencies above 8 cycles per second, and they also perceived a constriction or warmth in the chest (123). A few reported a "vital anxiety in the left chest," and screamed anxiously if the stimulation was repeated. Intense emotional reactions have been evoked by stimulation of the amygdaloid nucleus, but responses varied in the same patient even with the same parameters of stimulation. The effect was sometimes rage, sometimes fear. One patient explained, "I don't know what came over me. I felt like an animal" (100).

The sensation of fear without any concomitant pain has also been observed as a result of ESB of the temporal lobe (230). This effect may be classified as "illusion of fear" (174) because there was obviously no real reason to be afraid apart from the artificial electrical activation of some cerebral structures. In every case, however, fear is a cerebral interpretation of reality which depends on a variety of cultural and experiential factors with logical or illogical reasons. The fact that it can be aroused by stimulation of a few areas of the brain allows the exploration of the neuronal mechanisms of anxiety, and as a working hypothesis we may suppose that the emotional qualities of fear depend on the activation of determined structures located probably in the thalamus, amygdala, and a few other as yet unidentified nuclei. This activation usually depends on the symbolic evaluation of coded sensory inputs, but the threshold for this activation may be modified—and also reached—by direct application of ESB. Knowledge of intracerebral mechanisms of anxiety and fear will permit the establishment of a more rational pharmacological and psychiatric treatment of many suffering patients, and may also help us to understand and ameliorate the increasing level of anxiety in our civilization.

It is also known that in some tragic cases, abnormal neurological processes may be the causal factor for unreasonable and uncontrollable violence. Those afflicted may often hurt or even kill either strangers or close family members usually treated with affection. A typical example was J. P., a charming and attractive 20-year-old girl with a history of encephalitis at the age of eighteen months and many crises of temporal lobe seizures and grand mal attacks for the last ten years (60). Her main social problem was the frequent and unpredictable occurrence of rage which on more than a dozen occasions resulted in an assault on another person such as inserting a knife into a stranger's myocardium or a pair of scissors into the pleural cavity of a nurse. The patient was committed to a ward for the criminally insane, and electrodes were implanted in her amygdala and hippocampus for exploration of possible neurological abnormalities. As she was rather impulsive, confinement in the EEG recording room was impractical, and she became one of the first clinical cases instrumented with a stimoceiver, which made it possible to study intracerebral activity without restraint (see Figure 4). Depth recordings taken while the patient moved freely around the ward demonstrated marked electrical abnormalities in both amygdala and hippocampus. Spontaneous periods of aimless walking coincided with an increase in the number of high-voltage sharp waves. At other times, the patient's speech was spontaneously inhibited for several minutes during which she could not answer any questions although she retained partial comprehension and awareness. These periods coincided with bursts of spike activity localized to the optic radiation (Figure 17). Transitory emotional excitement was related with an increase in the number and duration of 16-cycles-per-second bursts; but the patient read papers, conversed with other people, and walked around without causing any noticeable alterations in the telemetered intracerebral electrical activity.

During depth explorations, it was demonstrated that crises of assaultive behavior similar to the patient's spontaneous bursts of anger could be elicited by radio stimulation of contact 3 in the right amygdala. A 1.2 milliampere excitation of this point was applied while she was playing the guitar and singing with enthusiasm and skill. At the seventh second of stimulation, she threw away the guitar and in a fit of rage launched an attack against the wall and then paced around the floor for several minutes, after which she gradually quieted down and resumed her usual cheerful behavior. This effect was repeated on two different days. The fact that only the contact located in the amygdala induced rage suggested that the neuronal field around

J.P. III-68

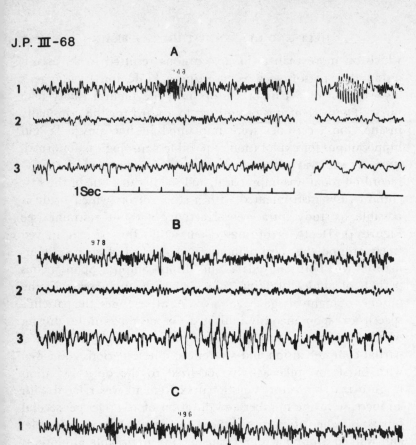

*Figure 17*

Telemetric recording of electrical activity of the brain in one of the patients shown in Figure 4. The location of the contacts was as follows: Channel 1: amygdaloid nucleus; Channel 2: anterior optic radiation; Channel 3: posterior optic radiation. A: spontaneous bursts appearing in Channel 1 were more prominent when the patient was psychologically excited. B: sudden spontaneous arrest of speech coincided with bursts of spikes in Channel 3. C: control recordings were unmodified by friendly behavior or by different types of motor activity such as walking and reading (60).

contact 3 was involved in the patient's behavior problem, and this finding was of great clinical significance in the orientation of subsequent treatment by local coagulation.

The demonstration that amygdaloid stimulation may induce violent behavior has also been provided by other investigators. King (128) has described the case of a woman with feelings of depression and alienation, with an extremely flat tone of voice and a facial expression which was blank and unchanging during interviews, who upon stimulation of the amygdala with 5 milliamperes had greatly altered vocal inflections and an angry expression. During this time she said, "I feel like I want to get up from this chair! Please don't let me do it! Don't do this to me. I don't want to be mean!" When the interviewer asked if she would like to hit him, the patient answered, "Yeah, I want to hit something. I want to get something and just tear it up. Take it so I won't!" She then handed her scarf to the interviewer who gave her a stack of paper, and without any other verbal exchange, she tore it into shreds saying, "I don't like to feel like this." When the level of stimulation was reduced to 4 milliamperes, her attitude changed to a broad smile, and she explained, "I know it's silly, what I'm doing. I wanted to get up from this chair and run. I wanted to hit something, tear up something—anything. Not you, just anything. I just wanted to get up and tear. I had no control of myself." An increase in intensity up to 5 milliamperes again resulted in similar aggressive manifestations, and she raised her arm as if to strike.

It is notable that although the patients seemed to be out of control in these two instances of electrically induced aggression, they did not attack the interviewer, indicating that they were aware of their social situation. This finding is reminiscent of the behavior of stimulated monkeys who directed their aggressiveness according to previous experience and social rank and did not dare to challenge the authority of well-established bosses. Apparently ESB can induce a state of increased violent reactivity which is expressed in accordance with individual structure and environmental circumstances. We may conclude therefore that artificially evoked emotional change is only one more factor in the constellation of behavioral determinants.

### Pleasurable Excitation of the Animal Brain

It is surprising that in science as well as in literature more attention has been paid to suffering than to happiness. The central theme of most novels is tragedy, while happy books are hard to find; excellent monographs have been published about pain, but similar studies of pleasure are nonexistent. Typically, in the monumental *Handbook of the American Physiological Society* (75), a full chapter is devoted to pain, and pleasure is not even listed in the general subject index. Evidently the pursuit of happiness has not aroused as much scientific interest as the fear of pain.

In psychological literature the study of reward is well represented, but even there it has been considered a second-rate sensation and perhaps an artifact of a diminution of pain. It has been postulated that a truly "pleasant" sensation could not exist because organisms have a continuous tendency to minimize incoming stimuli. Pleasure was thus considered a subjective name for the diminution of drive, the withdrawal of a strong stimulation, or the reduction of pain. This "pain reduction" theory (154) has been fruitful as a basis for psychological investigations, but it is gloomy to think that we live in a world of punishment in which the only reality is suffering and that our brain can perceive different degrees of pain but no real pleasure.

Interest in the earlier ideas of hedonism has been renewed by recent experimental studies. According to this theory, pain and pleasure are relatively independent sensations and can be evoked by different types of stimuli which are recognized by separate cerebral mechanisms. Behavior is considered to be motivated by stimuli which the organism tries to minimize (pain) or by stimuli which the organism tries to maximize (pleasure). The brain is thought to have different systems for the reception of these two kinds of inputs, and the psychological state of pleasure or reward can be determined not only by the termination of pain but also by the onset of primary pleasure. The discovery of two anatomically distinct mechanisms in the brain, one for punishment, as mentioned earlier, and one for reward, provides a physiological basis for the dualistic motivation postulated in hedonism (62, 165).

The surprising fact is that animals of different species, including rats, cats, and monkeys, have voluntarily chosen to press a lever which provides electrical stimulation of specific cerebral areas. The demonstrations are highly convincing because animals which initially pressed a lever to obtain the reward of sugar pellets later pressed at similar or higher rates when electrical stimulation was substituted for food. These experiments showed conclusively that the animals enjoyed the electrical impulses which were delivered only at their own demand. Watching a rat or monkey stimulate its own brain is a fascinating spectacle. Usually each lever pressing triggers a brief 0.5-to 1.0-second brain stimulation which can be more rewarding than food. In a choice situation, hungry rats ran faster to reach the self-stimulation lever than to obtain pellets, and they persistently pressed this lever, ignoring food within easy reach. Rats have removed obstacles, run mazes, and even crossed electrified floors to reach the lever that provided cerebral stimulation.

Not all areas of the brain involved in pleasurable effects appear equally responsive. The highest lever-pressing rates (of up to a remarkable 5,000 times per hour) were recorded by animals self-stimulating in the posterior hypothalamus; excitation of rhinencephalic structures (of only about 200 times per hour) was considered moderately rewarding; and in sensory or motor areas, animals self-stimulated at merely a chance level (of 10 to 25 times per hour), and these areas were classified as neutral. As should be expected, when stimulation was shifted from rewarding areas to nuclei in the punishment system in the same animals, they pressed the lever once and never went back, showing that in the brain of the same animal there were two different groups of structures, one rewarding and the other aversive.

A systematic analysis of the neuroanatomical distribution of pleasurable areas in the rat (164) shows that 60 per cent of the brain is neutral, 35 per cent is rewarding, and only 5 per cent may elicit punishing effects. The idea that far more brain is involved in pleasure than in suffering is rather optimistic and gives hope that this predominance of the potential for pleasurable sensations can be developed into a more effective behavioral reality.

Because of the lack of verbal communication with animals, any ideas about what kind of pleasure, if any, may be experienced during ESB is a matter of speculation. There are some indications, however, that the perceived sensations could be related to anatomical differentiation of primary rewards of food and sex, because hungry animals self-stimulated at a higher rate in the middle hypothalamus, while administration of sexual hormones to castrated rats increased their lever pressing of more lateral hypothalamic points.

The controversial issue of how these findings in animals may relate to human behavior and the possible existence of areas involved in pleasure in the human brain has been resolved by the information obtained in patients with implanted electrodes.

## Human Pleasure Evoked by ESB

On the basis of many studies during cerebral surgery, Penfield (174) has said of anger, joy, pleasure, and sexual excitement in the human brain that "so far as our experience goes, neither localized epileptic discharge nor electrical stimulation is capable of awakening any such emotion. One is tempted to believe that there are no specific cortical mechanisms associated with these emotions." This statement still holds true for the cerebral cortex, but studies in human subjects with implanted electrodes have demonstrated that electrical stimulation of the depth of the brain can induce pleasurable manifestations, as evidenced by the spontaneous verbal reports of patients, their facial expression and general behavior, and their desire to repeat the experience. In a group of twenty-three patients suffering from schizophrenia (98), electrical stimulation of the septal region, located deep in the frontal lobes, produced an enhancement of alertness sometimes accompanied by an increase in verbal output, euphoria, or pleasure. In a more systematic study in another group of patients, further evidence was presented of the rewarding effects of septal stimulation (20, 99). One man suffering from narcolepsia was provided with a small stimulator and a built-in counter which recorded the number of times that he voluntarily stimulated each of several selected points in his brain during a period of seventeen weeks. The highest score was recorded from one point in the septal region, and the patient declared that pushing this particular button made him feel "good" as if he were building up to a sexual orgasm, although he was not able to reach the end point and often felt impatient and anxious. His narcolepsia was greatly relieved by pressing this "septal button." Another patient with psychomotor epilepsy also enjoyed septal self-stimulation, which again had the highest rate of button pressing and often induced sexual thoughts. Activation of the septal region by direct injection of acetylcholine produced local electrical changes in two epileptic patients and a shift in mood from disphoria to contentment and euphoria, usually with concomitant sexual motivation and some "orgastic sensations."

Further information was provided by another group of sixty-five patients suffering from schizophrenia or Parkinson's disease, in whom a total of 643 contacts were implanted, mainly in the anterior part of the brain (201). Results of ESB were grouped as follows: 360 points were "Positive I," and with stimulation "the patients became relaxed, at ease, had a feeling of well-being, and/or were a little sleepy." Another 31 points were "Positive II," and "the patients were definitely changed . . . in a good mood, felt good. They were relaxed, at ease, and enjoyed themselves, frequently smiling. There was a slight euphoria, but the behavior was adequate." They sometimes wanted more stimulations. Excitation of another eight points evoked behavior classified as "Positive III," when "the euphoria was definitely beyond normal limits. The patients laughed out loud, enjoyed themselves, and positively liked the stimulation, and wanted more." ESB of another 38 points gave ambivalent results, and the patients expressed occasional pleasure or displeasure following excitation of the same area. From three other points, responses were termed "orgasm" because the patients initially expressed enjoyment and then suddenly were completely satisfied and did not want any more stimulation for a variable period of time. Finally, from about two hundred other points, ESB produced unpleasant reactions including anxiety, sadness, depression, fear, and emotional outbursts. One of the moving pictures taken in this study was very demonstrative, showing a patient with a sad expression and slightly depressed mood who smiled when a brief stimulation was applied to the rostral part of the brain, returning quickly to his usual depressed state, to smile again as soon as stimulation was reapplied. Then a ten-second stimulation completely changed his behavior and facial expression into a lasting pleasant and happy mood. Some mental patients have been provided with portable stimulators which they have used in self-treatment of depressive states with apparent clinical success.

These results indicate the need for careful functional exploration during brain surgery in order to avoid excessive euphoria or depression when positive or negative reinforcing areas are damaged. Emotional instability, in which the subject bursts suddenly into tears or laughter without any apparent reason, has been observed following some neurosurgical interventions. These major behavior problems might have been avoided by sparing the region involved in emotional regulation.

In our own experience, pleasurable sensations were observed in three patients with psychomotor epilepsy (50, 58, 109). The first case was V.P., a 36-year-old female with a long history of epileptic attacks which could not be controlled by medication.

Electrodes were implanted in her right temporal lobe and upon stimulation of a contact located in the superior part about thirty millimeters below the surface, the patient reported a pleasant tingling sensation in the left side of her body "from my face down to the bottom of my legs." She started giggling and making funny comments, stating that she enjoyed the sensation "very much." Repetition of these stimulations made the patient more communicative and flirtatious, and she ended by openly expressing her desire to marry the therapist. Stimulation of other cerebral points failed to modify her mood and indicated the specificity of the evoked effect. During control interviews before and after ESB, her behavior was quite proper, without familiarity or excessive friendliness.

The second patient was J.M., an attractive, cooperative, and intelligent 30-year-old female who had suffered for eleven years from psychomotor and grand mal attacks which resisted medical therapy. Electrodes were implanted in her right temporal lobe, and stimulation of one of the points in the amygdala induced a pleasant sensation of relaxation and considerably increased her verbal output, which took on a more intimate character. This patient openly expressed her fondness for the therapist (who was new to her), kissed his hands, and talked about her immense gratitude for what was being done for her. A similar increase in verbal and emotional expression was repeated when the same point was stimulated on a different day, but it did not appear when other areas of the brain were explored. During control situations the patient was rather reserved and poised.

The third case was A.F., an 11-year-old boy with severe psychomotor epilepsy. Six days after electrode implantation in both temporal lobes, his fourth tape-recorded interview was carried out while electrical activity of the brain was continuously recorded and 5-second stimulations were applied in a prearranged sequence at intervals of about four minutes. The interviewer maintained an air of friendly interest throughout, usually without initiating conversation. After six other excitations, point LP located on the surface of the left temporal lobe was stimulated for the first time, and there was an open and precipitous declaration of pleasure. The patient had been silent for the previous five-minute interval, but immediately after this stimulation he exclaimed, "Hey! You can keep me here longer when you give me these; I like those." He went on to insist that the ongoing brain tests made him feel good. Similar statements with an emphatic expression of "feeling good" followed eight of a total sixteen stimulations of this point during the ninety-minute interview. Several of these manifestations were accompanied by a statement of fondness for the male interviewer, and the last one was accompanied by a voluptuous stretch. None of these manifestations appeared during the control prestimulation period of twenty-six minutes or during the twenty-two minutes when other points were excited. Statistical analysis of the difference between the frequency of pleasurable expressions before and after onset of stimulations proved that results were highly significant ($P < 0.001$).

The open expressions of pleasure in this interview and the general passivity of behavior could be linked, more or less intuitively, to feminine strivings. It was therefore remarkable that in the next interview, performed in a similar manner, the patient's expressions of confusion about his own sexual identity again appeared following stimulation of point LP. He suddenly began to discuss his desire to get married, but when asked, "To whom?" he did not immediately reply. Following stimulation of another point and a one-minute, twenty-second silence, the patient said, "I was thinking—there's—I was saying *this* to you. How to spell 'yes'—y-e-s. I mean y-o-s. No! 'You' ain't y-e-o. It's this. *Y-o-u*." The topic was then completely dropped. The monitor who was listening from the next room interpreted this as a thinly veiled wish to marry the interviewer, and it was decided to stimulate the same site again after the prearranged schedule had been completed. During the following forty minutes, seven other points were stimulated, and the patient spoke about several topics of a completely different and unrelated content. Then LP was stimulated again, and the patient started making references to the facial hair of the interviewer and continued by mentioning pubic hair and his having been the object of genital sex play in the past. He then expressed doubt about his sexual identity, saying, "I was thinkin' if I was a boy or a girl—which one I'd like to be." Following another excitation he remarked with evident pleasure: "You're doin' it now," and then he said, "I'd like to be a girl."

In the interpretation of these results it is necessary to consider the psychological context in which electrical stimulation occurs, because the personality configuration of the subject, including both current psychodynamic and psychogenetic aspects, may be an essential determinant of the results of stimulation. Expression of feminine strivings in our patient probably was not the exclusive effect of ESB but the expression of already present personality factors which were activated by the stimulation. The balance between drive and defense may be modified by ESB, as suggested by the fact that after one stimulation the patient said without apparent anxiety, "I'd like to be a girl," but when this idea was presented to him by the therapist in a later interview without stimulation, the patient became markedly anxious and defensive. Minute-to-minute changes in personality function, influenced by the environment and by patient-interviewer relations, may modify the nature of specific responses, and these variables, which are difficult to assess, must be kept in mind.

### Friendliness and Increased Conversation Under Electrical Control

Human relations evolve between the two opposite poles of love and hate which are determined by a highly complex and little understood combination of elements including basic drives, cultural imprinting, and refined emotional and intellectual characteristics. This subject has so many semantic and conceptual problems that few investigators have dared to approach it experimentally, and in spite of its essential importance, most textbooks of psychology evade its discussion. To define friend-liness is difficult although its identification in typical cases is easy, and in our daily life we are continuously evaluating and classifying personal contacts as friendly or hostile. A smiling face, attentive eyes, a receptive hand, related body posture, in-tellectual interest, ideological agreement, kind words, sympa-thetic comments, and expressions of personal acceptance are among the common indicators of cordial interpersonal relations. The expression of friendship is a part of social behavior which obviously requires contact between two or more individuals. A mutually pleasurable relation creates a history and provides each individual with a variety of optic, acoustic, tactile, and other stimuli which are received and interpreted with a "friendly bias." The main characteristic of love and friendship is precisely that stimuli coming from a favored person are interpreted as more agreeable than similar stimuli originating from other sources, and this evaluation is necessarily related to neuronal activity.

Little is known about the cerebral mechanisms of friendliness, but as is the case for any behavorial manifestation, no emotional state is possible without a functioning brain, and it may be postulated that some cerebral structures are dispensable and others indispensable both for the interpretation of sensory in-puts as amicable and for the expression of friendship. Strong support for this idea derives from the fact, repeatedly proved in neurosurgery, that destruction of some parts of the brain, such as the motor and sensory cortices, produces motor deficits with-out modifying affective behavior, while ablation of the frontal lobes may induce considerable alteration of emotional per-sonality. Further support has been provided by electrical stim-ulation of the frontal lobes, which may induce friendly mani-festations.

In patient A. F., mentioned earlier in connection with pleas-urable manifestations, the third interview was characterized by changes in the character and degree of verbal output following stimulation of one point in the temporal cortex. Fourteen stimulations were applied, seven of them through point RP located in the inferolateral part of the right frontal lobe cortex, and the other seven through contacts located on the cortex of the right temporal lobe and depth of the left and right temporal lobes. The interview started with about five minutes of lively conversation, and during the next ten minutes the patient gradually quieted down until he spoke only about five seconds during every subsequent two-minute period. Throughout the interview the therapist encouraged spontaneous expression by reacting compassionately, by joking with, urging, and reassuring the patient, and by responding to any information offered. The attitude never produced more than a simple reply and often not even that.

In contrast to this basic situation, there were six instances of sharp increase in verbal communication and its friendly content. Each of these instances followed within forty seconds after stimulation of point RP. The only exception was the last excitation of this point when the voltage had been changed. The increases in verbal activity were rapid but brief and without any consistency in subject material, which was typical for the patient. Qualification and quantification of the patient's conversation was made by analyzing the recorded typescript which was divided into two-minute periods and judged independently by two investigators who had no knowledge of the timing or location of stimulations. Comparison of the two-minute periods before and after these stimulations revealed a verbal increase from seventeen to eighty-eight words and a greater number of friendly remarks, from six to fifty-three. These results were highly significant and their specificity was clear because no changes in verbalization were produced by stimulation of any of the other cerebral points. It was also evident that the evoked changes were not related to the interviewer's rather constant verbal activity. It was therefore concluded that the impressive increase in verbal expression and friendly remarks was the result of electrical stimulation of a specific point on the cortex of the temporal lobe.

# 15

# Hallucinations, Recollections, and Illusions in Man

Hallucinations may be defined as false perceptions in the absence of peripheral sensory stimulation, and they probably depend on two processes: (1) the recollection of stored information and (2) its false interpretation as an extrinsic experience entering through sensory inputs. Very little is known about the cerebral mechanisms responsible for these phenomena, but apparently the frontotemporal region of the brain is somehow involved because its electrical stimulation may evoke hallucinations.

In some patients electrical stimulation of the exposed temporal lobe has produced the perception of music. Occasionally it was a determined tune which could be recognized and hummed by the subject, and in some cases it was as if a radio or record were being played in the operating room. The sound did not seem to be a recollection but resembled an actual experience in which instruments of an orchestra or words of a song were heard (174). These artificially induced hallucinations were not static but unfolded slowly while the electrode was held in place. A song was heard from beginning to end and not all at once; in a dream, familiar places were seen and well-known people spoke and acted.

Like spontaneous memories, the recollections induced by ESB could bring back the emotions felt at the time of the original experience, suggesting that neuronal mechanisms keep an integrated record of the past, including all the sensory inputs (visual, auditory, proprioceptive, etc.) and also the emotional significance of events. Electrical stimulation activated only one memory without reawakening any of the other records which must be stored in close proximity. This fact suggests the existence of cerebral mechanisms of reciprocal inhibition which allow the orderly recall of specific patterns of memory without a flood of unmanageable amounts of stored information. In no case has brain stimulation produced two psychical experiences at the same time, and the responses have been on an all-or-nothing basis.

In one of our patients, complex sensory hallucinations were evoked on different days when the depth of the tip of the left temporal lobe was electrically stimulated. The patient said, "You know, I just felt funny, just now. . . . Right then all of a sudden somethin' else came to me—these people—the way this person talked. This married couple—as though the fellow came into my mind—as though like he was saying somethin' like oh my mind drifted for a minute—to somethin' foolish. . . . It seemed like he was coming out with some word—sayin' some word silly."

The fact that stimulation of the temporal lobe can induce complex hallucinations may be considered well established, and this type of research represents a significant interaction between neurophysiology and psychoanalysis (133). The mechanism of the evoked hallucinations, however, is far from clear, and it is difficult to know whether the experiences are new creations based on the recombination of items from memory storage and thus equivalent to psychotic hallucinations, or if the experiences are simply an exact playback of the past.

In either case, the applied electricity is not "creating" a new phenomenon but is triggering the orderly appearance at the conscious level of materials from the past, mixed in some cases with present perceptions. The order in the stream of perceived information is perhaps one of the most interesting qualities of this behavior because it indicates something about the mechanisms for storage of information in the brain. Memory does not seem to be preserved as single items but as interrelated collections of events, like the pearls on a string, and by pulling any pearl we have access to the whole series in perfect order. If memory were organized in this way, it would be similar to the strings of amino acids forming molecules of proteins and carrying genetic messages. Electrical stimulation may increase general neuronal excitability; and the memory traces which at this moment have a lower threshold may consequently be reactivated, reaching the perceptual level and forming the content of the hallucinatory experience while exerting a reciprocal inhibitory influence upon other traces. The excitability of individual traces may be modified by environmental factors and especially by the ideological content of the patient's thoughts prior to stimulation. Thus electrical excitation of the same point may produce a series of thematically related hallucinatory experiences with different specific details, as was the case in the patients that we have investigated.

All sensory inputs suffer distortion during the normal process of personal interpretation, which is determined to a great extent by past experience and depends heavily on cultural factors. A baby looking at the moon may extend his arms in an attempt to catch it without realizing the remoteness of celestial bodies. By comparing past and present experiences, we learn to evaluate distance, size, intensity, and other qualities of inputs. The mechanisms for these evaluations do not seem to be genetically determined and are related to neuronal activity which may be influenced by direct stimulation of the brain. We must remember that our only way to be in touch with external reality is by transducing physical and chemical events of the surroundings into electrical and chemical sequences at the sensory receptor level. The brain is not in touch with the environmental reality but with its symbolic code transmitted by neuronal pathways. Within this frame of personal distortion, our lives evolve within a range of "normality." Beyond this range, the distortion of perceptions qualifies as illusion. Illusions occur in a wide variety of regressed mental states, during moments of keen anticipation, and as a primary manifestation in some epileptic discharges. An hallucination is a false perception in the absence of sensory inputs, while an illusion requires an external sensory source which is misinterpreted by the individual. This distinction is convenient, and it will be observed in our discussion, although in practice the terms often overlap.

The following phenomena have been observed in patients: (1) illusions (visual, auditory, labyrinthine, memory or déjà vu, sensation of remoteness or unreality), (2) emotions (loneliness, fear, sadness), (3) psychical hallucinations (vivid memory or a dream as complex as life experience itself), and (4) forced thinking (stereotyped thoughts crowding into the mind). The first three groups of phenomena have been induced by different intracerebral stimulations. The most commonly reported effect has been the illusion of familiarity or déjà vu, which is characterized by surprise, interruption of conversation, and immediate spontaneous reporting that something unusual had just happened. For example, after a stimulation in the inferolateral part of the frontal lobe, one patient began to reply to the interviewer's question but suddenly stopped and said, "I was thinkin' —it felt like someone else was asking me that before." Occasionally a previously initiated statement would be completed, but there was always an overt desire to express the perceived experience. The effect was clearly felt as intrusive although not disturbing. After several of these experiences, the patient recognized the special quality of the phenomena and said, for example, "Hey—I had another strike. I have a feeling that someone once told me that before." The reliability of the response was remarkable, as was the consistency of its reporting, which was spontaneous and in most cases unsolicited. Each instance consisted usually of a reference to a remark made by the patient or the observer just before or during the moment of stimulation. The ideational content of the déjà vu was therefore dissimilar following each stimulation, but it always referred to the theme of the ongoing conversation.

The common feature was the sensation, expressed by the patient, that the words, ideas, or situation were similar to a previous experience. There was no new perception, only the interpretation of a novel input as one already known and familiar. There was no anxiety or fear in the perception of these illusions, and the apparent effect was one of interested surprise with a rather pleasant, amusing quality which made the patient more alert and communicative. He was eager to report that something similar had happened before, and the word "before" was used in reporting most of these incidents. No lasting traces could be detected, and after the sensation of familiarity had been expressed, the patient's behavior continued in the same vein as before stimulation.

Knowledge of the cerebral mechanisms of psychic activities is so elemental that it would not be wise to speculate about the neuronal causality of illusions of familiarity. However, the fact that they may be elicited with reliability indicates the probable existence of interpretive functions in a determined area of the brain and opens the way for further experimental studies of how sensory inputs are processed by the individual. Penfield supposes that the cortex of the temporal lobe has a ganglionic mechanism which is utilized in the personal assessment of experiential reality regarding distance, sound, sight, intensity, strangeness, or familiarity of sensory inputs. This mechanism would be relatively independent from the mechanism utilized in the recording of contemporary experience and could be affected by epileptic abnormality or by direct brain stimulation. If we accept this hypothesis, we may assume that artificial influencing of electrical and chemical neuronal physiology could play a decisive role in the interpretation of reality with some independence from past experience and personal structure.

# 16

# Inhibitory Effects in Animals and Man

The existence of inhibitory functions in the central nervous system was described in the last century by Sechenov (198), Pavlov (171), and other founders of Russian psychology. Inhibition is a well-known phenomenon, and it has been the main theme of several recent symposiums (14, 63, 77). In spite of its importance, information about inhibitory mechanisms has not yet been integrated into the general body of scientific knowledge, and no chapter is devoted to this subject in most neurophysiological, psychological, and pharmacological textbooks. This lack of interest is surprising because as Morgan (158) wrote eighty years ago, "When physiologists have solved the problem of inhibition they will be in a position to consider that of volition," and modern investigators maintain that inhibition and choice, rather than expression and learning, are the central problems of psychology (63). A shift in interest among scientists seems necessary to give inhibition its deserved importance, and the layman should also be aware of the decisive role of inhibition in the performance of most of our daily activities.

The sound of a theater crowd at intermission is a continuous roar without intelligible meaning. During the performance, however, noises and individual conversations must be inhibited so that the voices of the actors can be heard. The brain is like a monumental theater with many millions of neurons capable of sending messages simultaneously and in many directions. Most of these neurons are firing nearly continuously, and their sensitivity is like that of an enormous synaptic powder barrel which would explode in epileptic convulsions in the absence of inhibitory elements (122). During the organized performance of behavioral responses, most neurons and pathways must remain silent to allow meaningful orders to circulate toward specific goals. Inhibition is as important as excitation for the normal physiology of the brain, and some structures have specialized inhibitory functions. It should therefore be expected that, in addition to inducing the many types of activities described in previous sections, ESB can also block performance of such activities by exciting pools of neurons whose role is to inhibit these specific responses.

To behave is to choose one pattern among many. To think we must proceed in some orderly fashion repressing unrelated ideas; to talk we must select a sequence of appropriate words; and to listen we need to extract certain information from background noise. As stated by Ashby, we must "dispose once and for all of the idea . . . that the more communication there is within the brain the better" (6). As we know by personal experience, one of the problems of modern civilization is the confusion produced by a barrage of sensory inputs. We are optically and acoustically assaulted by scientific literature, news media, propaganda, and advertisements. The defense is to inhibit the processing of sensory stimuli. Conscious and unconscious behavioral inhibition should not be considered passive processes but active restraints, like holding the reins of a powerful horse, which prevent the disorderly display of existing energies and potentialities.

Within the central nervous system, the reticular formation seems to be especially differentiated to modulate or inhibit the reception of sensory impulses, and some other cerebral structures including the thalamus, septum, and caudate nucleus also possess important inhibitory properties which can be activated by ESB. Three types of inhibitory processes may be induced by electrical stimulation: (1) sleep, which usually starts slowly and can easily be interrupted by sensory stimuli; (2) general inhibition, which affects the whole body, starts as soon as ESB is applied, and persists in spite of sensory stimulation; and (3) specific inhibition, which appears immediately, affects only a determined pattern of behavior such as aggression or food intake, and may or may not be modified by sensory impulses.

One example of sleep induced in a monkey by application of ESB is shown in Figure 18. After 30 seconds of stimulation in the septal area, the animal's eyes started closing, his head lowered, his body relaxed, and he seemed to fall into a natural state of sleep. In response to noise or to being touched, the animal would slowly open his eyes and look around with a dull expression for a few seconds before falling asleep again. Similar results have been obtained in free-ranging monkeys stimulated by radio. In this situation there was a gradual diminution of spontaneous activity, and then the animals began to doze, closing their eyes and assuming a typical sleeping posture with heads down and bodies curved over the knees. Theoretically it should be possible to treat chronic insomnia by brain stimulation, or to establish an artificial biological clock of rest and activity by means of programed stimulation of inhibitory and excitatory areas of the brain, but these challenging possibilities still require further investigations.

Motor arrest is an impressive effect consisting of sudden immobilization of the experimental animal in the middle of ongoing activities, which continue as soon as stimulation is over. It is as if a motion picture projector had been stopped, freezing the subjects in the position in which they were caught. A cat lapping milk has been immobilized with its tongue out, and a cat climbing stairs has been stopped between two steps.

Other types of inhibitory effects are more specific and restricted to only one determined behavioral category. Typical examples are the inhibition of food intake, aggressiveness, territoriality, and maternal behavior. As these specific inhibitions do not influence general activities, they could pass unnoticed if the experimental situation was not properly arranged. Obviously inhibition of appetite cannot be demonstrated in the

*Figure 18*
Sleep induced by electrical stimulation of the brain is similar to spontaneous sleep. Above, control. Below, the monkey falls asleep under ESB.

absence of food, nor can changes in maternal behavior be investigated when no babies are present. One example of how a hungry monkey loses appetite under the influence of brain excitation is presented in Figure 19. At the sight of a banana, the animal usually shows great interest, leaning forward to take the fruit, which he eats voraciously and with evident pleasure. However, his appetite is immediately inhibited as soon as the caudate nucleus is electrically stimulated. Then the monkey looks with some interest at the banana without reaching for it, and may even turn his face away, clearly expressing refusal. During stimulation the animal is well aware of his surroundings, reacting normally to noises, moving objects, and threats, but he is just not interested in food. If a monkey is stimulated when his mouth is full of banana, he immediately stops chewing, takes the banana out of his mouth, and throws it away.

Close to the hunger inhibitory area there is a region which is involved in inhibition of aggressive behavior. When this part of the caudate nucleus is stimulated (Figure 20), the normally ferocious macacus rhesus becomes tranquil, and instead of grabbing, scratching, and biting any approaching object, he sits peacefully and the investigator can safely touch his mouth and pet him. During this time the animal is aware of the environment but has simply lost his usual irritability, showing that violence can be inhibited without making the animal sleepy or depressed. Identification of the cerebral areas responsible for ferocity would make it possible to block their function and diminish undesirable aggressiveness without disturbing general behavioral reactivity.

Similar results have been obtained in chimpanzees, and one example is presented in Figure 21. Chimpanzee Carlos was an affectionate animal who enjoyed playing with the investigators and had learned a variety of tricks including throwing and catching a ball. Enticed by an expected food reward, he sat voluntarily in the restraining chair where recordings and experiments were conducted. Like most chimpanzees, Carlos was

*Figure 19*
The normal reaction of a monkey is to stretch its arms and body to take an offered banana (above left). Appetite is immediately inhibited by stimulation of the caudate nucleus (below left). The monkey is not interested in food (above) and even turns away from the fruit (53). *Photo: Eric Schaal.*

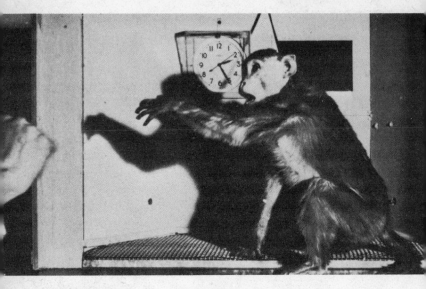

*Figure 20*

Rhesus monkeys are usually ferocious and will often launch attacks, trying to catch and bite the observers (above). This ferocity is inhibited during stimulation of the caudate nucleus, and then (below) it is safe to touch the animal, which extends its arm to meet the observer's hand without making any threatening gestures (53).

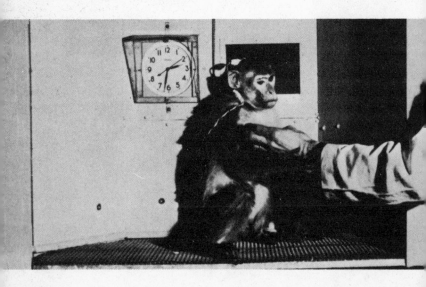

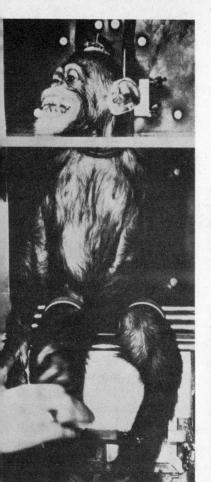

*Figure 21*

Chimpanzee Carlos reacts with offensive-defensive manifestations when touched by a stranger (left). During caudate stimulation, the chimpanzee is inhibited and can be teased without evoking any response.

rather temperamental and was easily provoked into a tantrum by being punished, frustrated, or merely teased. He liked to be touched by people he knew but not by strangers. Figure 21 (*left*) shows his defensive, anxious reaction when approached by an unfamiliar investigator. His fear and aggressive manifestations were, however, completely inhibited during electrical stimulation of the caudate nucleus, as shown in Figure 21 (*right*). The animal displayed no emotion, appeared peaceful, and could be teased without any resulting disturbance.

Other experiments in monkeys have also confirmed the pacifying possibilities of ESB. In the autocratic social structure of a monkey colony the boss enjoys a variety of privileges such as choosing female partners, feeding first, displacing other animals, and occupying most of the cage while the other monkeys avoid his proximity and crowd together in a far corner (see Figure 22). This hierarchical position is maintained by subtle communication of gestures and postures: a boss may look directly at a submissive member of the group who will glance only furtively at his superior, and the boss may paw the floor and threaten by opening his mouth or uttering a warning cry if any low-ranking animal does not keep a suitable distance. This social dominance has been abolished by stimulation applied for 5 seconds once a minute for one hour to the caudate nucleus in the boss monkey. During this period the animal's facial expression appeared more peaceful both to the investigator and to the other animals, who started to circulate freely around the cage without observing their usual respect. They actually ignored the boss, crowding around him without fear. During the stimulation hour, the boss's territoriality completely disappeared, his walking time diminished, and he performed no threatening or aggressive acts against other monkeys in the colony. It was evident that this change in behavior had been determined by brain stimulation because about ten minutes after ESB was discontinued, the boss had reasserted his authority and the other animals feared him as before. His territoriality was as well established as during control periods, and he enjoyed his customary privileges.

*Figure 22*

Monkey colonies form autocratic societies in which the territoriality of the boss is clearly shown. He occupies more than half of the cage (above). Radio stimulation of an inhibitory area of the brain (below) modifies the boss's facial expression, and the other monkeys crowd fearlessly around the former boss in his own corner.

The old dream of an individual overpowering the strength of a dictator by remote control has been fulfilled, at least in our monkey colonies, by a combination of neurosurgery and electronics, demonstrating the possibility of intraspecies instrumental manipulation of hierarchical organization. As shown in Figure 23, a monkey named Ali, who was the powerful and ill-tempered chief of a colony, often expressed his hostility symbolically by biting his hand or by threatening other members of the group. Radio stimulation in Ali's caudate nucleus blocked his usual aggressiveness so effectively that the animal could be caught inside the cage without danger or difficulty. During stimulation he might walk a few steps, but he never attempted to attack another animal. Then a lever was attached to the cage wall, and if it was pressed, it automatically triggered a five seconds' radio stimulation of Ali. From time to time some of the submissive monkeys touched the lever, which was located close to the feeding tray, triggering the stimulation of Ali. A female monkey named Elsa soon discovered that Ali's aggressiveness could be inhibited by pressing the lever, and when Ali threatened her, it was repeatedly observed that Elsa responded by lever pressing. Her attitude of looking straight at the boss was highly significant because a submissive monkey would not dare to do so, for fear of immediate retaliation. The total number of Ali's aggressive acts diminished on the days when the lever was available, and although Elsa did not become the dominant animal, she was responsible for blocking many attacks against herself and for maintaining a peaceful coexistence within the whole colony.

Appeasement of instinctive aggressiveness has also been demonstrated in an animal species which for generations has been bred to increase its ferocious behavior: the brave bull. Some races of bulls have been genetically selected for their aggressive behavior just as others have been bred for farm work or meat supply. Brave bulls are stronger and more agile than their tamer relatives, and these differences in appearance and behavior must be supported at the neurophysiological level by different

*Figure 23*

Above, Ali, the boss of the colony, expresses his ill temper by biting his own hand. Below, a submissive monkey, Elsa, has learned to press a lever which triggers radio stimulation of Ali, inhibiting his aggressive behavior (51).

mechanisms of responses. The sight of a person, which is neutral for a tame bull, will trigger a deadly attack in a brave one. If we could detect functional differences in the brains of these two breeds we could discover some clues about the neurological basis of aggression. This was the reason for implanting electrodes in the brains of several bulls. After surgery, different cerebral points were explored by radio stimulation while the animal was free in a small farm ring. Motor effects similar to those observed in cats and monkeys were evoked, including head turning, lifting of one leg, and circling. Vocalizations were often elicited, and in one experiment to test the reliability of results, a point was stimulated 100 times and 100 consecutive "moo's" were evoked.

It was also repeatedly demonstrated that cerebral stimulation produced inhibition of aggressive behavior, and a bull in full charge could be abruptly stopped, as shown in Figure 24. The result seemed to be a combination of motor effect, forcing the bull to stop and to turn to one side, plus behavioral inhibition of the aggressive drive. Upon repeated stimulation, these animals were rendered less dangerous than usual, and for a period of several minutes would tolerate the presence of investigators in the ring without launching any attack.

Maternal behavior is one of the instincts most widely shared by mammals, and a baby rhesus monkey enjoys the first months of his life resting in the arms of the mother, who spends most of her time hugging, nursing, grooming, and taking care of him. If the pair are forcibly separated, the mother becomes very disturbed and expresses her anxiety by prowling about restlessly, threatening observers, and calling to her baby with a special cooing sound. It is promptly reciprocated by the little one, who is also extremely anxious to return to the protective maternal embrace. This strong bond can be inhibited by ESB, as demonstrated in one of our colonies, consisting of Rose and Olga with their respective babies, Roo and Ole, plus a male monkey. Maternal affection was expressed as usual without being handicapped by the presence of electrodes implanted in both females (Figure 25). Several simple motor effects evoked by ESB (such as head turning or flexion of the arm) did not disrupt mother-infant relations, but when a 10-second radio stimulation was applied to the mesencephalon of Rose, an aggressive attitude was evoked with rapid circling around the cage and self-biting of the hand, leg, or flank. For the next eight to ten minutes, maternal instinct was disrupted, and Rose completely lost interest in her baby, ignoring his tender calls and rejecting his attempts to approach her. Little Roo looked rather disoriented and sought refuge and warmth with the other mother, Olga, who accepted both babies without hesitation. About ten minutes after ESB, Rose regained her natural maternal behavior and accepted Roo in her arms. This experiment was repeated several times on different days with similar disruptive results for the mother-infant relation. It should be concluded, therefore, that maternal behavior is somehow dependent on the proper functioning of mesencephalic structures and that short ESB applied in this area is able to block the maternal instinct for a period of several minutes.

Information about inhibitory effects induced by electrical stimulation of the human brain is more limited than our knowledge about inhibition in animals. The subject has great importance, however, because one of the primary aims of human therapy is to inhibit undesirable sensations or excessive neuronal activities. Some patients experience a type of "intractable pain" which cannot be alleviated by the usual analgesic drugs, and their unbearable suffering could be blocked by direct intervention in brain structures where sensations reach the perceptual level of consciousness. Illnesses such as Parkinson's disease and chorea are characterized by continuous involuntary movements maintained by neuronal discharges originating in specific cerebral structures which could be inhibited by suitable therapy. Assaultive behavior constitutes one of the most disturbing symptoms of a group of mental illnesses and is probably related to the abnormal reactivity of limbic and reticular areas of the brain. Epilepsy is caused by explosive bursts of electrical dis-

*Figure 24*
Brave bulls are dangerous animals which will attack any intruder into the arena. The animal in full charge can be abruptly stopped (above) by radio stimulation of the brain. After several stimulations, there is a lasting inhibition of aggressive behavior.

*Figure 25*
Above, maternal behavior is tenderly expressed by both mother monkeys, Rose and Olga, who hug, groom, and nurse their babies, Roo and Ole. Below, radio stimulation of Rose for ten seconds in the mesencephalon

evoked a rage response expressed by self-biting and abandoning her baby, Roo. For the next ten minutes Rose has lost all her maternal interest (above), ignoring the appealing calls of Roo who seeks refuge with the other mother. Below, Rose is sucking her foot and still ignoring her baby.

charges which might be inhibited at their original source. Anxiety poses very difficult therapeutic problems, and its basic mechanism might be traced to the increased reactivity of specific areas of the brain. All these disturbances could be cured, or at least diminished, if we had a better knowledge of their anatomical and functional bases and could inhibit the activity of neurons responsible for the phenomena.

In the near future, important advances may be expected in this field, and already we have some initial clinical information demonstrating that ESB can induce inhibitory effects in man. For example, ESB applied to the supplementary motor cortex has slowed down or completely arrested voluntary motor activity without producing pain or any concomitant loss of consciousness (174). In other cases, stimulation of the frontotemporal region has caused an "arrest response" characterized by sudden cessation of voluntary movements which may be followed by confusion, inappropriate or garbled speech, and overt changes of mood (128, 186). More interesting from the therapeutic point of view is the fact that abnormal hyperkinetic movements have been inhibited for the duration of the applied ESB, allowing patients to perform skilled acts which were otherwise impossible. In these cases, a small portable instrument could perhaps be used by the patient to stimulate his own brain in order to inhibit abnormal motility temporarily and restore useful skills (160).

Somnolence with inexpressive faces, tendency to lower the eyelids, and spontaneous complaint of sleepiness, but without impairment of consciousness, has been produced in some patients by stimulation of the fornix and thalamus (7, 199). In some cases, sleep with pleasant dreams has been induced, and occasionally sleep or awakening could be obtained from the same cerebral point by using a slow or high frequency of stimulation (96, 229). Diminished awareness, lack of normal insight, and impairment of ability to think have been observed by several investigators during excitation of different points of the limbic system (74, 120). Often the patients performed automatisms such as undressing or fumbling, without remembering the incidents afterward. Some of our patients said they felt as if their minds were blank or as if they had been drinking a lot of beer. These results indicate that consciousness may be related to specific mechanisms located in determined areas of the brain. They contrast with the full awareness preserved when other areas of the brain were stimulated.

Arrest of speech has been most common of all inhibitory effects observed during electrical stimulation of the human brain (8), and this fact is probably due to the extensive representation of the speech areas in the temporal lobe, and also to the facility of exploring verbal expression just by conversing with the patients. The most typical effect is cessation of counting. For example, one of our female patients was asked to count numbers, starting from one. When she had counted to fourteen, ESB was applied, and speech was immediately interrupted, without changes in respiration or in facial expression, and without producing fear or anxiety. When stimulation ceased seconds later, the patient immediately resumed counting. She said that she did not know why she had stopped; although she had heard the interviewer encouraging her to continue, she had been unable to speak. If the same stimulation was applied while the patient was silent, no effect could be detected by the observer or by the patient herself. In other cases, patients have been able to read and comprehend or to write messages that they were temporarily unable to verbalize (200).

It is known that ESB activation of pleasurable areas of the brain can inhibit pain perception in animals (42, 146), and similar results have also been reported in man, with an immediate relief of pain following septal stimulation (98). Because of the multiplicity of pathways in the nervous system which can transmit disagreeable sensations, it is often not possible to block all of them, and to alleviate unbearable suffering it may be easier to inhibit the cerebral structures involved in the psychological evaluation of pain, blocking the components of anxiety and diminishing the subjective sensation of unpleasantness.

There are also a few reports indicating that abnormal violence may be reduced by ESB: Heath has a movie showing a patient who self-stimulated his own brain in order to suppress an aggressive mood as it developed, and we have described a case in whom crises of antisocial conduct during which the patient attacked members of his own family were considerably diminished by repeated stimulations of the amygdaloid nucleus (60).

We are only at the beginning of our experimental understanding of the inhibitory mechanisms of behavior in animals and man, but their existence has already been well substantiated. It is clear that manifestations as important as aggressive responses depend not only on environmental circumstances but also on their interpretation by the central nervous system where they can be enhanced or totally inhibited by manipulating the reactivity of specific intracerebral structures.

Violence, including its extreme manifestation of war, is determined by a variety of economic and ideological factors; but we must realize that the elite who make the decisions, and even the individual who obeys orders and holds a rifle, require for their behavioral performance the existence of a series of intracerebral electrical signals which could be inhibited by other conflicting signals generating in areas such as the caudate nucleus. Inhibitory areas of the central nervous system can be activated by electrical stimulation as well as by the physiological impact of sensory inputs which carry messages, ideas, and patterned behavior. Reception of information from the environment causes electrical and chemical changes in the brain substance, and the stimuli shape the functional characteristics of individual interpretation and integration, determining the degree and quality of his reactions. Human relations are not going to be governed by electrodes, but they could be better understood if we considered not only environmental factors but also the intracerebral mechanisms responsible for their reception and elaboration.

Part IV

# EVALUATION OF
# ELECTRICAL CONTROL
# OF THE BRAIN

Because the brain controls the whole body and all mental activities, ESB could possibly become a master control of human behavior by means of man-made plans and instruments. In previous sections we have described methodology for brain stimulation and many effects evoked by ESB. This section will discuss the meaning of these results, the mechanisms involved, the expected limitations, and the problems facing investigators. How physiological or artificial is the electrical activation of neurons? How predictable? Who is responsible for acts performed under ESB—the stimulated subject or the scientist? Which benefits or risks may be expected in the future? Can we modulate perception and expression by electrical means? Can we expect that brain investigation will provide a new conception of the human mind? These and other questions confront the investigator while he is sending radio messages to induce a muscle to contract, a heart to beat faster, or a sensation to be felt. Evaluation of these experiments requires the formulation of appropriate theoretical concepts and the design of working hypotheses.

# 17

# Brain Stimulation Triggers Physiological
# Mechanisms

Electrical stimulation of the brain is in reality a rather crude technique based on the delivery of a monotonous train of pulses without modulation, without code, without specific meaning, and without feedback to the pool of neurons which by chance is located within the artificial electrical field created by stimulation. Temporal and spatial characteristics and the complexity of multisynaptic relays, delays, and convergent and divergent correlations are also absent. The intensity of several volts usually employed in ESB is hundreds of times higher than spontaneous neuronal potentials, which are measured in millivolts.

It is reasonable, therefore, that doubts have been expressed about the normality of responses obtained by brain stimulation. It is difficult to compare normal behavior with electrically evoked effects, considering the complications of operative trauma, artificiality of experimental conditions, and lack of specificity of ESB (4). "Electrical stimulus, unlike physiological excitation, unselectively affects all elements of a similar threshold that lie within the radius of action of the electrodes" (107), and in the majority of cases cortical stimulation "has failed to elicit anything but fragments of skilled movements" (224). Cobb (33) considers the greatest oversimplification the belief "among those not educated in physiology, that the electrical stimulation of a nerve or brain center closely resembles normal neuronal stimulation. Electrical stimulation, however, produces little that resembles the normal."

It is certainly true that many responses evoked by ESB are simple contractions of a small group of muscles without coordination, skill, or apparent purpose, and that many effects have abnormal characteristics far removed from the harmonious elegance of voluntary activities. It is also true, however, that with the development of technology to stimulate the brain in free subjects, many of the responses obtained in both animals and man are indistinguishable from spontaneous behavior. Sequential behavior, sexual activity, alimentary responses, walking, yawning, fighting, and many other effects documented in previous sections demonstrate conclusively that ESB can evoke purposeful, well-coordinated, skillful activities of great refinement and complexity. Patients have accepted evoked psychological changes, such as an increase in friendliness, as natural manifestations of their own personality and not as artificial results of the tests. The question to answer is not whether but how the application of a crude train of messageless electricity may result in the performance of a highly refined and complicated response.

To explain this apparent contradiction we must consider the normal mechanisms of physiological performance. In a simple act such as the flexion of a limb, the nerve impulse initiates a very complex process which includes well-organized, sequential, metabolic activities and structural changes in the myoproteins resulting in the shortening of muscle fibers. These processes do not depend on neural impulses and have been established by genetic determination as intrinsic properties of muscular tissue unfolding in a similar way under nervous command or direct electrical excitation. Electricity does not create muscle contraction; it simply activates a pre-established pattern of response. At the neurological level, flexion of a limb requires the propagation of many well-organized impulses from the brain to the different groups of muscles, the processing of proprioceptive information from many regions, the adjustments of servomechanisms, visceral adaptations, and many other electrical, thermal, chemical, mechanical, and physiological pre-established phenomena and correlations. The applied electricity is only the depolarizing trigger of a group of neurons; it starts processes which once activated are relatively independent of the initial cause. Evoked behavior is like a chain reaction in which the final result depends more on the structure and organization of the components than on the trigger. To understand the role of electrical stimulation, we may ask whether the finger of the person pushing a button to launch a man into orbit is responsible for the performance of the complicated machinery or for the sequence of events. Obviously the finger, like a simple electrical stimulus, is only the trigger of a programed series of interdependent events and cannot be accepted as the real cause of capsules orbiting around the earth.

A tentative explanation of some of the mechanisms involved in motor activities has been proposed in the theory of fragmental representation of behavior (53) which postulates that behavior is organized as fragments which have anatomical and functional reality within the brain, where they can be the subject of experimental analysis. The different fragments may be combined in different sequences like the notes of a melody, resulting in a succession of motor acts which constitute specific behavioral categories such as licking, climbing, or walking. The theory may perhaps be clarified with one example. If I wish to take a cookie from the table, this wish may be considered a force called "the starter" because it will determine the initiation of a series of motor acts. The starter includes drives, motivations, emotional perceptions, memories, and other processes. To take the cookie it is necessary to organize a motor plan, a mechanical strategy, and to decide among several motor choices, because the cookie may be taken with the left or right hand, directly with the mouth, or even by using the feet if one has simian skills. Choice, strategies, motor planning, and adjustments depend on a set of cerebral structures, "the organizer," which is different from the set employed by the starter, because the desire for cookies may exist in hungry people or in completely paralyzed patients, and the hands can move and reach the table for many different reasons even if there are no cookies. Finally, the actual contraction of muscles for the performance of the selected movement to reach the cookie—for example, using the right hand—depends on a cerebral set, "the performer," different from the previous two, because motor representation of hands, mouth, and feet is situated in different areas of the brain, and the choice of muscle group to be activated is under the supervision of a given organizer. Naturally, there is a close correlation among these three basic mechanisms, and also between them and other cerebral functions. The concept of a brain center as a visible anatomical locus is unacceptable in modern physiology, but the participation of a constellation of neuronal groups (a functional set) in a specific act is more in agreement with our present knowledge. The functional set may be formed by the neurons of nuclei far from one another, for instance, in the cerebellum, motor cortex, pallidum, thalamus, and red nucleus, forming a circuit in close mutual dependence, and responsible for a determined act such as picking up a cookie with the right hand.

If we accept the existence of anatomical representation of the three functional sets—starter, organizer, and performer—it is logical that they can be activated by different types of triggers, and that the evoked results will be related to the previous experiences linked to the set. The same set, evoking a similar behavioral response, may be activated by physiological stimuli, such as sensory perceptions and ideations, or by artificial stimuli, such as electrical impulses. When we stimulate the brain through implanted electrodes we can, depending on the location of contacts, activate the starter, the organizer, or·the performer of different behavioral reactions, so that natural and artificial stimuli may interplay with one another, as has been experimentally demonstrated.

# 18

# Electrical Activation of the "Will"

The theoretical considerations of the previous section may facilitate the understanding of so-called willful, free, or spontaneous behavior which to a great extent depends on pre-established mechanisms, some of them inborn and others acquired through learning. When a child takes his first steps or when an adult learns a new skill like tennis or typing, the initial movements are clumsy and require considerable attention and effort in every detail. Coordination progressively improves, unnecessary muscular tension diminishes, and the movements proceed with speed, economy, and elegance without being thought about. Acquisition of a skill means the automation of patterns of response with the establishment of spatial and temporal sequences. The voluntary aspects of willful activity are the purpose for it and the initiation of performance, while most of the details of complex movements and adaptation to changing circumstances are performed automatically. We may consider that *the role of the will is mainly to trigger previously established mechanisms.* Obviously the will is not responsible for the chemistry of muscular contraction, the electrical processes of neural transmission, or the intimate organization of responses. These phenomena depend on spindle discharges, cerebellar activation, synaptic junctions, reciprocal inhibitions, and many other mechanisms which are not only beyond consciousness but may be beyond our present knowledge and comprehension. The uniqueness of voluntary behavior lies in its initial dependence on the integration of a vast number of personal past experiences and present receptions.

Volition itself must be related to neuronal activities, and it may be asked whether either appropriate sensory perceptions or artificial electrical stimulation could induce neuronal pools involved in decision-making to discharge in a like manner. I shall not enter into the controversial issues of causality and determination of free behavior, but on the basis of experimental findings it is reasonable to assume that voluntary and electrical triggering can activate existing cerebral mechanisms in a similar way. If spontaneous and electrically evoked behavior involve participation of the same set of cerebral areas, then both types of behavior should be able to *interact* by modifying each others' inhibitory and excitatory influences. This possibility has been proved experimentally.

As described by Hess (107) and as observed also in our experiments, excitation of some points in the subthalamus of the cat induces a clockwise rotation of the head, and the effect of low intensity and low frequency (8 cycles per second) stimulation can be counteracted by the animal. The head starts rotating slowly and then is brought back to normal position by a quick voluntary jerk, the process repeating several times until stimulation ceases. If the intensity of stimulation is increased, the corrective movements disappear and rotation of the head progresses slowly but continuously, followed by rotation of the body on its longitudinal axis until the cat lies on its back. Then with a sudden jerk the animal abruptly completes the turn and springs to its feet. The explanation of these results may be as follows: During the initial part of the evoked head rotation, its abnormal position should produce normal proprioceptive and vestibular stimuli, starting a reflex reaction to slow down and counteract the electrically evoked effect. As soon as the cat is on its back, however, artificial and natural stimuli work together, the first to continue the turning, and the second to bring the animal to its usual horizontal position; the summation of these two actions would explain the sudden jerk. Interaction between evoked and spontaneous activity has also been observed during conditioning experiments with cats in which the animals often tried to suppress motor movements induced by ESB (89).

A clear example of algebraic summation between voluntary and evoked motility was observed in one of our cats with electrodes implanted in the left hidden motor cortex (48). Electrical stimulation induced an extension and raising of the right forepaw with proper postural adaptation. Offering of fish to the animal resulted in a similar extension and raising of the limb in order to seize the food. Simultaneous presentation of the fish and stimulation of the cortex produced a motor response of greater amplitude than usual; the cat miscalculated the necessary movement and overshot his target. He was unable to catch the food until he made a series of corrective adjustments, and then the fish was successfully captured and eaten. In addition to demonstrating the interrelation between evoked and spontaneous responses, this experiment also proved that the animal was aware of an artificial disturbance, and after a brief period of trial and error was able to correct its performance accordingly.

In the play of forces between spontaneous and evoked responses, which one is more powerful? Will one of them be prepotent over the other? Experimental results demonstrate that when there is a conflict in the response, the stronger stimulus dominates. For example, stimulation of the left sulcus presylvius with 0.6 milliamperes in a cat named Nero caused a small flexion of the right foreleg. When Nero was jumping from a table to the floor, the same excitation did not produce any visible effect, and the animal landed with perfect coordination, showing good voluntary control of all his limbs. Electrical flexion of the foreleg had therefore been completely inhibited by the peremptory need to use the musculature in the jump. If stimulation intensity was increased up to 1.8 milliamperes, flexion of the limb appeared even when Nero was air-borne in the middle of a jump, and landing was disrupted by the inability to use the right foreleg. In general, electrical stimulation of the brain was dominant over voluntary behavior, provided that its intensity was sufficiently increased.

It is known that reflexes are predictable responses, rigidly patterned and blindly performed. Similarly, electrical excitation of a peripheral motor nerve induces a stereotyped movement with little adaptation to external circumstances. In contrast, willful activity generally has a purpose, and its performance is adapted for the attainment of a determined aim, with a continuous processing of proprioceptive and exteroceptive sensory information, with the use of feedback mechanisms, with capacity for instantaneous readjustment of the central command to adapt to changes in the environment, and with prediction of the future which requires spatiotemporal calculation of speed, direction, and strategies of moving targets. Depending on the location of cerebral stimulation, the responses obtained by ESB may either be similar to a blind reflex or have all the above-mentioned characteristics of voluntary activity.

Stimulation of some points in the motor cortex and motor pathways in the cat, monkey, and other animals may produce simple movements, such as the flexion of a limb, which are completely stereotyped and lack adaptation. These effects may be interpreted as the activation of efferent structures where the pattern of response has already been decided. At this level, the neural functions are of conduction rather than of integration and organization, and only minor variations are possible in the circulating impulses, regardless of whether their origin was spontaneous or artificial. To the contrary, there is plenty of evidence that many of the effects evoked by ESB are oriented toward the *accomplishment of a specific aim* with adaptation of the motor performance to unexpected changes in environmental circumstances. The following examples substantiate this statement.

In the cat, electrical stimulation of the inferior part of the sulcus presylvius consistently induced licking movements with well-organized opening and closing of the mouth and phasic protrusion of the tongue. Under anesthesia, the licking was automatic and purposeless; but in the awake, free-moving animal the response was directed toward some useful purpose, and the cat searched for a target to lick—food, the hands of the experimenter, the floor, or its own fur. In this case, motor performance and posture of the whole body adapted to the experimental setting, and in order to lick the investigator's hand, for example, the cat advanced a few steps and approached the hand even if it moved slowly away. Another example of adaptation to the environment is the "avoidance of obstacles" (48). Stimulation of the middle part of the presylvian sulcus in the cat induced a contralateral turning of the head in the horizontal plane. The effect was reliable, but when the movement was interrupted by placing an obstacle such as a book in its path, the animal modified its performance and raised its head to avoid the interposed obstacle before continuing the evoked head turning.

The adaptability of artificially induced cerebral responses to changes in the environment has been clearly demonstrated by rhesus monkeys' aggressive behavior which was selectively directed by the animals against their natural enemies within the group with a motor pattern of chasing and fighting which continuously changed according to the unpredictable strategies of those under attack. In this case, ESB evidently did not evoke a predetermined motor effect but an emotional state of increased aggressiveness which was served by pre-established motor skills and directed according to the previous history of social relations (53).

Similar experiments have been performed in roosters (111). If the bird was alone, motor restlessness was the only observable effect of ESB, while the same stimulation of a rooster in a group produced a state of increased aggressiveness and attacks on other birds. Sharp fighting ensued with perfectly coordinated, typical patterns of attack and defense in the group.

We may conclude that ESB can activate and influence some of the cerebral mechanisms involved in willful behavior. In this way we are able to investigate the neuronal functions related to the so-called will, and in the near future this experimental approach should permit clarification of such highly controversial subjects as "freedom," "individuality," and "spontaneity" in factual terms rather than in elusive semantic discussions. The possibility of influencing willful activities by electrical means has obvious ethical implications, which will be discussed later.

# 19

# Characteristics and Limitations
# of Brain Control

The possibility of man's controlling the thoughts of other men has ranked as high in human fantasy as the control over transmutation of metals, the possession of wings, or the power to take a trip to the moon. Our generation has witnessed the accomplishment of so many nearly impossible tasks that today we are ready to accept almost anything. In the world of science, however, speculation and fantasy cannot replace truth.

There is already abundant evidence that ESB can control a wide range of functions, including motor activities and mental manifestations, in animals and in man. We know that by electrical stimulation of specific cerebral structures we can make a person friendlier or influence his train of thought. In spite of its spectacular potential, ESB has practical and theoretical limitations which should be delineated.

## Predictability

When we get into a car and press the starter, the motor will almost certainly begin to run in a few seconds. The brain, however, does not have the simplicity of a machine. When electrodes are introduced into a cerebral structure and stimulation is applied for the first time, we really cannot predict the quality, localization, or intensity of the evoked effects. We do not even know that a response will appear. This is especially true for complex structures, like the amygdaloid region, which have great functional multiplicity; but it is also the case in relatively simple areas like the motor cortex. The anatomical and functional variability of the brain are factors which hinder prediction of ESB results (53). The importance of these limiting factors is compounded by alterations in regional activity related to changes in local, general, and environmental circumstances. We know that certain functions are represented in specific cerebral structures, but the precise location of a desired target requires careful exploration, and implantation of only a few contacts may be rather disappointing. After repeated explorations of a selected area in several subjects, predictability of the observed responses in that area for that species can be assessed with a higher degree of confidence. Present information about functional mapping in most cerebral areas is still rather incomplete.

## Functional Monotony

Electrical stimulation is a nonspecific stimulus which always activates a group of neurons in a similar way because there is no coded neural message or feedback carried to the stimulating source. The responses, therefore, are repeated in a monotonous way, and any variability is related to changes in the stimulated subject. This functional monotomy rules out the possibility that an investigator could direct a subject toward a target or induce him, like a robot, to perform any complex task under remote-controlled orders.

Science fiction has already imagined men with intracerebral electrodes engaged in all kinds of mischief under the perverse guidance of radio waves sent by some evil scientist. The inherent limitations of ESB make realization of this fantasy very remote. The flexion of a limb can be radio controlled and an emotional state could also be set remotely, but the sequences of responses and adaptation to the environment depend on established intracerebral mechanisms whose complexity cannot be duplicated by ESB. Even if we could stimulate different points of the brain through twenty or thirty channels, it would be necessary to have sensory feedback and computerized calculations for the programing of simple spatiotemporal sequences. Induced performance of more complex acts would be far beyond available methodology. It should be clarified that I am talking about directing each phase of a response, and not about complex behavior such as lever pressing or fighting, which may be triggered by ESB but develops according to individual experiential circumstances which are beyond electrical control.

## Skillful Performance

Many of the activities elicited by ESB certainly can be categorized as skillful. Pressing a lever, climbing a cage wall, and looking for a fight require good motor coordination and suitable processing of information. Walking on two feet, which has been repeatedly elicited in monkeys during stimulation of the red nucleus (Figure 12), is another example of refined coordination and equilibrium seldom observed in spontaneous behavior.

These facts demonstrate that ESB may result in different types of skillful performance, but it must be understood that these responses represent the manifestation of skills already familiar to the subject. Motor learning requires the reception of sensory inputs not only from the environment but also from the performing muscles, and a relatively lengthy process of motor training is required to perfect reactions related to each type of performance and to store the appropriate ideokinetic formulas in the brain for future reference and use. Much of the brain participates in learning, and a monotonous train of pulses applied to a limited pool of neurons cannot be expected to mimic its complexity. The acquisition of a new skill is theoretically and practically beyond the possibilities of electrical stimulation, but ESB can create the desire to perform certain acts which may be skillful.

## Individual Stability

Personal identity and reactivity depend on a large number of factors accumulated through many years of experience interacting with genetic trends within the complexity of neuronal networks. Language and culture are among the essential elements of individual structure. All these elements cannot be substituted for by the delivery of electricity to the brain. Memories can be recalled, emotions awakened, and conversations speeded up by ESB, but the patients always express themselves according to their background and experience. It is possible to disturb consciousness, to confuse sensory interpretations, or to elicit hallucinations during excitation of the brain. It is also possible to induce fear, pleasure, and changes in aggressive behavior, but these responses do not represent the creation of a new personality—only a change in emotionality or reactivity with the appearance of manifestations closely related to the previous history of the subject.

ESB cannot substitute one personality for another because electricity cannot replicate or influence all the innumerable factors which integrate individual identity. Contrary to the stories of science fiction writers, we cannot modify political ideology, past history, or national loyalties by electrical tickling of some secret areas of the brain. A complete change in personality is beyond the theoretical and practical potential of ESB, although limited modification of a determined aspect of personal reactions is possible. In spite of important limitations, we are certainly facing basic ethical problems about when, why, and how some of these changes are acceptable, and especially about who will have the responsibility of influencing the cerebral activities of other human beings.

## Technical Complexity

Electrical stimulation of the central nervous system requires careful planning, complex methodology, and the skillful collaboration of specialists with knowledge and experience in anatomy, neurophysiology, and psychology. Several prerequisites, including construction of the delicate multilead electrodes and refined facilities for stereotaxic neurosurgery, are necessary. The selection of neuronal targets and appropriate parameters of stimulation require further sophistication and knowledge of functional brain mapping as well as electronic technology. In addition, medical and psychiatric experience is necessary in order to take care of the patient, to interpret the results obtained, and to plan the delivery of stimulations. These elaborate requirements limit the clinical application of intracerebral electrodes which like other modern medical interventions depends on team work, equipment, and facilities available in only a few medical centers. At the same time, the procedure's complexity acts as a safeguard against the possible improper use of ESB by untrained or unethical persons.

## Functions Beyond the Control of ESB

We are in the initial steps of a new technology, and while it is difficult to predict the limits of unknown territory, we may suppose that cerebral manifestations which depend on the elaboration of complex information will elude electrical control. For example, reading a book or listening to a conversation involves reception of many messages which cannot be mimicked by ESB. A pattern of behavior which is not in the brain cannot be organized or invented under electrical control. ESB cannot be used as a teaching tool because skills such as playing the piano, speaking a language, or solving a problem require complex sensory inputs. Sequential behavior or even elemental motor responses cannot be synthetized by cerebral stimulation, although they are easily evoked if they have already been estab-lished in the excited area as ideokinetic formulas. Since electri-cal stimulation does not carry specific thoughts it is not feasible as a technique to implant ideas or direct behavioral performance in a specific context. Because of its lack of symbolic meaning, electricity could not induce effects comparable to some post-hypnotic performances.

# 20

# Medical Applications

The discovery of new therapies has been—and still is—a more pressing need in cerebral disorders than in other fields of medicine because of their greater consequences for the mental and somatic well-being of patients. Unfortunately, advances in this area have been relatively slow, partly because of the intrinsic complexity of the problems involved, and partly because of a traditional fear and reluctance to disturb or deal directly with the material substratum of mental activities. At the beginning of the century, the public was generally hostile to surgery and considered it almost obscene for a surgeon to look into the most intimate depths of the body (185). With cultural and scientific advances this prejudice has slowly receded, and the study of the human body is now recognized as essential for the advance of medicine. Sexual taboos have diminished, and even the scientific investigation of the phases and details of human intercourse has at last been undertaken. All of the organs of the body, including the heart, genitals, and brain, have been accepted as suitable subjects for research.

Implantation of electrodes inside the human brain is like installing a magic window to reveal the bursts of cellular discharges during functional activation of specific structures. The meaning of these bursts is often difficult to decipher, but some correlations between electrical patterns and behavioral effects have already been firmly established. The electrical line of communication has also been used to send simple messages to the depth of the brain in order to arouse dormant functions or to appease excessive neuronal firing. A new method was thus found to impose therapeutic order upon disorderly activity.

In spite of the tremendous potential offered by the direct access to the brain, medical applications were received with suspicion and strong criticism and have progressed rather slowly. The growing acceptance of even experimental surgical interventions in most organs including the human heart is in sharp contrast with the generally cold reception to the implantation of wires in the human brain, even though this procedure has been used in animals for forty years and has proved to be safe. The reasons are to a great extent related to the persistence of old taboos, in scientists as well as in laymen, and to the more logical fear of opening some Pandora's box.

As experience overcomes opposition, cerebral explorations are being extended to different hospitals around the world, as shown by several recent symposia (159, 182, 216).

## Diagnosis

The spontaneous electrical activity of the brain (electroencephalogram or EEG) can be recorded by means of surface electrodes attached by conductive paste to the outside of the scalp. This is a standard procedure used for diagnostic purposes in several cerebral illnesses, such as epilepsy, which is characterized by episodes of increased amplitude and synchronization of neuronal activity which can be recorded and identified. Strong electrical disturbances may, however, be present in structures located in the depth of the brain which cannot be detected by scalp EEG (57), and in this case the use of intracerebral electrodes may provide essential diagnostic information. For example, psychomotor epilepsy has been alleviated by surgical removal of the tip of the temporal lobe where seizure activity originated, and in these cases it is imperative to identify the source of the fits and especially to decide whether they are unilateral or present on both sides of the brain. In spite of some controversial problems about the location, multiplicity, and migration of epileptic foci, there is general agreement that depth recordings through implanted electrodes can give valuable data unobtainable by any other means.

The expected correlations between scalp EEG and mental disturbances have failed to materialize in experimental studies, although some mentally ill patients have exhibited electrical abnormalities. Depth recordings have also failed to provide decisive information about these patients, and for example, the suggestion that septal spikes might be typical of schizophrenia (98) has not been confirmed (57). The absence of significant data must be attributed to the lack of refinement of present methodology. Disturbed functions must have a background of altered neuronal physiology which should be detectable if more knowledge of the mechanisms involved and more sophisticated techniques were available. One step in this direction is the analysis of electrical activity by means of autocorrelation and cross-correlation (23) in order to recognize periodicity of patterns among the noise of other signals. Computer analysis of power and spectral analysis of frequencies are also new tools which will increase the future scientific and diagnostic usefulness of electrical recordings. Depth recordings may also be used for localization of tumors inside the unopened skull to detect abnormally slow potential shifts from the tissue surrounding the neoplasm and the lack of spontaneous waves within the mass of tumoral cells.

In addition to knowledge derived from the study of spontaneous brain waves, other valuable information may be obtained by recording the alterations evoked in intracerebral electrical activity following application of sensory stimulation or ESB. Presentation of flashes of light with a stroboscope, or of auditory clicks, activates the corresponding cerebral analyzers and may unveil areas of excessive reactivity. Epileptic patients are especially sensitive to repeated flashes and may respond with an activation of dormant electrical abnormalities or even with a convulsive seizure. Administration of single or repeated electrical shocks may also help in the localization of malfunctioning neuronal fields. Systemic administration of drugs which increase or decrease brain excitability (such as metrazol or phenobarbital) can be used in conjunction with evoked potentials in order to test the specific pharmacological sensitivity of a patient, thus orienting his medical or postsurgical therapy.

Electrical stimulation of the brain during surgical interventions, or during therapeutical destruction of limited cerebral areas, is necessary in order to test local excitability and determine the functional localization of areas which must be spared. This is particularly important during the surgical treatment of Parkinson's disease, which requires freezing of cerebral tissue around the pallidum or thalamus, close to motor pathways in the internal capsule. Identification of these pathways is imperative in order to avoid their accidental destruction and the subsequent permanent motor paralysis of the patient.

## Therapy

The cerebral tissue around the electrode contact may be destroyed by electrocoagulation, passing a suitable amount of direct current. The main advantages of using implanted electrodes for this purpose, instead of open brain surgery, are that careful functional explorations are possible before and after the brain lesion is placed and, more importantly, that coagulation can be controlled and repeated if necessary over a period of days or weeks, according to the therapeutic results obtained. The procedure has been used for therapy of involuntary movements, intractable pain, focal epilepsy, and several mental disturbances including anxiety, fear, compulsive obsessions, and aggressive behavior. Some investigators report a remarkable therapeutic success in obsessive patients; others are more skeptical about the usefulness of depth electrodes and electrocoagulations in treating mental illness.

Electrical stimulation of specific structures has been used as a therapeutic procedure, and beneficial effects have been obtained in schizophrenic patients by repeated excitation of the septum and other areas which produce pleasurable sensations (99, 201, 233). In other cases of intractable pain, considerable improvement has also been reported, and some patients have been allowed to stimulate their own brains repeatedly by means of portable stimulators. In one patient, spontaneous bursts of aggressive behavior were diminished by brief periods of repeated stimulation of the amygdaloid nucleus (60).

One of the promising medical applications of ESB is the programing of long-term stimulations. Animal studies have shown that repeated excitations of determined cerebral structures produced lasting effects and that intermittent stimulations could be continued indefinitely. Some results in man have also been confirmatory. It should be emphasized that brain lesions represent an irreversible destruction while brain stimulations are far more physiological and conservative and do not rule out placing of lesions if necessary. One example may clarify the potential of this procedure. Nashold (160) has described the case of one patient, suffering from very severe intention tremor associated with multiple sclerosis, in whom stimulation of the dentate nucleus of the cerebellum produced an inhibition of the tremor with marked ipsilateral improvement of voluntary motility. The speculation was that a cerebral pacemaker could be activated by the patient himself when he desired to perform voluntary movements.

Many other possible applications could be explored including the treatment of anorexia nervosa by stimulation of the feeding centers of the lateral hypothalamus, the induction of sleep in cases of insomnia by excitation of the center median or of the caudate nucleus, the regulation of circulating ACTH by activation of the posterior hypothalamus, and the increase of patients' communication for psychotherapeutic purposes by excitation of the temporal lobe.

A two-way radio communication system could be established between the brain of a subject and a computer. Certain types of neuronal activity related to behavioral disturbances such as anxiety, depression, or rage could be recognized in order to trigger stimulation of specific inhibitory structures. The delivery of brain stimulation on demand to correct cerebral dysfunctions represents a new approach to therapeutic feedback. While it is speculative, it is within the realm of possibility according to present knowledge and projected methodology.

### Circumvention of Damaged Sensory Inputs

The miracle of giving light to the blind and sound to the deaf has been made possible by implantation of electrodes, demonstrating the technical possibility of circumventing damaged sensory receptors by direct electrical stimulation of the nervous system.

Brindley and Lewin (24) have described the case of a 52-year-old woman, totally blind after suffering bilateral glaucoma, in whom an array of eighty small receiving coils were implanted subcutaneously above the skull, terminating in eighty platinum electrodes encased in a sheet of silicone rubber placed in direct contact with the visual cortex of the right occipital lobe. Each receiving coil was tuned to a frequency of 6 or 9.5 megahertz and could be activated by pressing a transmitting coil against the scalp. With this type of transdermal stimulation, a visual sensation was perceived by the patient in the left half of her visual field as a very small spot of white light or sometimes as a duplet or a cluster of points. The effects produced by stimulation of contacts 2.4 millimeters apart were easily distinguished, and simultaneous excitation of several electrodes evoked the perception of predictable simple visual patterns. The investigators suppose that by implanting six hundred tiny electrodes it would be possible for blind patients to discriminate visual patterns; they could also achieve a normal reading speed by using electrical signals from an automatic page scanner.

Using a different approach, the Mexican investigator del Campo (26) has designed an instrument called an "amaroscope," consisting of photoelectric cells, to transform luminous images into electrical impulses which are modulated and fed through electrodes placed over the skin above the eyes to stimulate the supraorbital branches of the trigeminal nerve. Impulses are thus carried to the reticular system and the cerebral cortex. The instrument is not too sophisticated and its neurophysiological principles are controversial, but its experimental testing in more than 100 persons has proved that visual perceptions may be electrically produced in blind patients, even in some who have no eyes at all.

Auditory sensations have also been produced in a deaf person by electrical stimulation of the auditory nerve through permanently implanted electrodes. Simmons et al. (208) studied a 60-year-old male who had been totally deaf in his right ear for several years and nearly deaf in the left for several months. Under local anesthesia, a cluster of six electrodes was implanted on the right auditory nerve with a connector anchored to the skull just beneath the right ear. Two weeks after surgery, electrical stimuli were able to produce perception of different kinds of auditory sensations. Pitch varied with the point stimulated and also depended on the electrical parameters used. For example, 3 to 4 pulses per second were heard as "clicks," 10 per second as "telephone ringing," 30 per second as "bee buzz," and 100 to 300 per second could not be discriminated. Loudness was related to amplitude of stimulation and to pulse duration, and was less affected by its frequency.

To evaluate these studies we must understand that the refinement of the senses cannot be duplicated by electronic means because receptors are not passive transducers of energy but active modulators and discriminators of impulses. The reciprocal feedback between peripheral and central neurons and the processes of filtering and cross-correlation of information which takes place during afferent transmission of impulses are absent in the instrumental reception of inputs. It is doubtful that refined perceptions comparable to physiological ones can be provided by electronic means, but the perception of sensations—even if crude—when hope had been lost is certainly encouraging and demands the continuation of research efforts.

## Brain Viability

The clinical distinction between life and death was not too difficult to establish in the past. When respiration and palpitations of the heart had ceased, a person was pronounced dead, and there was little that a doctor could do. It is true that in some extraordinary cases the signs of death were only apparent, and a few patients have revived spontaneously, creating quite a shock for their doctors, relatives, and for themselves, but these fantastic stories are the very rare exceptions.

A new situation has been created in recent years because medical technology has often taken the determination of human death away from natural causality. Respiratory arrest is no longer fatal, and many poliomyelitic victims have survived with the help of iron lungs; cardiac block does not necessarily signal the end of life because heart beats may be artificially controlled by pacemakers; kidney failure will not poison the patient if dialysis machines are available to clean his blood. To the growing collection of ingenious electromechanical instruments a new methodology has recently been added: the cross-circulation between a sick human being and a healthy baboon in order to clear the human blood. This procedure was first tested in December, 1967, by Dr. Hume at the Virginia Medical College Hospital to treat a woman patient in deep hepatic coma with jaundice and edema. A 35-pound baboon was anesthetized, cooled, and its blood completely washed out with Ringer solution and replaced with human blood matched to the patient's. Then a cross-circulation was established from the ape's leg to the patient's arm. In twelve hours the patient had excreted about 5 liters of fluid through the baboon's kidney and regained consciousness. Twenty-two days later the patient went home, and the baboon was alive and healthy. A similar procedure was successfully used later in other cases (21).

Today the lives of many patients do not depend completely on the well-being of their own organic functions but on the availability of apes, organ donors, the voltage of a battery, integrity of electronic circuits, proper management of pumps, and teamwork of doctors and technicians. In certain cases death can be delayed for weeks or months, and current technology has placed upon doctors the tremendous responsibility, the nearly deific power, of deciding the duration of patients' survival. A heated controversy, reaching the public and the British Parliament, was created by the recent disclosure that in London's Neasden Hospital the records of patients over sixty-five years of age and suffering from malignant tumors or other serious chronic diseases were marked "NTBR" ("not to be resuscitated") in case of cardiac arrest. Artificial prolongation of human life is time consuming and expensive in terms of instrumentation and personnel, and it imposes added stress on the patients and their families. Because resources are limited, it is materially impossible to attempt to resuscitate all the patients who die every day, and it is necessary to select those who have the best chance of prolonged and useful survival. Why should life be maintained in unconscious patients with irreversible brain damage and no hope of recovery?

This dramatic decision between individual life and death illustrates both man's recently acquired power and the necessity to use it with intelligence and compassion. To make the situation even more complex, the recent development of organ transplantation is creating a literally "vital" conflict of interests because a person kept alive artificially owns many good working organs—including kidneys, pancreas, heart, and bones —that are needed by other dying patients.

Death, personality, and biological human rights must be redefined in view of these new scientific advances. Possessions to be disposed of after death include not only real estate, stocks, and furniture, but teeth, corneas, and hearts as well. This prospect involves many ethical and legal questions and sounds altogether gruesome and uncomfortable, but that is only because it is unfamiliar. Giving blood to be transfused, skin to be grafted, spermatozoas for artificial insemination, and kidneys to be transplanted are more acceptable practices because they do not depend on the death of the donor; but when death cannot be avoided, the idea of the transfer and survival of some organs should be considered reasonable.

The possibility of piecemeal survival of functions and organs introduces the basic question of what part of the organism to identify with human personality. There is general agreement that the organ most fundamental to individual identity is not the stomach, the liver, or even the heart, but the brain. In the necessary redefinition of death it has been proposed that in difficult cases when circulation, digestion, metabolic exchange, and other functions are still active, the decisive information about whether a  person should be considered alive—entailing the decision to continue or to withdraw artificial support for survival—must come from the viability of the brain. In some hospitals the ultimate arbiter of death is the EEG machine, and at the Massachussetts General Hospital, Dr. Robert Schwab has proposed that death should be determined by flat lines on all EEG leads for twenty minutes of continuous recordings and lack of response to sensory and mechanical stimuli. In the absence of EEG activity tested twenty-four and forty-eight hours later, death is presumed to have occurred even if (as happens in rare cases) the heart is still beating normally.

In the near future it will be necessary to examine this question in greater detail in order to determine the parts of the brain considered essential for the survival of human personality. We already know that portions of the brain may be destroyed or taken away with negligible or only moderate psychic changes. Destruction of the motor cortex produces paralysis; ablation of the temporal lobe may affect recent memory; and destruction of the frontal lobes may modify foresight and affective reactions, but in all these cases the patient's behavior is recognized as human. Destruction of the hypothalamus or reticular formation, however, may induce permanent loss of consciousness, and in this case it is questionable whether personal identity persists. The possible piecemeal survival of psychological functions will make the definition of man more difficult and will perhaps increase the present problem of deciding what human life is. From the examination of these questions, however, a deeper understanding of the essential qualities of being human—and of the direction of their evolution with intelligent purpose—will emerge.

# 21

# Ethical Considerations

Placing electrodes inside of the brain, exploring the neuronal depth of personality, and influencing behavior by electrical stimulation have created a variety of problems, some of them shared with general medical ethics and others more specifically related to moral and philosophical issues of mental activity.

## Clinical Use of New Procedures

One of the main objectives of animal research is the discovery of new principles and methods which can be applied for the benefit of man. Their potential advantages and risks cannot be ascertained until they have been extensively tested in human subjects, and preliminary trials must always be considered experimental. Evidence that penicillin or any other new drug may be therapeutically effective is obtained initially in vitro and then in different species of mammals, but the conclusive demonstration of its clinical safety and efficacy requires application to man. In spite of established safeguards, there is an inherent possibility that unforeseen, slowly developing side effects may have serious consequences. A thorium product used in the early thirties as a contrast medium for X-ray analysis of the liver was found to be radioactive and caused the slow death of hundreds of patients. A supposedly innocuous drug, the ill-famed thalidomide given as a sedative, had damaging effects on fetal development, creating the tragedy of children born with severe physical deformities. Accidents like these have promoted more stringent regulations, but the gap between animal and human biology is difficult to fill and in each case a compromise must be reached between reasonable precautions and possible risks.

The historical demonstration by Fulton and Jacobsen (81) that frustration and neurotic behavior in the chimpanzee could be abolished by destruction of the frontal lobes was the starting point of lobotomy, which was widely used for treatment of several types of mental illness in human patients. This operation consisted of surgical disruption of the frontal lobe connections and demonstrated the important fact that psychic manifestations can be influenced by physical means as bold as the surgeon's knife. The Nobel Prize bestowed on the first neurosurgeon to perform human lobotomies, Egas Moniz, recognized the significance of the principle that the mind was not so unreachable as formerly believed, and that it could be the object of experimental investigation.

In spite of initial acclaim, lobotomy was soon severely criticized as a therapeutic procedure because it often produced concomitant undesirable alterations of personality, and more conservative treatments were actively sought in order to provide a "less damaging, less sacrificial means of dealing with mental disorders than are lobotomy, leucotomy, gyrectomy, thalamotomy, and other intentional destructions of nervous structures" (145). Among these efforts, implantation of electrodes in the brain offered promising possibilities. In monkeys, stimulation or limited destruction of the caudate nucleus produced several of the symptoms of frontal lobotomy with more discrete behavioral changes (191). Implantation of electrodes in man permitted access to any cerebral structure for recording, stimulation, or destruction. Their potential clinical application raised controversial issues about risks, rationale, and medical efficacy, but there is general agreement that depth recordings may provide significant information which cannot be obtained by other means and is essential for the proper diagnosis and

treatment of patients with some cerebral disturbances. Therapeutic use of electrodes in cases of mental illness has been more
doubtful and must still be considered in an experimental phase.

Recordings and stimulations in a patient equipped with intracerebral leads provide basic information about neurophysiological mechanisms in man which may be of great value for the
patient himself, for the welfare of other patients, and for the
advance of science. In addition, they provide a unique opportunity to obtain important data about neuronal functions which
may not be directly related to the patient's illness. In this case
we are facing ethical issues of human research which must be
carefully considered.

### Human Experimentation

While medical practice has generally accepted guidelines based
on the Hippocratic oath—to do what "I consider best for my
patients, and abstain from whatever is injurious"—research
with human subjects has lacked traditional codes and has followed the investigator's personal criteria—which have not always
been correct. According to Beecher (12), leading medical schools
and renowned doctors have sometimes conducted unethical
research. Extremely high doses of a drug have been adminis-
tered, with resulting behavioral disturbances, in order to evaluate the toxicity of the product; placebos have been given instead
of a well-known beneficial drug, with a resulting increase in the
incidence and severity of illness; live cancer cells have been
injected under the skin of twenty-two elderly patients without
telling them what the shots were, at New York's well-respected
Sloan-Kettering Institute. Beecher does not believe that these
studies demonstrate a willful disregard of the patient's rights,
but a thoughtlessness in experimental design.

Although no formal ethical code has been universally accepted
for the performance of research in man, basic guidelines have
been formulated by the American Psychological Association
(43); by the judges of the Nuremberg war crime trials (218); by

the World Medical Association (246); and by the Medical Research Council of Britain (153). A 1966 editorial in the *New England Journal of Medicine* (161) states that in medicine and in human investigations the welfare of the sick patient or the experimental subject has traditionally been of prime importance. "This implies clearly that therapeutic or theoretical experiments with significant risk of morbidity or mortality are undertaken only with a view to the immediate benefit of the patient; for the experimental subject to whom no benefit may accrue, the most meaningful possible informed and unforced consent must be secured." In the summer of 1966, the United States Public Health Service issued regulations for their sponsored research involving humans, specifying the need for full consent by the participating subjects and careful review of the projects by an *ad hoc* committee. In a detailed discussion, Wolfensberger (245) clarified the meaning of informed consent: The experimental subject understands all the essential aspects of the study, the types and degrees of risks, the detrimental or beneficial consequences, if any, and the purpose of the research.

One of the main ethical issues is the conflict of interest between science, progress, and society, and the rights of the individual. The principles of personal dignity, privacy, and freedom are often waived—voluntarily or forcefully—in favor of the group. Firemen, policemen, and soldiers may risk or lose their lives for the benefit of the community. Civilized activities are full of regulations which limit behavioral freedom. We are obliged to reveal our income, to pay taxes, and to serve in the army. We cannot walk around naked, take flowers from public gardens, or leave our cars where we please. We are searched when crossing borders and put in jail if our conduct is considered antisocial by the law. Although respect for the individual is highly prized and accepted in theory, in practice it is often challenged and curtailed. The balance between social duties and individual rights is decided not by the individual but by customs and laws established by the group.

In the case of medical research, it is difficult to write an ethical code. As the Panel of Privacy and Behavioral Research concluded in 1967, "legislation to assure appropriate recognition of the rights of human subjects is neither necessary nor desirable," and "because of its relative inflexibility, legislation cannot meet the challenge of the subtle and sensitive conflict of values under consideration." Ethical decisions in science require not only moral judgment but also factual information, technical knowledge, and experience, especially in the evaluation of risks and benefits. In order to decide to undergo open heart surgery, a patient must have a medical evaluation of his condition and of the state of the surgical art, a judgment which the doctor, but rarely the patient, is prepared to make. In medical research, consent is certainly essential, but the main responsibility still lies with the investigator and his institution. The request for consent from a patient—or from a student participating in a research project—carries a heavy weight of moral authority and a degree of coercion, and granting of it does not relieve the director of full responsibility in the experimental design and consequences. The simple request to perform a dubious procedure must be considered unethical because it represents psychological stress for the patient. Children and adults with mental disturbances cannot give proper consent, and relatives must be consulted. Their decisions, however, are easily influenced by the picture presented by the attending physician, thus increasing his responsibility which preferably should be shared by a group of three or more professional consultants.

There is one aspect of human research which is usually overlooked: the existence of a moral and social duty to advance scientific knowledge and to improve the welfare of man. When important medical information can be obtained with negligible risk and without infringing on individual rights, the investigator has the duty to use his intelligence and skills for this purpose. Failure to do so represents the neglect of professional duties in some way similar to the negligence of a medical doctor who does not apply his full effort to the care of a patient. Subjects with implanted electrodes provide a good example, because the use of telemetry and video tape recordings in them makes possible many studies concerning the sources of normal and abnormal activities, spectral analysis of electrical waves, conduction time, evoked potentials, and electrobehavioral correlations. This type of research may provide data of exceptional value—available only from man—without any risks or even demands on a patient's time or attention. Information can be obtained while the subject is engaged in spontaneous normal activities like reading a paper, watching television, or sleeping. Only the recording equipment and research team need to be alert and working. Methodology for the telemetric study of the brain is very new, and it will take some time before its potential and practicality are recognized and its use spreads to different hospitals. In my opinion this research is both ethical and desirable.

However, procedures which represent risk or discomfort for the patient should be ruled out. The implantation time of electrodes cannot be prolonged unnecessarily, and administration of drugs, injections, or catheterizations for research purposes are not acceptable. Any contemplated exception to this rule should be very carefully evaluated and clearly explained to the experimental subject.

When a patient needs to have electrodes in his brain for a period of weeks or months, the medical doctors in charge face a dual responsibility, first not to do anything harmful or unpleasant for the sake of science, and second to do as much research as possible provided it is safe and comfortable for the patient.

The use of healthy volunteers in medical research is controversial, partly because they are usually recruited from prisons, the military services, universities, or other groups which are more or less bound to authority and therefore have a diminished capacity for free choice. One of the most famous experiments was a study of antimalarial drugs which had to be performed in man. In a well-planned research project 1,000 army volunteers in Australia were deliberately infected with malaria. This study was later continued in several federal penitentiaries in the

United States. A most dramatic and successful mass experiment was the application of poliomyelitis vaccine to thousands of school children a few years ago, statistically demonstrating the effectiveness of a new vaccine. Decisions about experiments like these must be reached by careful consideration of the factors involved, with the basic ethical guidelines clearly in mind.

Individual volunteers have greater freedom of choice, and I have received letters from many people offering themselves as "human guinea pigs" for implantation of electrodes in their brains. For both ethical and practical reasons their offers cannot be accepted, but it is interesting to note the varied motivations behind these proposals. They included pure scientific interest, hopes for monetary reward or fame, manifestations of psychotic disturbances, and also a most generous intent: Some people wished to donate their brains for study in the hope that information could be obtained leading to the cure of loved ones whose brain dysfunctions could not be cured by standard therapies. The most articulate expression of this wish to contribute one's own brain for scientific research was that of a most distinguished investigator, Dr. David Rioch, who at the close of a conference about the unanesthetized brain, held in Washington, D.C., in 1957, declared:

When I come to retire . . . I might quite reasonably approach an experimental neurosurgeon in whose work and scientific orientation I had confidence and say "Let us do an experiment together, as there are a number of things both you and I would like to find out." I would be considerably intrigued to know what "attitudes" and "sensations" a good experimenter could evoke electrically from my amygdala and even more intrigued to check personally on the sense of euphoria and the sense of disphoria (185).

## Electrical Manipulation of the Psyche

The most alarming aspect of ESB is that psychological reactivity can be influenced by applying a few volts to a determined area of the brain. This fact has been interpreted by many people as a disturbing threat to human integrity. In the past, the individual could face risks and pressures with preservation of his own identity. His body could be tortured, his thoughts and desires could be challenged by bribes, by emotions, and by public opinion, and his behavior could be influenced by environmental circumstances, but he always had the privilege of deciding his own fate, of dying for an ideal without changing his mind. Fidelity to our emotional and intellectual past gives each of us a feeling of transcendental stability—and perhaps of immortality—which is more precious than life itself.

New neurological technology, however, has a refined efficiency. The individual is defenseless against direct manipulation of the brain because he is deprived of his most intimate mechanisms of biological reactivity. In experiments, electrical stimulation of appropriate intensity always prevailed over free will; and, for example, flexion of the hand evoked by stimulation of the motor cortex cannot be voluntarily avoided. Destruction of the frontal lobes produced changes in affectiveness which are beyond any personal control.

The possibility of scientific annihilation of personal identity, or even worse, its purposeful control, has sometimes been considered a future threat more awful than atomic holocaust. Even physicians have expressed doubts about the propriety of physical tampering with the psyche, maintaining that personal identity should be inviolable, that any attempt to modify individual behavior is unethical, and that methods—and related research —which can influence the human brain should be banned. The prospect of any degree of physical control of the mind provokes a variety of objections: theological objections because it affects free will, moral objections because it affects individual responsibility, ethical objections because it may block self-defense mechanisms, philosophical objections because it threatens personal identity.

These objections, however, are debatable. A prohibition of scientific advance is obviously naive and unrealistic. It could not be universally imposed, and, more important, it is not knowledge itself but its improper use which should be regulated. A knife is neither good nor bad; but it may be used by either a surgeon or an assassin. Science should be neutral, but scientists should take sides (242). The mind is not a static, inborn entity owned by the individual and self-sufficient, but the dynamic organization of sensory perceptions of the external world, correlated and reshaped through the internal anatomical and functional structure of the brain. Personality is not an intangible, immutable way of reacting, but a flexible process in continuous evolution, affected by its medium. Culture and education are meant to shape patterns of reaction which are not innate in the human organism; they are meant to impose limits on freedom of choice. Moral codes may vary completely from civilization to civilization. Polygamy was acceptable in biblical times, and it is still practiced among Moslems, but it is rejected by many other civilizations with strong social, legal, religious, and educational pressures to make behavior monogamous. Of course there is no physical impediment to the acquisition of half a dozen wives—at least until the law or the ladies catch up—but then we enter into a play of forces, into the dynamic equilibrium among all of the elements which determine behavioral choice. If there are very strong reasons to react in a particular way (for example, to have only one wife), the chance of living by a different custom is so slim as to be negligible.

This is precisely the role of electrical stimulation of the brain: to add a new factor to the constellation of behavioral determinants. The result as shown experimentally in animals is an algebraic summation, with cerebral stimulation usually prepotent over spontaneous reactions. It is accepted medical practice to try and modify the antisocial or abnormal reactions of mental patients. Psychoanalysis, the use of drugs such as energizers and tranquilizers, the application of insulin or electroshock, and other varieties of psychiatric treatment are all aimed at influencing the abnormal personality of the patient in order to change his undesirable mental characteristics. The possible use, therefore, of implanted electrodes in mental patients should not pose unusual ethical complications if the accepted medical rules are followed. Perhaps the limited efficiency of standard psychiatric procedures is one reason that they have not caused alarm among scientists or laymen. Psychoanalysis requires a long time, and a person can easily withdraw his cooperation and refuse to express intimate thoughts. Electroshock is a crude method of doubtful efficacy in normal people. Although electrical stimulation of the brain is still in the initial stage of its development, it is in contrast far more selective and powerful; it may delay a heart beat, move a finger, bring a word to memory, or set a determined behavioral tone.

When medical indications are clear and the standard therapeutic procedures have failed, most patients and doctors are willing to test a new method, provided that the possibility of success outweighs the risk of worsening the situation. The crucial decision to start applying a new therapeutic method to human patients requires a combination of intelligent evaluation of data, knowledge of comparative neurophysiology, foresight, moral integrity, and courage. Excessive aggressiveness in a doctor may cause irreparable damage, but too much caution may deprive patients of needed help. The surgical procedure of lobotomy was perhaps applied to many mental patients too quickly, before its dangers and limitations were understood; but pallidectomy and thalamotomy in the treatment of Parkinson's disease encountered formidable initial opposition before attaining their present recognition and respected status.

While pharmacological and surgical treatment of sufferers of mental illness is accepted as proper, people with other behavioral deviations pose a different type of ethical problem. They may be potentially dangerous to themselves and to society when their mental functions are maintained within normal limits and only one aspect of their personal conduct is socially unacceptable. The rights of an individual to obtain appropriate treatment must be weighed with a professional evaluation of his behavioral problems—and their possible neurological basis—which necessitates a value judgment of the person's behavior in comparison with accepted norms. One example will illustrate these considerations.

In the early 1950s, a patient in a state mental hospital approached Dr. Hannibal Hamlin and me requesting help. She was an attractive 24-year-old woman of average intelligence and education who had a long record of arrests for disorderly conduct. She had been repeatedly involved in bar brawls in which she incited men to fight over her and had spent most of the preceding few years either in jail or in mental institutions. The patient expressed a strong desire as well as an inability to alter her conduct, and because psychiatric treatment had failed, she and her mother urgently requested that some kind of brain surgery be performed in order to control her disreputable, impulsive behavior. They asked specifically that electrodes be implanted to orient possible electrocoagulation of a limited cerebral area; and if that wasn't possible, they wanted lobotomy.

Medical knowledge and experience at that time could not ascertain whether ESB or the application of cerebral lesions could help to solve this patient's problem, and surgical intervention was therefore rejected. When this decision was explained, both the patient and her mother reacted with similar anxious comments, asking, "What is the future? Only jail or the hospital? Is there no hope?" This case revealed the limitations of therapy and the dilemma of possible behavioral control. Supposing that long-term stimulation of a determined brain structure could influence the tendencies of a patient to drink, flirt, and induce fights; would it be ethical to change her personal characteristics? People *are* changing their character by self-medication through hallucinogenic drugs, but do they have the right to demand that doctors administer treatment that will radically alter their behavior? What are the limits of individual rights and doctors' obligations?

As science seems to be approaching the possibility of controlling many aspects of behavior electronically and chemically, these questions must be answered. If, as in the case of this patient, the deviation of behavior conflicts with society so seriously as to deprive her of her personal freedom, medical intervention could be justified. The case of habitual criminal conduct is another example of this type of problem. Therapeutic decisions related to psychic manipulation require moral integrity and ethical education. Scientific training concentrates mainly in natural sciences and often neglects the study and assimilation of ethical codes, considering them beyond the realm of science. Perhaps it is often forgotten that the investigator needs a set of convictions and principles, not only to administrate grant money, to give proper credit to the work of others, and to be civilized with his colleagues, but especially to direct his life and his research, and to foresee the implications of his own discoveries.

# 22

# Social Implications

From ancient times, man has tried to control the destiny of other human beings by depriving them of liberty and submitting them to obedience. Slaves have been forced to work and to serve the caprices of their masters; prisoners have been chained to row in the galleys; and men were and still are inducted into the armed forces and sent thousands of miles away to create havoc, take lives, and lose their own.

Biological assault has also existed throughout recorded history. In ancient China, the feet of female children were bound to reduce their size. In many countries thieves have been punished by having their hands cut off; males have been castrated to inhibit sexual desire and then placed as eunuchs in charge of harems; and in some African tribes it was customary to ablate the clitoris of married females to block their possible interest in other men and insure their fidelity. These barbaric practices belong to the past, but the forceful imposition of biological changes still continues in our age. Sterilization of human beings by surgery or radiation has been legally imposed in some lands as a punishment for sexual crimes or a preventive measure to avoid the spread of genetic defects. In the face of the real danger of population explosion, several scientists have proposed government enforced regulations to control fertility, and it is expected that in the next few years an antifertility drug, which can be added to the water supplies of cities, will be developed. According to Ketchel (126), "Voluntary methods are to be preferred but only if they work. If they do not, then involuntary controls must be imposed. . . . Such measures are preferable to the starvation and misery resulting from overpopulation."

When an individual's behavior is judged unfit by members of a society, the consequences may be forceful deprivation of liberty and incarceration. If the individual is confined to a mental hospital, his undesirable conduct may cause the authorities to administer drugs, by forceful injection if necessary, in order to change or control his behavioral responses. In the early 1950s an historical precedent was established for the deliberate destruction of part of the brain as a legal treatment for criminals (130). A man apprehended in Pittsburgh after committing a series of robberies was given the alternative of a long jail sentence or submission to frontal lobe surgery which might curb or eliminate his future criminal behavior. Lobotomy was performed, and although initially the patient appeared better adjusted socially, several months later he committed more thefts. When he realized that the police were closing in, he wrote a letter to the surgeon expressing appreciation for his efforts and regret that the operation had not been successful. Hoping that the study of his case might help others, he donated his brain to the surgeon and committed suicide by shooting himself through the heart. In spite of this therapeutic failure, the possibility of surgical rehabilitation of criminals has been considered by several scientists as more humane, more promising, and less damaging for the individual than his incarceration for life.

Even if our conduct is entirely within the law, we cannot escape the intervention of the state in our private lives and in our most intimate biology. In general, we are not even aware of it. Many "free" societies, including the United States, do not allow a bride and groom to marry legally until blood has been drawn from their veins and a medical officer has certified the absence of syphilis, a procedure which casts a rather insulting doubt on their past integrity and intelligence. In order to cross international borders, it is necessary to document that our skin has recently been scarified and injected with smallpox. In many cities, by governmental regulations, the drinking water floods our bodies with chlorine for safety reasons and with fluoride for strengthening our teeth. The table salt that we buy is usually fortified with iodine to aid the proper physiology of our thyroid gland. These intrusions into our private blood, teeth, and glands are accepted, practiced, and enforced. Naturally they have been legally introduced, are useful for the prevention of illness, and generally benefit society and individuals, but they have also already established the precedent of official manipulation of our personal biology.

To evaluate the rationale of governmental intervention in our bodies, we must realize that civilization represents a considerable degree of biological artificiality, mainly the intelligent escape from a primitive natural fate which was characterized by the death of countless babies, the short span of life, and the high incidence of illness and physical misery. Human health has improved in a spectacular way precisely because official agencies have had the knowledge and the power to influence our personal biology, and it should be emphasized that health regulations are similar in dictatorial and in democratic countries.

Our own existence from birth to death must be properly certified to be officially recognized, and we are surrounded by government-regulated industrial manipulations which extend to the food we eat, the water we drink, and the conditioned air we breathe. We are in a highly organized age where social and individual needs often conflict, and social ruling usually prevails. From the medical point of view this organization is highly beneficial, but the loss of personal self-determination is one of the problems of civilized life which must be carefully confronted if we are to reach reasonable compromises. Even if we agree that individual freedom should in general bow to community welfare, we enter into a new dimension when considering the social implications of the new technology which can influence personal structure and behavioral expression by surgical, chemical, and electrical manipulation of the brain. We may tolerate the practicality of being inoculated with yellow fever when visiting Asiatic countries, but shall we accept the theoretical future possibility of being forced to take a pill or submit to an electric shock for the socially protective purpose of making us more docile, infertile, better workers, or happier? How can we decide the limits of social impositions on individual rights?

It is convenient to remember that the art of mental escape from reality has been practiced from ancient times, especially by using drugs. Opium, for example, has probably been known since the Stone Age, and its extensive use in the Near and Far East has sometimes been encouraged by local rulers, partly because populations under opium habituation were more apathetic and easier to govern. Peyote also has a long history, being known to the Mexican Indians since pre-Columbian times and revered by some as a link to the divine. A substance closely related to peyote alkaloids is LSD (d-lysergic acid diethylamide tartrate), which has powerful effects on behavioral reactivity at a microgram dose, and which, along with marijuana, has contributed to changes in the mental and behavioral attitudes of recent generations. During the last fifteen years, a large number of tranquilizers, energizers, and other psychoactive drugs have been discovered, and their use has changed the atmosphere of mental hospitals and the practice of psychiatry. They are highly beneficial both for patients and for relatively normal persons who need pharmacological help to cope with the pressures of civilized life. The widespread use of psychoactive substances including alcohol, caffeine, nicotine, opium, chlorpromazine, and LSD may have an incalculable impact on the social behavior of large population groups. Administration of a chemical mist in order to subdue hostile crowds has already been used as a strategic weapon by armies and by local police. There is no doubt that even more selective and powerful psychodrugs will be discovered in the near future and that decisions must be made to regulate their use and to prevent their abuse.

The history of ESB is very recent, but already there is abundant information about its effectiveness and fears about the dangers of its social misuses. Could a ruthless dictator stand at a master radio transmitter and stimulate the depth of the brains of a mass of hopelessly enslaved people? This Orwellian possibility may provide a good plot for a novel, but fortunately it is beyond the theoretical and practical limits of ESB. By means of ESB we cannot substitute one personality for another, nor can we make a behaving robot of a human being. It is true that we can influence emotional reactivity and perhaps make a patient more aggressive or amorous, but in each case the details of behavioral expression are related to an individual history which cannot be created by ESB. The classical methods of punishment and reward through normal inputs are more effective in inducing purposeful changes in behavorial activity than the modifications of emotional tuning evoked by cerebral stimulation. Several of the psychoactive drugs may be nearly as effective and are far simpler to use.

Both medical benefits and social implications of cerebral research depend on the acquisition of knowledge about brain physiology, the possibility of investigating the mechanisms of the mind experimentally, the new approach to the understanding of the determinants of reward and punishment in relation to human emotions and desires, and the unveiling of the neuronal basis of personal identity.

Understanding of biology, physics, and other sciences facilitated the process of ecological liberation and domination. Man rebelled from natural determination and used his intelligence and skills to impose a human purpose on the development of the earth. We are now on the verge of a process of mental liberation and self-domination which is a continuation of our evolution. Its experimental approach is based on the investigation of the depth of the brain in behaving subjects. Its practical applications do not rely on direct cerebral manipulations but on the integration of neurophysiological and psychological principles leading to a more intelligent education, starting from the moment of birth and continuing throughout life, with the preconceived plan of escaping from the blind forces of chance and of influencing cerebral mechanisms and mental structure in order to create a future man with greater personal freedom and originality, a member of a psychocivilized society, happier, less destructive, and better balanced than present man (55).

# 23

# Neurophysiology and Mental Activities

The scientific study and possible prediction of human behavior have been challenged by several authors who questioned the existence of a cause-effect relationship and even claimed that analysis of intelligent goal-seeking activities, which are so typically human, requires methodology completely different from that used in physical sciences (179). For many years, Bertalanffy (17), in agreement with last century's German idealistic philosophy, supported the view that organisms are more than the sum of their parts. He favored a new conception of man based on his faculties of symbolic expression and offered an organismal approach different from that of "hard science." Criticizing the stimulus-response paradigm, Bertalanffy identified it with the "robot model" which Koestler has called "the ratomorphic view of man" (129).

Controversy about the possible physicochemical determination of human behavior is important because it involves the concepts of free will and responsibility. Its philosophical history begins before Democritus and passes through Aristotle, Spinoza, Claude Bernard, and many other well-known authorities. In a brief and lucid review, Grünbaum (90) has outlined the four main arguments against causality of human behavior: (1) Since each individual is unique, his behavior is not predictable or amenable to causal description. (2) Human behavior is so complex that it eludes analysis of a problematic causality. (3) Human behavior is oriented toward future goals and is not determined by past facts as in the physical sciences. (4) The acceptance of behavioral causality and predictability would deny responsibility, remorse, and possible choice of good and evil. Grünbaum rejects these four arguments on logical and scientific bases, but the best proof that most of us believe in at least a degree of behavioral predictability is that we teach our children to talk, to use the toilet, and to live in a civilized society, and that within a range of variability we do succeed in educating them.

Modern cerebral physiology, which is fully deterministic, provides a new set of arguments. It has been demonstrated that when perception of sounds is totally blocked, the auditory neurons of the inferior colliculus are impoverished in specific chemicals such as RNA. Lights, shapes, or moving shadows presented to the eye produce specific electrical waves which can be recorded in the occipital lobes and which are causally related to the optic phenomena. Brain stimulation determines sensation, movement, or emotion depending on the activated structure. The material presented in this book includes many examples of cause-effect between ESB and behavioral responses.

Against this experimental determinism it has been argued that spontaneous behavior is different from laboratory phenomena and, more important, that the gap between neuronal physiology and mental activities is still immense. How can we relate electrical spikes or ionic changes in the cells with the reality of enjoying music, being in love, or writing a book? Are mental activities and neuronal physiology as unrelated to each other as the message of a painting and the chemical structure of colors and canvas? Kety (127) has indicated that there is no valid physicochemical model to explain the phenomena of consciousness, and little likelihood of developing one. The sensation of a blue sky cannot be understood or even described in terms of changes in the retina, or spikes traveling through the optic nerve, occipital cortex, and association areas.

To clarify this discussion let us review a classical experiment. In a cat under deep anesthesia, electrodes can be placed in the inner ear and connected with an electrical amplifier and a loudspeaker. The spectacular result is that if we whisper in the cat's ear, "How are you?" the loudspeaker will reproduce "How are you?" The interpretation of this phenomenon is not that the cat has learned to speak English but that its ear has worked as a microphone, transducing sound into electricity. The vibrations of the air produced by the human voice are received by the tympanic membrane and give rise to electrical signals in the cochlea which are picked up by the recording electrodes. The cochlea functions as an acoustic analyzer which generates "all or none" spikes in single nerve fibers, sending coded messages to the brain. Sensory inputs impinging on different sensory receptors like the ear, eye, or skin originate patterns of electrical signals which can be recorded at ascending levels of the central nervous system.

In the attempt to correlate physicochemical events of the brain with psychological phenomena, we must differentiate three groups of neuronal functions: (1) *Basic metabolic changes* are necessary to keep the nerve cells alive, receptive, and reactive. These processes, which include ionic exchange, oxidation of chemicals, and consumption of energy, are absolutely necessary but are unspecific and not directly correlated with psychological responses. They allow the traffic of signals independently of their quality. (2) *A material carrier* of coded signals is needed to circulate information through the central nervous system. This carrier is represented by chemical changes and electrical impulses which can be recorded, identified, and measured. Without senses, without neural conductors, or without basic metabolic activity, reception of information is not possible, but these mechanisms are to a great extent unlearned and automatic. At these levels there is no understanding of messages, and the signals have not yet been decoded. A gross similarity may be found in a record player where the pickup cartridge transforms the irregularities of record grooves into electrical patterns traveling through the electronic circuitry of the amplifier where they can be mixed, delayed, or changed in tonality. At these levels, the material carrier is formed by electrical pulses with a voltage which can be measured and a pattern which can be seen in the oscilloscope, even without knowing that there is a musical message. In order to perceive the notes of the melody, a suitable decoding mechanism, the loudspeaker, is necessary. One more element is needed to understand the musical sounds: a suitable sensor, a human being with previous training to recognize music. (3) *The symbolic meaning* of a message is not intrinsic in the object or in the material carrier. Its understanding is not provided automatically by inborn mechanisms within the brain. Recognition of messages *must be learned* and is related to the experiential history of each individual. When we show a pencil to a monkey, a savage, and a cultured man, the visual sensory inputs are transformed into electrical patterns and transmitted through optic pathways. In all three cases this initial process is probably comparable and the transmitted electrical signals are probably similar, but the interpretation will be different. For a monkey and for a savage, the pencil is only a little stick; but for a writer the pencil has many uses and meanings, and it conveys a multitude of associations. Symbolism is not in the pencil or in the receptive brain but in their previous encounters and relations.

The distinction between material carrier and symbolic meaning is important for the clarification of the limitations of electrophysiological studies of the brain. Even if our methodology for recording electrical codes of transmitted signals were highly sophisticated, we would only be able to detect the carrier, and not the meaning. We could identify the shape of a stick circulating in visual pathways, but not its history. Symbolism cannot be deciphered by any instrument when the reference point of past experience is unknown. The frame of reference which must be examined to capture a meaning is the individual experience stored inside the brain by means of special material carriers of information, probably stereochemical combinations of amino-acids and other substances forming the nucleoproteic structure of memory traces. Symbolism is found by recalling experience from memory storage and comparing it with the received inputs.

Two events are therefore taking place: comparative evaluation and temporal correlation. This constitutes the physiochemical basis of individual reactivity, and it is a matter of definition whether these processes are considered as *material* (because essential material events are involved) or as *immaterial* (because the processes depend on comparison and temporal correlation). It is more important to understand the terms of discussion than to decide on a definition.

The human newborn brain has, among other qualities, the capacity *to learn* languages, abstract thinking, and moral judgment, but *not to create them*. With the ideological materials received during childhood and the initial training in how to use them, a more adult brain may find new combinations and new ideas, but only in reference to information received from the outside. In each individual, conscious or subconscious understanding of messages is probably dependent upon progressive steps of chemical and electrical subcoding of sensory inputs, with the resulting creation of new material carriers and codes which activate a new series of electrical and chemical phenomena, involving constellations of specialized neurons. These ideas are hypothetical but they have the advantage of being useful working hypotheses that can be tested experimentally.

While recording of electrical activity in the brain provides information limited to the carriers, it should be expected that electrical stimulation of neuronal fields may activate intracerebral processes related to both initial material carriers and subsequent subcarriers of symbolic meaning and past experiences stored in the brain. In this way we could differentiate between the cerebral mechanisms responsible for simple transmission of inputs and for the cognitive processing of received information. At the present moment we still lack neurophysiological understanding of how we enjoy music or recognize a pencil, but at least we have methodologies and working hypotheses to investigate the problem, and already we can create musical and optic hallucinatory perceptions by direct stimulation of some areas of the brain.

# Part V

# TOWARD A PSYCHO-CIVILIZED SOCIETY

Since war begins in the minds of men, it is in the minds of men that the defences of peace must be constructed.

—UNESCO Constitution

# 24

# Social Dependence and Individual Freedom

It was a blow to human pride when Copernicus and other astronomers discovered that the planet earth is neither the center of the universe nor the center of the solar system, not even unique among celestial bodies, but only an insignificant bit of matter in the immensity of galaxies, many of which may contain other highly developed planets (66, 113). The modesty of the spaceship earth is a reality, and we must accept it and adapt to it. Only then can we understand our universe and start planning to conquer the stars.

Darwin gave our pride a second blow and made an historical step toward understanding ourselves. Man had embellished fantasies about his unique origin as a descendent of gods, made master of a world graciously created for his enjoyment and fulfillment. Shattering this wishful thinking, Darwin developed the ideas of Anaximander, Lamarck, and his own grandfather, Erasmus, and proposed the doctrine of evolution. The different forms of life developed gradually from a common ancestry through a struggle for existence and survival of the fittest. Homo sapiens was not created *de novo* by special design and was only the remarkable product of a long process of biological evolution. Man is different from monkeys and lizards, just as monkeys and lizards differ from worms and amoebas. All are links in the evolutionary process. A biological memory of ancient times is preserved as functional traces in higher organisms. The chemical composition of the blood of mammals, for example, has a strong resemblance to sea water where life probably originated. Antecedents of a thinking brain may be found in lower animals, and in varying degrees, mental abilities like memory, learning, and problem solving are shared by octopus, rat, and man. By accepting this reality we can perceive our continuing evolution and become more motivated to influence the destiny of the human race.

We may now be approaching a third equally momentous discovery about ourselves. The analysis of mental activities in the context of brain physiology indicates that our own self, our ego, is not so unique or even independent, as Freud pointed out many years ago. Study of the elements which constitute personal identity reveals the two classical factors of nature and nurture. These factors are given to, and not chosen by, the individual. The amino acids which form the genes are selected and assembled in the helix by natural chance, without intervention of the desires of the owner or the donors, and according to laws related to the history of protozoas, fishes, and apes, beyond the control or awareness of man. Genetically we are not the masters but the slaves of millenniums of biological history.

The other factors which form personality originate in the environment and are initially received by each baby without any possible choice. The baby does not select his parents, country of birth, or the language spoken around him. Personality is formed by a constellation of borrowed elements related to ideological, behavioral, and cultural systems, and dependent on a continuous stream of sensory inputs. This is reality, and we must accept it and adapt to it. Only then can we apply our intelligence to the investigation and conquering of the human mind. Only then can we contemplate development of a future psychocivilized human being, a less cruel, happier, and better man. The concept of individuals as self-sufficient and independent entities is based on false premises.

In the Copernican universe, our planet and man himself were demoted from their original geocentric position, but there was still a comfortable sensation of security based on law and order, and as Newton explained, the most complex celestial phenomena could in fact be reduced to relatively simple formulas. Similar laws could be applied to falling apples or to the attraction and repulsion of planets floating in the immensity of sidereal space. Reality, however, was still more complex and less stable, and a new understanding of the universe was provided by the quantum theory of Planck and the uncertainty principle of Heisenberg, culminating in the ideas of relativity formulated by Einstein. Time and distance lost their former absolute values and appeared to have a different meaning to different observers.

The problem is that the universe has no center. Everything is relative and all that we can do is to compare the relations among given sets of values and express the result by mathematical formulas. If the size of all existing materials in the earth was suddenly reduced (or increased) 100 times (or any other amount), no human being would be able to detect the spectacular change because of the lack of units of reference. Two cars traveling at the same speed are motionless with respect to each other. While inside a jet airplane flying at 1,000 kilometers per hour, we may take a slow walk down the aisle at a speed of 1 meter per second. To say then that we are moving at 1,003.6 kilometers per hour would be meaningless unless we specified our points of reference. We do not have any absolute and immutable yardstick. The limitation of the world of physics is that it can be perceived only as the relativity of one value compared with another.

These well-known concepts of physics have a direct application to the understanding of mental functions, to which some absolute values were erroneously attributed in the past. The mind also lacks a center, and in reality its functions are based on the relativistic comparison of information which has not been created by cerebral neurons but which originates in the environment and is perceived through sensory reception of data as a temporal sequence of experiences which are processed by cerebral neurons and stored, to be used as future frames of reference.

After all, the acceptance of relativity in physics is only a consequence of the physiological properties of our brain, which lacks the intrinsic capability for absolute measurement of time or space.

We must formulate similar questions in psychology, knowing that the brain is not able to produce absolute thoughts, to create absolute values, or to unveil intrinsic principles of ethics. There is a *psychological relativity* parallel to the physical one, and our task is not to discover "true" personalities, because the search for absolute values is fantasy, but rather to investigate the origin, reception, intracerebral circulation, and behavioral manifestations of the sets of values which form the relative frame of reference of each individual. The importance of this approach is that in rejecting the immutability of values we also reject the fatal determination of destiny, and instead of accepting natural fate, we may gain a new personal freedom by using intelligence, considering that the systems of ideology and behavioral reactivity are only relative human creations which can be modified by the feedback of reason.

Man may be considered a provisional collection of matter and information, both provided by the environment, constituting relative frames of reference to be compared, within the limitations and under the terms of the human mind, with other frames of reference.

We know that atoms of oxygen, carbon, hydrogen, nitrogen, and other elements which form part of organic and inorganic compounds, such as water, vegetables, and animal proteins, have been combined in a special manner to constitute membranes, cells, and other parts of living beings, without the help of "vital spirits" or other metaphysical mysteries. Our living body is only a transitory organization of chemical compounds. We may place a radioactive tag in sodium or potassium ions, to follow their metabolic pathways as they enter the body, circulate through it, take part in specific activities, and are stored in some organ or excreted to the outside. Every single ion which forms our flesh pre-existed in nature. A small number of them, a minor fraction of the immense total, form part of each organism during its relatively brief span of existence, and all of these "personal" atoms, which in reality lack any individual specificity, will revert back to the environment. Atoms, organization, and time are the only factors which constitute the organisms, and nobody should be disturbed or offended by the fact that he has not invented or consciously chosen the ions that integrate his anatomical structure. It is true that the astonishing unique properties of awareness, thinking, and behaving are new qualities which did not exist among the properties of the single ions, and that their appearance is related to a tremendously complex organization which we still do not comprehend. In order to understand and accept this fact it may be helpful to consider that water has different physical and chemical properties than its constituent elements of hydrogen and oxygen. The complexity of organization may determine the emergence of new properties nonexistent in the simpler building blocks.

To establish a psychophysical parallel, we may consider that words, concepts, information, patterns of response, and other elements indispensable for mental activities pre-exist in culture before each individual is born. These elements enter the organism by impinging on sensory inputs, and then circulate through the central nervous system, taking part in specific mental activities and finally being stored as memories and perhaps exteriorized as part of behavioral expression. The gamut of words, symbols, and information necessary for ideological processes must be provided from the outside, and only a small portion of the existing immensity is used to structure the individual mind. No one should be disturbed by the fact that he is borrowing most of his mental constituents and that he has not invented the alphabet, mathematics, ethics, history, or any of the many subjects filling our brains.

We are provided with frames of mental reference and by necessity our reactions—and personal identity—will be related to this given frame. Individual uniqueness is merely the unique chance in the acquisition, combination, and modulation of available elements, and the relative central axis is not the individual but the elements originating in the outside. There is not much more merit—or responsibility—in learning to walk or in speaking our native tongue than there is in growing hair.

Unless we are taught to think with critical evaluation of the perceived reality and we understand the principle of psychological relativity, it will be very difficult to escape from the ideological and behavioral imprinting of early childhood. The individual may think that the most important fact of reality is his own existence, but this is only his personal point of view, a relative frame of reference which is not shared by the rest of the living world. This self-importance also lacks historical perspective, for the brief existence of one person should be considered in terms of the world population, mankind, and the whole universe. It is quite reasonable to feel that "I" am the most important creature that ever existed, but unless I realize the egocentric relativity of my appreciation at the same time, I am ignoring many other frames of reference, as valuable as my own, which are essential in order to understand my position both among other living beings and in the context of cosmic evolution. Understanding of the relative value of personal existence from the individual and cosmic points of view as complementary aspects of the same reality may facilitate the personal adaptation to the environment. It may also provide feedback possibilities of influencing this reality by using intelligent purpose to modify natural causality.

In Sartre's (194) dualism of being-in-itself (a stone is a stone, which being static always coincides with itself) and being-for-itself (the realm of consciousness perpetually beyond itself), the second aspect represents our existence as continuously *flowing out,* preventing us from possessing our being the way we can possess a static object, and creating the essential conflict and anxiety over our desire for the security of being a stable entity. This important concept should be supplemented by recognition of the essential need for a continuous *flowing in* of sensory inputs. Self-realization, after all, derives from the processing of information coming from the environment, and accomplishment is a feedback which establishes a congruence between a drive and the sensory perception of a behavioral performance. The existential flowing out cannot occur without a previous flowing in, and what flow in and out are merely information, cultural symbols, and behavioral patterns created not by the individual but by the collective effort of many men—most of them dead—accumulated through many thousands of years and graciously given to each of us.

A clearer understanding of our continuous environmental and social dependence will increase our interest in identifying and investigating the factors, reasons, and mechanisms of this dependence. Realization that the elements which form our personality and originate in the surroundings are so essential may promote the establishment of stronger intellectual and emotional bonds with the cultural source, increasing our motivation to enhance the environment which is the provider of our personal building blocks. *Social integration* may be improved when it is understood that society forms the basis of each individual and that personal destiny is related to and in large part dependent on the destiny of the whole group. Alienation from established cultural forms and lack of social responsibility could be diminished by an increased awareness of our social dependence.

In primitive societies there was a limited choice of sensory inputs, provided mainly by surrounding nature. As man was bound to a small piece of territory, he had very few opportunities for ecological, sociological, or ideological change, and natural chance was the principle source of information. In present civilized societies, many sensory inputs originate in the technological surroundings created by man. Because of mass communications, important events are shared around the world. The tragic death of one man, once an incident of local significance, may now be reported globally and felt as a personal loss by millions of distant people. The work of one person who discovers electricity or antibiotics may now transform the quality of life in all countries. Different technologies, arts, sciences, and political and religious ideologies affect the lives of most men. In principle, adults can select their country, climate, and culture and any setting from the sensory isolation of a psychologist's experimental cubicle to the sensory assault of a metropolis.

But the desires and mechanisms for choice are determined mainly by early childhood experiences, cultural imprinting, and learned patterns of response. Newborn babies are completely dependent on parental care for the quality and quantity of sensory inputs as well as for food and warmth. The elements offered by the environment are almost infinite, but only a limited number are used to structure each individual. Their selection depends on chance, which among many variables includes the presence and behavior of parents and teachers. We must recognize that initially an individual has no control over the sensory inputs which mold his mind, and that during the decisive years of childhood, when each of us receives emotional impacts, behavioral formulas, and ideological frameworks, we are unable to search independently for alternatives. Our initial personality is structured in a rather automatic way when our capacity for intelligent choice has not developed.

If we accept that early experience is decisive for the establishment of personal identity, then we must accept that individual mental structure is not self-determined but heterodetermined by the interaction of genes received from our ancestors and information received from the environment and culture. Where, then, is the freedom to construct personal identity? To clarify these ideas, let us remember that liberal societies are based on the principle of individual self-determination, with the assumption that each human being is *born free* and has the *right* to develop his own mind, to construct his own ideology, to shape his own behavior, and to express his personality without external pressures or indoctrination. The role of education, which involves both parents and schools, is to help these processes evolve with due respect for the individual. One of the main goals in these societies is "to find ourselves," and to develop our potential while remaining independent and self-sufficient. Privacy has a high priority in its intellectual, emotional, material, and territorial aspects, and personal freedom stops with interference in the rights of others.

This kind of liberal orientation has great appeal, but unfortunately its assumptions are not supported by neurophysiological and psychological studies of intracerebral mechanisms. The brain of the newborn lacks the stored information, neurronal circuits, and functional keyboards prerequisite to the formulation of choice. The infant may have the right to be free, but he has neither the option nor the biological mechanisms for free behavior. Confrontation with a multiplicity of choices may create confusion and anxiety in a child who does not yet possess the necessary mental sophistication to choose. This frustrating situation of inadequacy may have a traumatic and deforming effect rather than a constructive and positive one. The brain of an adult usually possesses the capacity to select a response but even it is not self-sufficient; for the brain needs constant environmental inputs in order to preserve mental normality, and a flow of information is necessary to make each judgment against the background of experience.

The decisive importance of children's education has been recognized in pedagogy, psychology, and sociology, and the permissive or authoritarian orientation has been a highly controversial subject. Without entering directly into this debate, I would like to point out the fallacy in the theory that permissiveness develops the "true" and "free" personality of the child. Permissiveness, like any other educational approach to human relations, imposes a type of response which influences the processing of sensory inputs and establishes a pattern of behavior. Education has consequences predictable within a range of variability. Obviously if we were not expecting some result, we would not educate. We may argue that the personality developed through permissiveness is better adapted to present times, or that it will have less—or more—psychological and social conflicts. We should understand, however, that a permissively structured child is as much the product of his parents' manipulation as the child of the most authoritarian mother. The choice is the parents', not the child's.

The brain, per se, with all its genes, is not sufficient for the development of a mind in the absence of external information, and the content of this information is decisive in the establishment of mental structure. Even the withdrawal of parental care is a factor which can irrevocably shape future behavior of the young, as demonstrated by Harlow's neurotic motherless monkeys and by the emotional and mental handicap suffered by homeless children.

When a parent passively accepts violent behavior, insulting words, or physical assault from his child, he is positively reinforcing this kind of reaction and is facilitating the establishment of aggressive patterns which may be generalized to other social situations later on. While physical aggression is rare in four year olds, by six years of age a child has developed sufficient motor skills and curiosity to engage in social interaction and competition with his peers. Studies have shown that at this point intermittent or differential reinforcing of antisocial behavior is the most effective method for establishing patterns of aggression (9). Some tendencies are inborn, but the quality and quantity of their expression depend on experience. Repression of violence may create undesirable conflicts and frustrations only when the pattern of violence has already been created by previous learning. A basic inborn drive like sex is a blind force dependent on symbols, experience, and cultural patterns of response.

Whatever we do or fail to do when we are in charge of a baby will influence his future mental structure. Our attitude, therefore, should not be to close our eyes and accept chance, but to investigate the extracerebral and intracerebral elements which intervene in the formation of personality. To study what is going on inside of the brain is as important as to consider the other aspects of education and behavior.

These remarks are intended both to demonstrate that we

should not base our interpersonal relations on false or unproved assumptions and to indicate the need to study these problems experimentally within the framework of intracerebral physiology. As our power to influence the mental structure of man continually increases, we face the question of the kind of people we would like to create. We must realize that parents and educators are imprinting and manipulating the minds and personalities of young people in any case, and that we are responsible for giving coherent form and ethical purpose to the psychogenetic elements transmitted to the child. The issue is whether violence and other behavioral patterns are inborn and inevitable or whether they are mainly related to a cultural learning which may be influenced by intelligent planning.

Ecological forces cannot be ignored or destroyed. Liberation from and domination of the environment became possible when we discovered the laws of nature and directed them with our intelligence. We cannot ignore the biological laws of the mind either. We should use our intelligence to direct our behavior, rather than accept its determination by unknown forces. Through education we should provide awareness of the elements, including intracerebral mechanisms, which intervene in the formation of personal identity, and we should teach the processes of decision-making and intelligent choice. Personal freedom is not a biological gift but a mental attribute which must be learned and cultivated. To be free is not to satisfy sexual drive, to fill an empty stomach, or to quarrel with our wives because of our repressed fears or mother-infant relations. Freedom requires the recognition of biological drives and their intelligent direction through processes of sublimation, substitution, postponement, or simply their satisfaction with civilized refinement and enjoyment. Individual freedom will increase when we understand the setting of our personality in early childhood and when we develop means for the intelligent evaluation and emotional interpretation of the information reaching us from the environment.

We should try to establish, at the earliest possible moment

of the baby's life, a program of *psychogenesis*, meaning the use of available physiological, psychological, and psychiatric knowledge for the formation of the child's personality. Courses on psychogenesis should be taken by parents and educators as well as by children as a part of the school curriculum. The postulates of psychogenesis are: (1) The mind does not exist at the moment of birth. (2) The mind cannot appear in the absence of sensory inputs. (3) Individual identity and personal behavior are not properties of the brain which will unfold automatically through neuronal maturation, but are acquired functions which must be learned and therefore depend essentially on the reception of sensory inputs. (4) The purpose of education is not the unveiling of individual mental functions but *the creation, the genesis of them.* (5) Symbols from the environment will be physically integrated within the brain as molecular changes in the neuronal structure. (6) Man is not born free but subservient to genes and education. (7) Personal freedom is not inherited nor is it a gift of nature, but one of the highest attainments of civilization which requires awareness and intellectual and emotional training in order to process and choose consciously and intelligently among environmental alternatives. (8) Education should not be authoritarian because then mental flexibility is reduced, handicapping creativity and forcing behavioral conformity or producing hyperreactive rejection and rebellion. Education should not be permissive either, because then other kinds of automatisms are being developed, determined by the blind chance of environmental circumstances. In a permissive atmosphere, the individual may be a slave of his own emotions, while an authoritarian upbringing creates a tyranny of inhibitions and conformism. Both extremes are undesirable and it is preferable to direct mental and behavioral development toward a self-determination of goals, knowing that if we want to create free individuals, we must teach them to be so (210). Understanding of the cerebral mechanisms involved in behavioral responses provides a feedback which modifies these mechanisms, introducing elements of conscious determination.

In recent generations, there has been an anxious search for freedom and personal identity, an attempt to escape from the faceless mass of a technological society, and a rebellion against traditional morality, ethical principles, and ideological clichés. In this challenge to established values, sensory stimulation has grown louder, men's hair longer, skirts shorter, and rebellion has become the goal—to be free from family, teachers, and society; to let the mind float, searching for the depth of the self, perhaps with psychedelic aids, perceiving a stream of uninhibited messages and dreams; to live a natural life without the artificial pressures of schedules and obligations; to have free speech, free expression, artistic creativity without established rules, and a multiperception of feelings flooding the senses.

In this attitude, which is responsible for many of the present conflicts and maladjustments, there is a fallacy similar to the fallacy of permissive education. We cannot be free from parents, teachers, and society because they are the extracerebral sources of our minds, and to resent or deny this reality is not going to change it. A young person can be proud of working hard, but he cannot take credit for being smart: studies have shown that IQ is determined by the environment, and that the intellectual and motor skills required for success must be taught by the guardians of childhood. The persistence of dependence on an initial source of emotions and information, like the mother, can be undesirable, but this problem should not be confused with the existence of bonds and education provided by the mother and by society.

We may disagree with the system of values and ideology given to us, and subsequently we may espouse a different philosophy and try to assume another identity. Great alterations are possible, and we may cherish or curse our past, but its cultural elements will be forever our frame of reference. In the depth of our minds we are going to discover only the remains of what we have learned and experienced.

The young Americans who have taken refuge in Ibiza or Crete seldom identify with the customs or ideology of their adopted lands. They enjoy nature but do not participate in local culture. They admit to feeling "American," although they may reject the present economic or political values of the United States. Their basic emotional patterns of response were established during early childhood and their later changes are limited. This fact is in part related to the progressive loss of neuronal plasticity through age.

The old temple inscription "Know Thyself" is often repeated today, but perhaps it is not adequate. It should declare "Construct Thyself" as well. Shape your mind, train your thinking power, and direct your emotions more rationally; liberate your behavior from the ancestral burden of reptiles and monkeys— be a man and use your intelligence to orient the reactions of your mind.

The human being is a functional trinity of sensory inputs and behavioral responses connected by the essential link of intra-cerebral processes. The three aspects are equally essential, even if only the first two were considered important in the past. Today we have begun to unravel the secrets of cerebral activities, and a new perspective for the understanding of man is emerging from the experimental complexities of neurobehavioral data.

# 25

# Natural Causality and Intelligent Planning in the Organization of Human Behavior

Perhaps the most important quality of civilization is the substitution of intelligent planning for natural chance. Today our lives are not regulated by hunting needs, darkness of night, or seasonal variations. We may request food by telephone, flip a switch for light, or adjust a dial to obtain a room temperature. At the same time that we have gained freedom from natural elements, we have become increasingly dependent on coordinated technical planning. The accomplishments in outer space travel are an outstanding example. Escape from gravity abolished man's historical bond to the earth; day and night rhythms were drastically changed; time and space took on new dimensions; the horizon vanished; the cardinal points lost meaning, and a totally new system of references and computations had to be created in order to navigate and survive orbiting around and beyond the earth. It is symbolic that man's new found celestial freedom required the greatest imaginable social dependence. Every single bit of each space vehicle represented the combined thinking and material efforts of thousands of men. Even the air to be breathed inside the capsule had to be carefully calculated and stored.

Manipulation of natural elements for the benefit of mankind is usually accepted as highly desirable, and most of us are rather proud of the colossal engineering efforts involved in changing the course of a river, joining oceans formerly separated by land, or reaching distant stars with our instruments. These wonderful realities are considered a logical consequence of our present cultural system, although they would have been impossible to materialize or even to conceive of several thousand years ago. Can we imagine the attitude of primitive man about tampering with the eternal stability of the rivers or about capturing the sparks of lightning with a metallic rod? The suggestion would have been rejected as foolish and impossible, if not sacrilegious. "Reaching for the moon" was the expression for striving for an unattainable goal, although that actual goal has now been realized.

We may wonder whether man's still ingrained conceptions about the untouchable self are not reminiscent of the ancient belief that it was completely beyond human power to alter omnipotent nature. We are at the beginning of a new ideological and technological revolution in which the objectives are not physical power and control of the environment, but direct intervention into the fate of man himself.

The fact that the human brain is learning to influence its own material and functional substratum should not be interpreted as a foolish attempt to modify "cosmic design," or to change "God's will," but simply as the appearance of a new mechanism determined by the normal evolution of natural chance. Human domination of ecological forces should not be taken as a victory against natural fate but as a result of it, in the same way that the flight of a bird against gravity is not in defiance of physical laws. Nature, not man, deserves credit for creating a thinking brain. Natural evolution provided the cerebral properties of originality, foresight, and awareness. The process was probably comparable to the needs of warm-blooded animals which required the development of a neuronal thermostat, located in the hypothalamus, in order to regulate complex vasomotor and metabolic mechanisms to keep body temperature within narrow limits. The newcomer in the series of warm mammals seems to be developing a novel and most useful homeostatic mechanism which in the future will perhaps be referred to as the "psychostat," meaning the intelligent neuronal adaptation for the maintenance of mental stability in spite of changes in external and internal demands. Natural evolution should favor the development of this mechanism which certainly has great survival value in the present world of tensions and conflicts. Natural evolution is, however, too slow, and if we recognize the decisive importance of the new development, we may be able to facilitate the feedback of cognitive behavior upon its own material basis of cerebral physiology.

When atomic energy was discovered, its destructive capabilities were developed much faster than its constructive applications, and the blame for this tragedy must be placed on the lack of human reason—on the functional inadequacy of our little brains which have not yet learned to solve their behavioral conflicts reasonably. The danger of atomic misuse may, hopefully, be solved by new ideas produced by better brains to come, while the risks derived from behavioral control may be created and at the same time avoided by the same subject of inquiry, the mind, which contains within itself all the elements for search and for decision and cannot expect any external help. As Dobzhansky (65) has said, "In giving rise to man, the evolutionary process has, apparently for the first and only time in the history of the Cosmos, become conscious of itself. This opens at least a possibility that evolution may some day be directed by man, and that prevalence of the absurd may be cut down."

The phrase "control of human behavior" is emotionally loaded, in part because of its threat to the "inviolability of the ego" and in part because of unpleasant associations with dictatorships, brainwashing, and selfish exploitation of man. Well-known novels like Huxley's *Brave New World* (114), Orwell's *1984* (168), and Condon's *The Manchurian Candidate* (40) are exposés of utopian societies with obedient, soma-drugged, satisfied individuals whose activities are planned by the master minds of the ruling council. These satires are meant to shock the reader, but other novels also based on cultural design and behavioral engineering, such as Skinner's *Walden Two* (209), have more messianic tones. The problem of external controls was well expressed by Skinner (210) when he described

a world in which there is food, clothing, and shelter for all, where everyone chooses his own work and works on the average only 4 hours a day, where music and the arts flourish, where personal relationships develop under the most favorable circumstances, where education prepares every child for the social and intellectual life which lies before him, where—in short—people are truly happy, secure, productive, creative, and forward looking. What is wrong with it? Only one thing: someone "planned it that way."

The concern about external planning depends to a great extent on learned attitudes, and the circular problem is that arbiters of ethical values are so biased by ideas of the prevailing, self-perpetuating cultural system that they cannot objectively evaluate their own evaluations. To own slaves was considered a respectable manifestation of social status not too long ago. Inculcation of honesty, loyalty, bravery, and self-sacrifice is the custom in many cultures, but by adding obedience and mobilizing the population for aggressive action against other groups, all these excellent qualities are perverted.

The dangers inherent in the control of human behavior are recognized by Skinner as well as by most investigators, and the hope that the new power acquired by the behavioral sciences will be restricted to the scientists or to some benevolent elite is little supported by either recent or distant history. Faith in science has been shattered when the stupendous discoveries of physics have been applied to kill several hundred thousand human beings in a single blow, when teams of investigators have been applying their skills to find more efficient napalm oils to burn villages, when civilized countries are stockpiling deadly gases, germs, and megatons of lethal power, and when governmental elites are using computers and "think centers" to calculate a game of destruction and retaliation. Greater efficiency in behavioral control could be only a more subtle and dangerous weapon. No wonder that Berkner (15) has posed the question "Is there intelligent life on earth?" while Cole (38) expressed universal concern by asking, "Can the world be saved?"

These very serious problems must be recognized and solutions must be found. Danger has never stopped progress; the risk is not in the acquisition of knowledge but in its improper use; notwithstanding problems and concerns, atomic investigations will continue their explosive development, and control of human behavior will advance rapidly in methodology and applicability. We must accept the reality that different degrees of behavioral control have been practiced since immemorial times, are widely used at present, and will expand in the future. Man is a social animal and interpersonal relations are a form of mutual control. The mother certainly teaches her baby. The policeman imposes order on city traffic. To discuss whether human behavior can or should be controlled is naive and misleading. We should discuss what kinds of controls are ethical, considering the efficiency and mechanisms of existing procedures and the desirable degree of these and other controls in the future.

Available techniques can be classified in two groups: (1) Use of chemical and physical agents to induce modifications in neurophysiological activity. This category includes psychoactive drugs and direct electrical manipulation of the brain. (2) Use of positive or negative social reinforcements, based on the sensory relations between the subject and his environment, mainly other human beings who are the suppliers of stimuli. This category includes subliminal stimulation, conditioning, social pressure, psychotherapy, hypnosis, sensory deprivation, and brainwashing. In these situations the behavior of one individual is planned or at least purposefully influenced by another.

In the control of behavior through psychotherapy, the doctor uses his own experience and scientific knowledge in order to influence the reactions of the patient who has consented to the general procedure. In this situation, there is a communication of values and behavioral characteristics, and it has been pointed out that "whether or not the analyst is consciously tempted to act as a teacher, model and ideal to his patients, he inevitably does so to a greater or lesser extent; and this is a central aspect of the psychoanalytic process" (152). Patients who improve after psychotherapy have often changed their moral values on sex, aggression, and authority to conform to those of the therapist, but there is much less modification in the patients who have not improved (189). The overwhelming experimental evidence shows that human behavior can be controlled by psychological means (131), and the new approach of physical manipulation of the brain is only one more aspect of possible behavioral control.

The widely accepted principle that "all men are born free and equal" is cherished as the backbone of democratic societies and the basis of human dignity. If we interpret the statement as an ideal for social organization or as a symbolic expression of human rights, the principle is certainly commendable. If we analyze its biological basis, however, we realize that freedom of the newborn is only wishful thinking, and that literal acceptance of this fallacy may cause frustrations and conflicts. Expecting freedom, we may be puzzled by the reality of biological determination and early imprinting compounded by the servitude to a mechanized and organized society. This dilemma would be eased if we realized that liberty is not a natural, inborn characteristic of human expression but a product of awareness and intelligent thinking which must be acquired by conscious individual and collective efforts. Civilization has accelerated the elaboration of human potential including the possibility for greater freedom, but its fulfillment is contingent on purposeful efforts to escape from the countless elements of behavioral determination.

Heredity is established by pure chance—not chosen by parents or by the individual—and this genetic determination represents the potential to be a genius or an idiot. Denying the existence of mental functions in the newborn, emphasizing the essentiality of extracerebral elements for the appearance of the mind, and accepting that the baby lacks the capacity to search for and to choose the decisive initial inputs leads to the conclusion of the possibility and convenience of intelligent planning as superior to blind chance. The poet needs words—which he did not invent—to write a poem; the mason needs bricks, constructed by someone else, to build a house; the thinker needs ideas, provided by readings and experience, in order to develop new concepts; and the baby, who is the first state of poets, masons, and thinkers, has the absolute need of cultural inputs in order to become a man.

The "personal identity" of the newborn is a question of definition, because initially he has potentialities rather than realities. Being left- or right-handed, more or less excitable, possessing a white or black skin, and the faculty—or inability—to learn are genetically determined characteristics. After the baby is born, the choices are: *who* is going to provide the necessary information and training, *what and how much* will be provided, and the *techniques* to be used. The ideological vacuum of the newborn brain cannot be filled by autochthonous neuronal spikes but by experiences and cultural inputs. The unfortunate circumstance is that the baby, for whom the consequences of these choices are so important, is totally unable to participate in the discussion.

The elements which form the frame of reference for individual mental structure include, among others, language, knowledge, beliefs, and patterns of response, but the number of existing cultural elements is enormous and only a few are received by each person. This requires a process of selection which is influenced by (1) natural chance, represented, for example, by country of birth, social environment, and economic factors; (2) national organization which uses mass media to communicate facts, news, and ideology with a variable degree of bias (and which also controls the educational system and may deprive people of specific knowledge and experiences by means of social and political pressure, censorship, and repression); (3) family and friends, who represent the most important sources of information in early childhood; and (4) the individual himself, who may choose cultural elements, but only after he has acquired the power of reason and choice, and within the limits of available information. This power will be considerably biased by the three previous groups of factors.

Let us accept that the structure of mental qualities and their behavioral manifestations depend on genetic, neurophysiological, and cultural factors which can be investigated, known, and modified by intelligent planning. Let us accept also that the necessary methodology is available or will soon be developed. The most important question then is how we shall use this power. How should the human mind be structured? Which mental qualities and behavioral responses should be favored or inhibited? Who will be the human artifact created by intelligent manipulation? As Rogers has asked, "Who will be controlled? Who will exercise control? What type of control will be exercised? Most important of all . . . toward what end or what purpose, or in the pursuit of what value, will control be exercised?" (188).

Powerful cultural determination is already being imposed on the behavior of children and adults, but as history shows it has not been too successful in preventing or solving human conflicts. Our predicament is that the power to control behavior is progressing very rapidly in both knowledge and technology, while we still do not know in which direction to use it. Skinner, who is the main proponent of cultural design, has listed the specifications for a behavioral technology as follows: "Let men be happy, informed, skillful, well behaved, and productive" (210), but in a later publication (211) he has not been so definite about these goals; and the implicit assumption is that behavioral control will bring "a far better world for everyone."

The contention that an ideal society should be "well behaved" may be disputed by many and in any case requires a clarification of meaning. In some old plantations slaves behaved very well, worked hard, were submissive to their masters, and were probably happier than some of the free blacks in modern ghettos. In several dictatorial countries the general population is skillful, productive, well behaved, and perhaps as happy as those in more democratic societies. It is doubtful, however, that slavery or dictatorship should be our models. To outline a formula for the future ideal man is not easy. This is partly due to the fact that if man is identified by his mental qualities, our difficulty is increased because we do not know these qualities well, and they are evolving entities with an unpredictable future. How would it have been possible 100 years ago to foresee the biological convenience of resisting radiation or gravitational forces? These concepts were beyond the thinking range of the epoch. How can we outline the mental requirements for a mankind in search of another planet to inhabit when the earth loses its warmth and can no longer support life? Our present problem is far from clear although it requires immediate action: How should we orient human behavior in the present and in the next few decades?

The confusion about behavioral goals contrasts sharply with the relative clarity of material needs. Food, clothing, and shelter may be accepted as the most basic requirements, to which we may add health, education, and leisure. The puzzling reality is that the excellent material accomplishment of our present civilization has not only failed to solve human conflicts and clashes but has increased their destructive efficiency, creating additional and unexpected problems such as alienation and ecological pollution without increasing human happiness. The new generations of affluent societies experience growing restlessness and escalating explosions of rebellion which may be interpreted as an anxious search for identity and purpose. The complaint is spiritual more than material, a rejection of the established order with its "false" values, without, however, reaching the creative crisis of a better cause. It is a wishful yearning for freedom while remaining chained to behavioral patterns of the group: contempt for television, automobiles, and detergents; contempt for affiliations with the church, state, or military. This attitude often leads the alienated to seek sex without love and the artificial paradise of mental distortion provided by drugs; to live aimlessly for today while feeling the emptiness of the future.

They search for the independent self without realizing its essential biological and ideological dependence.

Some of our present problems derive from the lack of balance between material and mental evolutions. We are civilized in our physical ecological accomplishments but barbaric in our psychological responses. Within some limits we can control atoms, trees, and animals, while we have not learned to control ourselves. New solutions are needed in order to civilize our psyche, consciously to organize our efforts to develop a future psychocivilized society.

Recognizing that we must do something in order to understand the human mind better and to improve the human condition is not very original. This idea was expressed before Platonic and Aristotelian times. What is surprising is the limited practicality of the solutions proposed in the past. Why after several thousand years of civilization are human beings continuing to torture and kill each other? Why do we agree in our efforts to understand and dominate natural forces, while we disagree on the organization of mankind? Why have some countries reached a considerable degree of physical comfort without enjoying a comparable degree of personal happiness?

One aspect of the problem is certainly that the many factors involved are not well known and may be in conflict. Another is that philosophy, sociology, and the behavioral sciences have been limited to the outside of organisms, ignoring the internal organization which is responsible for behavioral activity. The tremendous possibilities introduced by new methodologies will allow the exploration of the depth of functioning brains and the influencing of their physiological mechanisms. Knowledge acquired through this approach will permit a more realistic and precise understanding of the human mind and of its behavioral consequences, and it will also permit the introduction of a greater amount of awareness and intelligence in the determination of behavioral responses. This orientation should not be identified with authoritarian control. To the contrary, "awareness of our own needs and attitudes is our most effective instrument for maintaining our own integrity and control over our own reactions" (187). Awareness is a major element in defense against external manipulation. "Throughout the course of his life . . . an individual is an active participant in the creation of his own mind, the development of his own self, and more generally speaking, his own reality world" (28).

How much reason we use to influence our personal fate is up to us. Even the most deterministic doctrine must accept the role of individual intelligence as a feedback in the constellation of behavioral determinants. Planning the organization of mental functions in children—and in adults—may be oriented toward an increase in the awareness of the cultural elements and neurological mechanisms involved in decision-making. Increasing the participation of conscious evaluation diminishes the automatism of responses, increases responsibility, augments individual differentiation of reactivity, and permits enjoyment of a greater degree of freedom because the choices are more thoughtful and in accord with personal evaluation of the circumstances. One of the aims of the planners of psychocivilization should be to expose and avoid the psychological traps being built into our increasingly organized societies. We should try to avoid the present trend to dehumanize our behavior, in which social relations are effective but not affective. Services in hospitals, schools, and shops are progressively automatized and depersonalized, so that now merchandise, information, words, and money may be exchanged between people without personal contact.

These problems must be identified and understood at their many sociological, psychological, and neurophysiological levels in order to make decisions about how to face them. The psychocivilized trend should avoid the inculcation of rigid patterns of response while favoring the power of reason through better knowledge of the intervening factors, including intracerebral functioning. To pontificate about moral codes or to impose restrictive measures may be less desirable—and less effective—than to clarify the reasons for individual choice. A very important decision to make is whether we are going to accept the prevailing orientation of human life toward construction of more automobiles and designing of orbital bombs, or whether we would prefer to dedicate greater social effort to investigating and directing our own minds, which must create and interpret our circumstances.

The fundamental question of who is going to exert the power of behavioral control is easy to answer: everybody who is aware of the elements involved and understands how they act upon us will have that power. It is therefore essential that relevant information not be restricted to a small elite but be shared by all. In this way, solutions will be the product of collective thinking, and more importantly, the individual will be provided with a critical sense which will diminish his dependence on group decisions and allow the search for new personal solutions and therefore greater individual freedom.

# 26

# A Tentative Plan

A new technology has been developed for the exploration of cerebral mechanisms in behaving subjects, and it has already provided data about the intracerebral correlates of learning, memory, drives, performance, and other aspects of mental functions. This methodology has proved that movements, sensations, emotions, desires, ideas, and a variety of psychological phenomena may be induced, inhibited, or modified by electrical stimulation of specific areas of the brain. These facts have changed the classical philosophical concept that the mind was beyond experimental reach.

To study psychic mechanisms it is convenient to identify and to investigate the elements responsible for the initiation of mental activity at birth and for its continuation throughout life. The newborn baby lacks detectable mental activity, and the reception of sensory information from the environment is absolutely necessary for the development of psychic manifestations. The adult is also dependent on a continuous reception of sensory inputs for the preservation of mental normality.

Understanding and study of the essential and continuous dependence of the mind on sensory reception will favor man's social integration because it shows that we cannot live alone and that we need constant inputs of information and sensations from the environment for our mental survival. At the same time, understanding and experimental investigation of the genetic, environmental, and intracerebral elements which determine mental structure will favor the intelligent selection of these elements, and thus increase the basis for individual differentiation and personal freedom.

Many scientists have already been attracted by the potential of the neurobehavioral sciences. Brain research institutes flourish, publications are increasing in number, and the International Brain Research Organization (IBRO) was recently founded to promote study of the central nervous system and to encourage international collaboration in this field. The social sciences, which have a behavioral rather than a physiological orientation, are also in rapid development, partly because of increasing public awareness of ghettos, juvenile violence, educational problems, and general social unrest. Social scientists investigate interpersonal and intergroup relations, considering factors like the emotions, economy, culture, and working conditions, all of which are involved in man's adaptation to his ever more complex surroundings. The source of behavioral interactions, however, and the mechanisms underlying anxiety, violence, drives, and motivations depend on mental activities, which are usually excluded from these studies. Both the neurobehavioral and the social sciences are very active fields, but their present rate of growth is too slow and their objectives too limited to give adequate support to the ambitious project of improving the present imbalance of civilization.

I am well aware that although learning has detectable electrical correlates in the brain and emotional behavior may be controlled by cerebral radio stimulation in monkey colonies, these and similar facts are rather distant from the problems created and the solutions required by juvenile delinquency or by international tensions. We must realize, however, that the potential of new fields must be evaluated by the importance of the newly discovered principles and their possible future applications.

When Papin saw the lid of a pot being raised by boiling water and expressed this phenomenon as a physical law, it would have been difficult to foresee electricity being produced by steam-driven turbines or ocean liners crossing the seas. The experimental reality was a daily household occurrence; understanding the potential applications of the principle was transcendental. If we could modify mental mechanisms intelligently, the consequences would be far more important than the consequences of extending man's life span or limiting his birth rate, because to influence mental processes is to influence the source of all human activities.

To increase significantly the manpower and resources devoted to neurobehavioral sciences it will be necessary first to make the public as well as the scientific and political authorities aware that an effort of unusual proportions is essential, explaining the reasons for this effort along with the consequences and possible individual and social gains. Second, it should be made known that the necessary technology is already available and that significant results have already been obtained. Third, a strategy should be developed to mobilize public opinion, talent, and resources. This strategy requires interdisciplinary collaboration in order to organize a general plan of action which should include the following aspects.

## Scientific Investigation

Acquisition of new knowledge is the cornerstone of scientific advance, and a massive increase in research into the cerebral mechanisms of mental activity could be initiated simply by applying the available technology on a larger scale. This effort, however, cannot be generated by the scientists themselves but must be promoted and organized by governmental action declaring "conquering of the human mind" a national goal at parity with conquering of poverty or landing a man on the moon. National agencies should be created in order to coordinate plans, budgets, and actions just as NASA in the United States has directed public interest and technology, launching the country into the adventures and accomplishments of outer space. Fortunately brain research is much less expensive, and rather than building up new industrial empires, it is necessary to create neurobehavioral institutes with the specific purpose of investigating the mechanisms of the behaving brain, while more basic neurophysiological research continues at its normal rate of growth. These institutes require interdisciplinary organization because their main purpose will be to correlate genetics, anatomy, physiology, biochemistry, and psychopharmacology with behavioral, mental, and sociological phenomena. The main aim is to establish a scientific foundation for the creation of a future psychocivilized society based on a better understanding of mental activities, on the liberation from the domination of irrational mental determinants, on the establishment of personal freedom through intelligent choice, and on a balance between the material and mental development of civilization with the power of reason directing the use of increasing technological control of our physical environment. The research will be oriented toward its application to psychology, psychiatry, and education without excluding philosophical implications.

The project of conquering the human mind could be a central theme for international cooperation and understanding because its aim is to know the mechanisms of the brain, which make all men behave and misbehave, which give us pleasure and suffering, which promote love and hate. The differences in genetic potential among men are magnified grotesquely, like shadows on a wall, by the educational environment in which they find themselves. Even if political ideas, cultural values, and behavioral reactivity vary, the basic physical, intellectual, and emotional needs of man are the same and must have similar neurophysiological mechanisms which can be investigated. Hate and destruction are not functional properties of the brain but elements introduced through sensory inputs into the neuronal reactivity; they originate not within the person, but in the environment.

## Communication

Interdisciplinary communication is always important, but it is even more essential in the neurobehavioral sciences because they are at the crossroads of diverse disciplines. Cross-communication should involve investigators not only in related biological fields but also in areas which ordinarily have less contact with neural sciences, like sociology, pedagogy, and philosophy. At present there is an important body of knowledge about cerebral physiology and behavioral responses that has not been absorbed into general scientific texts and has not evoked the philosophical repercussions it deserves. Specialists usually recognize the need to communicate beyond their own discipline, but in practice they often neglect to do so, and this should be one of the purposes of the neurobehavioral institutes.

## Manpower Shift

In free enterprise systems, a shift in manpower requires the attraction and training of the corresponding personnel, and this is usually accomplished by offering intellectual, economic, and social incentives. With this procedure, talented workers have been attracted to newly developing fields such as electronics and outer space technology, and it will be necessary in the neurobehavioral field as well. In this case, however, something else is needed because a plan designed to modify the orientation of civilization and to improve the balance between mechanization and mentalization must be based on suitable education of youth, beginning with elementary schools and continuing through the highest levels.

## Education of Youth

Educators and psychologists have recognized that the intellectual and emotional impact of training received at an early age is decisive for the rest of one's life. Important conceptions about mental activities and the functioning of the brain which will have great influence on the student's future development should be introduced as early as possible—just as today's child is confronted with information about man's escape from his terrestrial environment via interplanetary flights. These subjects should continue with greater sophistication at secondary school and college levels, competing for teaching time with all other subjects. What I am proposing is a modification of the curriculum to introduce the discipline of "psychogenesis." Its purpose would be to teach factual scientific material about cerebral mechanisms, to increase the student's awareness of his own mental and behavioral activity, and to show him how to use his intelligence to decide which behavioral determinants to accept and which to reject. The present orientation of courses in psychology and sociology should be adapted and expanded according to this plan.

## Social Education

Understanding of the mechanisms of individual and social behavior could be an important feedback factor for the modulation of behavioral responses because this understanding will simultaneously increase the importance of individual intellect and decrease the power of irrational automatisms. Education of the general public would be facilitated by the natural interest in understanding the activity of our own minds. The mass media must be mobilized for this purpose, and preparation of entertaining and informative programs should be encouraged and promoted by the neurobehavioral institutes.

## Related Problems

A host of medical, ethical, legal, and political questions are involved in the possibility of intelligent choice among behavioral determinants and their control. Each of these aspects deserves careful study and should form part of the general plan of action.

I want to emphasize that human happiness is a relative value and depends as much on mental interpretation as on environmental reality. A better understanding of mental mechanisms will favor the pursuit of happiness and diminish the unnecessary suffering of human beings. The direction of the colossal forces discovered by man requires the development of mental qualities able to apply intelligence not only to the domination of nature but also to the civilization of the human psyche.

# Bibliography

1. AHFELD, J. F. Beiträge zur Lehre vom Uebergange der intra-uterinen Athmung zur extrauterinen. Pp. 1–32 in: "Beiträge zur Physiologie, Festschrift zu Carl Ludwig, zu seinem 70. Geburtstage gewidmet von seinen Schülern." Leipzig: Vogel, 1890.

2. ALBERTS, W. W., E. W. WRIGHT, JR., G. LEVIN and B. FEINSTEIN. Types of responses elicited by electrical stimulation of certain nuclei of the thalamus and basal ganglia in the human. EEG clin. Neurophysiol., 12:546, 1960.

3. ALTMAN, J. Autoradiographic and histological studies of post-natal neurogenesis. II. J. comp. Neurol., 128:431–473, 1967.

4. ANDERSON, B., P. A. JEWELL and S. LARSSON. An appraisal of the effects of diencephalic stimulation of conscious animals in terms of normal behaviour. Pp. 76–89 in: "Neurological Basis of Behaviour," G. E. W. Wolstenholme and C. M. O'Conner, (eds.) Boston: Little, Brown & Co., 400 pp., 1958.

5. ANGULO Y GONZÁLEZ, A. W. Is myelinogeny an absolute index of behavioral capability? J. comp. Neurol., 48:459–464, 1929.

6. ASHBY, W. R. "Design for a Brain." 2nd Ed. New York: Wiley, 286 pp., 1960.

7. AUSTT, GARCIA E., R. ARANA, E. MIGLIARO, M. T. SANDE and J. P. SEGUNDO. Changes in the EEG and in the tendon jerks induced by stimulation of the fornix in man. EEG clin. Neurophysiol., 6:653–661, 1954.

8. BALDWIN, M. Electrical stimulation of the mesial temporal region. Pp. 159–176 in: "Electrical Studies on the Unanesthetized Brain," E R. Ramey and D. S. O'Doherty, (eds.) New York: Paul B. Hoeber, 423 pp., 1960.

9. BANDURA, A. A social learning interpretation of psychological dysfunctions. Pp. 293–344 in: "Foundations of Abnormal

Psychology," P. London and D. Rosenhan, (eds.) New York: Rinehart and Winston, 644 pp., 1968.

10. BARRETT, W. "Irrational Man. A Study in Existential Philosophy." New York: Doubleday, 278 pp., 1958.

11. BEACH, F. A. The perpetuation and evolution of biological science. Amer. Psychologist, 21:943–949, 1966.

12. BEECHER, H. K. Ethics and clinical research. New Eng. J. Med., 274:1354–1360, 1966.

13. BENNETT, E. L., M. C. DIAMOND, D. KRECH, and M. R. ROSENZWEIG. Chemical and anatomical plasticity of brain. Science, 146:610–619, 1964.

14. BERITOFF, J. S. "Neural Mechanisms of Higher Vertebrate Behavior." Trans. from Russian and Edited by W. T. Liberson. Boston: Little Brown, 384 pp., 1965.

15. BERKNER, L. V. Man versus technology. Population Bull., 22:83–94, 1966.

16. BERLYNE, D. E. "Conflict, Arousal, and Curiosity." New York: McGraw-Hill, 350 pp., 1960.

17. BERTALANFFY, L. VON. "Robots, Men and Minds." New York: Braziller, 150 pp., 1967.

18. BEXTON, W. H., W. HERON and T. H. SCOTT. Effects of decreased variation in the sensory environment. Canad. J. Psychol., 8:70–76, 1954.

19. BICKFORD, R. G., M. C. PETERSEN, H. W. DODGE, JR. and C. W. SEM-JACOBSEN. Observations on depth stimulation of the human brain through implanted electrographic leads. Proc. Mayo Clin., 28:181–187, 1953.

20. BISHOP, M. P., S. T. ELDER and R. G. HEATH. Intracranial self-stimulation in man. Science, 140:394–396, 1963.

21. BOSMAN, S. C. W., J. TERBLANCHE, S. J. SAUNDERS, G. G. HARRISON, and C. N. BARNARD. Cross-circulation between man and baboon. Lancet, ii:583–585, 1968.

22. BRATTGÅRD, S.-O. The importance of adequate stimulation for the chemical composition of retinal ganglion cells during early post-natal development. Acta radio., Suppl. 96, 80 pp., 1952.

23. BRAZIER, M. A. B. "A History of the Electrical Activity of the Brain. The First Half Century." London: Pitman med. Publ., 119 pp., 1961.

24. BRINDLEY, G. S. and W. S. LEWIN. The sensations produced by

electrical stimulation of the visual cortex. J. Physiol., 196:479–493, 1968.

25. CAJAL, S. RAMON Y. "Histologie du Système Nerveux de L'homme et des Vertébrés." Vol. I & II. Paris: Malorie, 1909–1911.

26. DEL CAMPO, A. Blind can "see" the shape of things. Med. World News, Oct. 7, 142–143, 1966.

27. CANESTRINI, S. Uber das Sinnesleben des Neugeborenen. Monogr. Gesamtgeb. Neurol. Psychiat., No. 5. Berlin: Springer, 104 pp., 1913.

28. CANTRIL, H. Sentio, ergo sum: "motivation" reconsidered. J. Psychol., 65:91–107, 1967.

29. CANTRIL, H. and W. K. LIVINGSTON. The concept of transaction in psychology and neurology: J. indiv. Psychol., 19:3–16, 1963.

30. CARMICHAEL, L. The onset and early development of behavior. Pp. 60–185 in: "Manual of Child Psychology," L. Carmichael, (ed.). New York: John Wiley, 2nd Ed., 1295 pp., 1960.

31. CASPARI, E. Genetic basis of behavior. Pp. 103–127 in: "Behavior and Evolution," A. Roe and G. G. Simpson, (eds.) New Haven: Yale Univ. Press, 557 pp., 1958.

32. CHASE, W. P. Color vision in infants. J. exp. Psychol., 20:203–222, 1937.

33. COBB, S. Foreword. Pp. vii–viii in: "Electrical Stimulation of the Brain," D. E. Sheer, (ed.) Austin, Univ. Texas Press, 641 pp., 1961.

34. COGHILL, G. E. VI. The mechanism of integration in Amblystoma punctatum. J. comp. Neurol., 41:95–152, 1926.

35. COGHILL, G. E. Correlated anatomical and physiological studies of the growth of the nervous system of Amphibia: IX. The mechanism of association of Amblystoma punctatum. J. comp. Neurol., 51:311–375, 1930a.

36. COGHILL, G. F. The structural basis of the integration of behavior. Proc. nat. Acad. Sci., 16:637–643, 1930b.

37. COGHILL, G. E. X. Corollaries of the anatomical and physiological study of Amblystoma from the age of earliest movement to swimming. J. comp. Neurol., 53:147–168, 1931.

38. COLE, L. C. Can the world be saved? BioScience, 18:679–684, 1968.

39. COMPAYRÉ, G. "The Intellectual and Moral Development of the

Child: Part I. (Trans. by M. E. WILSON). New York: Appleton, 1896.

40. CONDON, R. "The Manchurian Candidate." New York: McGraw-Hill, 311 pp., 1959.

41. CONEL, J. L. "The Postnatal Development of the Human Cerebral Cortex." Vol. I, 114 pp. Vol. II, 136 pp. Vol. III, 158 pp. Cambridge, Harvard Univ. Press: 1939, 1941, 1947.

42. COX, V. C. and E. S. VALENSTEIN. Attenuation of aversive properties of peripheral shock by hypothalamic stimulation. Science, 149:323–325, 1965.

43. CRANBERG, L. Ethical code for scientists? Science, 141:1242, 1963.

44. DE CRINIS, M. Die Entwicklung der Grosshirnrinde nach der Geburt in ihren Beziehungen zur intellektuellen Ausreifung des Kindes. Wien. Klin. Wschr., 45:1161–1165, 1932.

45. CRUCHET, R. La mésure de l'intelligence chez l'enfant de la naissance. J. méd. Bordeaux, 107:951–960, 1930.

46. DECARLO, C. R. Perspectives on technology. Pp. 8–43 in: "Technology and Social Change." E. Ginzberg, (ed.) New York: Columbia Univ. Press, 158 pp., 1964.

47. DELGADO, J. M. R. Permanent implantation of multilead electrodes in the brain. Yale J. Biol. Med., 24:351–358, 1952a.

48. DELGADO, J. M. R. Hidden motor cortex of the cat. Amer. J. Physiol., 170:673–681, 1952b.

49. DELGADO, J. M. R. Chronic implantation of intracerebral electrodes in animals. Pp. 25–36 in: "Electrical Stimulation of the Brain," D. E. Sheer, ed.), Austin: Univ. Texas Press, 641 pp. 1961.

50. DELGADO, J. M. R. Emotional behavior in animals and humans. Psychiat. Res. Rep., 12:259–271, 1960.

51. DELGADO, J. M. R. Cerebral heterostimulation in a monkey colony. Science, 141:161–163, 1963.

52. DELGADO, J. M. R. Electrodes for extracellular recording and stimulation. Pp. 88–143 in: "Electrophysiological Methods," Vol. V, Part A: "Physical Techniques in Biological Research." N. L. Nastuk, (ed.), New York: Academic Press, 460 pp., 1964a.

53. DELGADO, J. M. R. Free behavior and brain stimulation. Pp. 349–449 in: "International Review of Neurobiology," Vol. VI. C. C. Pfeiffer and J. R. Smythies, (eds.) New York: Academic Press, 476 pp., 1964b.

54. DELGADO, J. M. R. Sequential behavior repeatedly induced by red nucleus stimulation in free monkeys. Science, 148:1361–1363, 1965.

55. DELGADO, J. M. R. Brain technology and psychocivilization. Pp. 68–92 in: "Human Values and Advancing Technology. A New Agenda for the Church in Mission." C. P. Hall (ed.), New York: Friendship Press, 175 pp., 1967.

56. DELGADO, J. M. R. Aggression and defense under cerebral radio control. Pp. 171–193 in: "Aggression and Defense. Neural Mechanisms and Social Patterns." UCLA Forum in Medical Sciences, No. 7, Vol. V, C. D. Clemente and D. B. Lindsley, (eds.), Berkeley: Univ. Cal. Press, 361 pp., 1967.

57. DELGADO, J. M. R. and H. HAMLIN. Surface and depth electrography of the frontal lobes in conscious patients. EEG clin. Neurophysiol., 8:371–384, 1956.

58. DELGADO, J. M. R. and H. HAMLIN. Spontaneous and evoked electrical seizures in animals and in humans. Pp. 133–158 in "Electrical Studies on the Unanesthetized Brain." Estelle R. Ramey and Desmond S. O'Doherty, (eds.) New York: Paul B. Hoeber 432 pp., 1960.

59. DELGADO, J. M. R., H. HAMLIN and W. P. CHAPMAN. Technique of intracranial electrode implacement for recording and stimulation and its possible therapeutic value in psychotic patients. Conf. neurol., 12:315–319, 1952.

60. DELGADO, J. M. R., V. MARK, W. SWEET, F. ERVIN, G. WEISS, G. BACH-Y-RITA, and R. HAGIWARA. Intracerebral radio stimulation and recording in completely free patients. J. nerv. ment. Dis., 147:329–340, 1968.

61. DELGADO, J. M. R. and D. MIR. Infatigability of pupillary constriction evoked by stimulation in monkeys. Neurology, 16:939–950, 1966.

62. DELGADO, J. M. R., W. W. ROBERTS, and N. E. MILLER. Learning motivated by electrical stimulation of the brain. Amer. J. Physiol., 179:587–593, 1954.

63. DIAMOND, S., R. S. BALVIN, and F. R. DIAMOND. "Inhibition and Choice. A Neurobehavioral Approach to Problems of Plasticity in Behavior." New York: Harper & Row, 456 pp., 1963.

64. DOBZHANSKY, TH. Genetics, society and evolution. Bull. N.Y. Acad. Med., 38:451–459, 1962.

## 268     BIBLIOGRAPHY

65. Dobzhansky, Th. "Mankind Evolving. The Evolution of the Human Species." New Haven: Yale Univ. Press, 381 pp., 1962.

66. Dobzhansky, Th. Changing man. Science, 155:409–415. 1967.

67. Drever, J. "A Dictionary of Psychology." Baltimore, Md.: Penguin Books, Inc., 316 pp., 1952.

68. DuBois-Reymond, E. Untersuchungen über thierische Elektricität. Vol. I. Berlin: Reimer, 1848. Vol. II, 1849.

69. Dubos, R. "The Torch of Life." New York: Trident Press, Simon & Schuster, 140 pp., 1962.

70. Dunbar, F. "Emotions and Bodily Changes. A Survey of Literature on Psychosomatic Interrelationships 1910-1953." New York: Columbia Univ. Press, 1192 pp., 4th Ed., 1954.

71. Eccles, J. C. "The Neurophysiological Basis of Mind." Oxford: Clarendon Press, 314 pp., 1953.

72. Erlanger, J. E. and H. S. Gasser. "Electrical signs of Nervous Activity." Philadelphia: Univ. Penn. Press, 221 pp., 1937.

73. Ervin, F. Participant in "Brain Stimulation in Behaving Subjects." Neurosciences Research Program Workshop, Dec., 1966.

74. Feindel, W., W. Penfield and H. Jasper. Localization of epileptic discharge in temporal lobe automatism. Trans. Amer. Neurol. Assoc., 14–17, 1952.

75. Field, J., H. W. Magoun, and W. E. Hall (eds.). "Handbook of Physiology. Section 1: Neurophysiology." Washington, D.C.: Amer. Physiol. Soc., Vol. I, 1959, Vols. II & III, 1960.

76. Flechsig, P. E. "Gehirn und seele." Leipzig: Veit & Co., 112 pp., 1896.

77. Florey, E. (ed.). "Nervous Inhibition." Proc. Second Friday Harbour Symp. New York: Pergamon Press, 475 pp., 1961.

78. Forbes, A. The interpretation of spinal reflexes in terms of present knowledge of nerve conduction. Physiol. Rev., 2:361–414, 1922.

79. Forbes, H. S. and H. B. Forbes. Fetal sense reaction: hearing. J. comp. Psychol., 7:353–355, 1927.

80. Freud, S. (1856–1939) "The Basic Writings of Sigmund Freud." Trans. and edited by A. A. Bull. New York: Modern Library, 1001 pp., 1938.

81. Fulton, J. F. and C. F. Jacobsen. The functions of the frontal lobes, a comparative study in monkeys, chimpanzees and man. Advances in mod. Biol. (Moscow), 4:113–123, 1935.

82. FURFEY, P. H., M. A. BONHAM, and M. K. SARGENT. The mental organization of the newborn. Child Develpm., 1:48–51, 1930.

83. GALVANI, L. De viribus electricitatis in motu musculari. Commentarius. Proc. Acad. Bologna, 7:363–418, 1791.

84. GAMPER, E. Bau und Leistungen eines menschlichen Mittelhirnwesens (Arhinencephalie mit Encephalocele). Z. ges. Neurol. Psychiat., 102:154–235, 1926.

85. GEERTZ, C. The impact of the concept of culture on the concept of man. Bull. atom. Sci., 22:2–8, 1966.

86. GENZMER, A. Utersuchungen über die Sinneswahrnehmungen des neugeborenen Menschen. (Dissertation, 1873). Halle: Niemeyer, 1882.

87. GERARD, M. W. Afferent impulses of the trigeminal nerve. The intramedullary course of the painful, thermal and tactile impulses. Arch. Neurol. Psychiat. (Chicago), 9:306–338, 1923.

88. GESELL, A. L. "Infancy and Human Growth." New York: Macmillan, 418 pp., 1928.

89. GRASTYÁN, E., K. LISSÁK and F. KÉKESI. Facilitation and inhibition of conditioned alimentary and defensive reflexes by stimulation of the hypothalamus and reticular formation. Acta physiol. Acad. Sci. hung., 9:133–151, 1956.

90. GRUNBAUM, A. Causality and the science of human behavior. Amer. Sci., 40:665–676, 1952.

91. HAMBERGER, C. A. and H. HYDÉN. Production of nucleoproteins in the vestibular ganglion. Acta oto-laryng., Suppl. 75:53–81, 1949.

92. HARLOW, H. F. Love in infant monkeys. Sci. Amer., 200:68–74, 1959.

93. HARLOW, H. F., and M. K. HARLOW. Learning to think. Sci. Amer., 181:36–39, 1949.

94. HARLOW, H. F. and M. K. HARLOW. Social deprivation in monkeys. Sci. Amer., 207:136–146, 1962.

95. HARLOW, H. F., M. K. HARLOW, and D. R. MEYER. Learning motivated by a manipulation drive. J. exp. Psychol., 40:228–234, 1950.

96. HASSLER, R. Ueber die Bedeutung des pallidären Systems für Parkinsonsyndrom und Psychomotorik nach Erfahrungen bei gezielten Hirnoperationen. Brussels: 1st int. Congr. Neurosurg., 1:171–178, 1957.

270        BIBLIOGRAPHY

97. HASSLER, R. and T. REICHERT. Clinical effects produced by stimulations of different thalamic nuclei in humans. EEG clin. Neurophysiol., 6:518, 1954.

98. HEATH, R. G., "Studies in Schizophrenia. A multidisciplinary Approach to Mind-Brain Relationships." Cambridge: Harvard Univ. Press, 619 pp., 1954.

99. HEATH, R. G. Electrical self-stimulation of the brain in man. Amer. J. Psychiat., 120:571–577, 1963.

100. HEATH, R. G., R. R. MONROE and W. MICKLE. Stimulation of the amygdaloid nucleus in a schizophrenic patient. Amer. J. Psychiat., 111:862–863, 1955.

101. HEBB, D. O. The innate organization of visual activity: I. Perception of figures by rats reared in total darkness. J. genet. Psychol., 51:101–126, 1937.

102. HEBB, D. O. "A Textbook of Psychology." Philadelphia: Saunders, 276 pp., 1958.

103. HERON, W. The pathology of boredom. Sci. Amer., 196:52–56, 1957.

104. HERRICK, C. J. "Neurological Foundations of Animal Behavior." New York: Hafner, 334 pp., 1962.

105. HESS, W. R. Stammganglien-Reizversuche. (Verh. Dtsch. physiol. Ges., Sept., 1927). Ber. ges. Physiol., 42:554–555, 1928.

106. HESS, W. R. "Beitrage zur Physiologie d. Hirnstammes I. Die Methodik der lokalisierten Reizung. und Ausschaltung subkortikaler Hirnabschnitte." Leipzig: Georg Thième, 122 pp., 1932.

107. HESS, W. R. "The Functional Organization of the Diencephalon." New York: Grune & Stratton, 180 pp., 1957.

108. HESS, W. R. "Hypothalamus und Thalamus. Experimental-Dokumente." Stuttgart: Georg Thieme Verag, 77 pp. 1968.

109. HIGGINS, J. W., G. F. MAHL, J. M. R. DELGADO and H. HAMLIN. Behavioral changes during intracerebral electrical stimulation. Arch. Neurol. Psychiat., (Chicago), 76:399–419, 1956.

110. HINSIE, L. E. and R. J. CAMPBELL. "Psychiatric Dictionary." New York: Oxford Univ. Press, 3rd Ed., 788 pp., 1960.

111. HOLST, E. VON and U. VON SAINT PAUL. Electrically controlled behavior. Sci. Amer., 206:50–59, 1962.

112. HOOKER, D. Fetal behavior. Res. Publ. Ass. nerv. ment. Dis., 19:237–243, 1939.

113. HUANG, S. Life in space and humanity on the earth. Amer. Scientist, 53:288–298, 1965.

114. HUXLEY, A. "Brave New World." New York: Harper & Brothers, 311 pp., 1932.

115. HYDEN, H. Satellite cells in the nervous system. Sci. Amer., 205:62–70, 1961.

116. IRWIN, O. C. Infant responses to vertical movements. Child Develpm., 3:167–169, 1932.

117. IRWIN, O. C. Can infants have IQ's? Psychol. Rev., 49:69–79, 1942.

118. JAKOB, C. El lobulo frontal. Folia Neurobiol. Argentina, 3:1–141, 1943.

119. JAMES, W. "Principles of Psychology." New York: Dover Publ., Vols. I & II, 688 pp. ea., 1950.

120. JASPER, H. H. and T. RASMUSSEN. Studies of clinical and electrical response to deep temporal stimulation in man with some considerations of functional anatomy. Res. Publ. Ass. nerv. ment. Dis., 36:316–334, 1958.

121. JENNINGS, H. S. "The Biological Basis of Human Nature." New York: Norton, 384 pp., 1930.

122. JUNG, R. Discussant. P. 198 in: "Brain Mechanisms and Consciousness." J. F. Delafresnaye, (ed.). Springfield, Ill.: C. C. Thomas, 1954.

123. JUNG, R. and R. HASSLER. The extrapyramidal motor system. Pp. 863–927 in: "Handbook of Physiology," Section 1: Neurophysiology Vol. II, J. Field, H. W. Magoun and V. E. Hall, (eds.) Baltimore, Md.: Williams & Wilkins, pp. 781–1439, 1960.

124. JUNG, R., T. REICHERT u. R. W. MEYER-MICKELEIT. Ueber intracerebrale Hirnpotentialableitungen bet hirnchirurgischen Eingriffen. Dtsch. Z. Nervenheilk., 162:52–60, 1950.

125. KASATKIN, N. I., and A. M. LEVIKOVA. On the development of early conditioned reflexes and differentiations of auditory stimuli in infants. J. exp. Psychol., 18:1–19, 1935.

126. KETCHEL, M. M. Should birth control be mandatory? Med. World News, Oct. 18:66–71, 1968.

127. KETY, S. A biologist examines the mind and behavior. Science, 132:1861–1870, 1960.

128. KING, H. E. Psychological effects of excitation in the limbic

system. Pp. 477–486 in: "Electrical Stimulation of the Brain," D. E. Sheer (ed.) Austin: Univ. Texas Press, 641 pp., 1961.

129. KOESTLER, A. "The Ghost in the Machine." New York: Macmillan, 384 pp., 1968.

130. KOSKOFF, Y. D. Personal Communication.

131. KRASNER, L. Behavioral control and social responsibility. Amer. Psychologist, 17:199–204, 1964.

132. KRECH, D., M. R. ROSENZWEIG and E. L. BENNETT. Environmental impoverishment, social isolation and changes in brain chemistry and anatomy. Physiology and Behavior, 1:99–104, 1966.

133. KUBIE, L. Some implications for psychoanalysis of modern concepts of the organization of the brain. Psychoanalyt. Quart., 22:21–68, 1953.

134. KUHLENBECK, H. "Mind and Matter. An Appraisal of Their Significance for Neurologic Theory." Basel: S. Karger, 548 pp., 1961.

135. KUSSMAUL, A. "Utersuchungen über das Seelenleben des neugeborenen Menschen." Leipzig: Winter, 1859.

136. LANE, H. H. The correlation between structure and function in the development of the special senses of the white rat. Univ. Okla. Bull (N. S. no. 140), pp. 1–88, 1917.

137. LANGE, F. A. "History of Materialism." 1873 (Trans. by E. C. Thomas). New York: Harcourt Brace, 1925.

138. Langworthy, O. R. A correlated study of the development of reflex activity in fetal and young kittens and the myelinization of tracts in the nervous system. Contr. Embryol., Carnegie Inst. Wash., 20, No. 114, 127–171, 1929.

139. LANGWORTHY, O. R. Development of behavior patterns and myelinization of the nervous system in the human fetus and infant. Contr. Embryol. Carneg. Inst., 24: No. 139, 1933.

140. Lashley, K. S. Studies of cerebral function in learning: VI. The theory that synaptic resistance is reduced by the passage of the nerve impulse. Psychol. Rev., 31:369–375, 1924.

141. LEIDERMAN, P. H., J. H. MENDELSON, D. WEXLER and P. SOLOMON. Sensory deprivation: clinical aspects. Arch. int. Med., 101:389–396, 1958.

142. LÉVI-STRAUSS, C. "A World on the Wane." Trans. by J. Russell. London: Hutchinson & Co., 404 pp., 1961.

143. LIFTON, R. J. "Thought Reform and the Psychology of Totalism: A Study of "Brainwashing" in China." New York: W. W. Norton, 510 pp., 1961.

144. LILLIE, R. S. "Protoplasmic Action and Nervous System." Chicago, Ill.: Univ. Chicago Press, 2nd Ed., 417 pp., 1932.

145. LILLY, J. C. Discussion of "Studies in Schizophrenia." Pp. 528–532, in "Studies in Schizophrenia," Cambridge: Harvard Univ. Press, 619 pp., 1954.

146. LILLY, J. C. Learning motivated by subcortical stimulation: the start and stop patterns of behavior. Pp. 705–721, in: "Reticular Formation of the Brain," Henry Ford Hosp. int. Symp., H. H. Jasper, et al. (eds.). Boston: Little Brown, 766 pp., 1958.

147. LOCKE, J. "Essay Concerning Human Understanding." (1690). Cambridge: Harvard Univ. Press, 306 pp., 1931.

148. LORENZ, K. Ritualized fighting. Pp. 39–50 in: "The Natural History of Aggression." J. D. Carthy and F. J. Ebling, (eds.) New York: Academic Press, 159 pp., 1964.

149. LORENZ, K. "On Aggression." New York: Harcourt, Brace & World, 306 pp., 1966.

150. MAHL, G. F., A. ROTHENBERG, J. M. R. DELGADO and H. HAMLIN. Psychological responses in the human to intracerebral electric stimulation. Psychosom. Med., 26:337–368, 1964.

151. MARCUSE, H. One Dimensional Man. Boston: Beacon Press, 1964.

152. MARMOR, J. Psychoanalytic therapy as an educational process: Common denominators in the therapeutic approaches of different psychoanalytic "schools." Paper presented to the Acad. Psychoanal., Chicago, May, 1961.

153. MEDICAL RESEARCH COUNCIL. Responsibility in investigations on human subjects. Brit. med. J., 2:178–179, 1964.

154. MILLER, N. E. Learnable drives and rewards. Pp. 435–472 in: "Handbook of Experimental Psychology," S. S. Stevens, (ed.) New York: John Wiley, 1436 pp., 1951.

155. MINKOWSKI, M. Sur les mouvements, les réflexes, et les réactions musculaires du foetus humain de 2 à 5 mois et leur rélations avec le système nerveux foetal. Rev. neurol., 37:1105–1118, 1235–1250, 1921.

156. MITTELMANN, B. Motility in infants, children, and adults: pat-

terning and psychodynamics. Psychoanal. Study of the Child, 9:142–177, 1954.

157. MONTAGU, A. "On Being Human." New York: Hawthorne Books, Inc., 128 pp., 2nd Ed., 1966.

158. MORGAN, C. "Animal Life and Intelligence." London: Arnold, 512 pp., 1890–91.

159. NASHOLD, B. S. and W. V. HUBER (eds.). Second Symposium on Parkinson's Disease. J. Neurosurg., 24:117–481, 1966.

160. NASHOLD, B. S. Personal communication.

161. New England J. Med. Editorial: New Eng. J. Med., 275:785–786, 1966.

162. NISSEN, H. W., S. MACHOVER, and E. F. KINDER. A study of performance tests given to a group of native African Negro Children. Brit. J. Psychol., 25:308–355, 1935.

163. OKUMA, T., Y. SHIMAZONO, T. FUKUDA and H. NARABAYASHI. Cortical and subcortical recordings in non-anesthetized and anesthetized periods in man. EEG clin. Neurophysiol. 6:269–286, 1954.

164. OLDS, J. Hypothalamic substrates of reward. Physiol. Rev., 42:554–604, 1962.

165. OLDS, J. and P. MILNER. Positive reinforcement produced by electrical stimulation of the septal area and other regions of the rat brain. J. comp. physiol. Psychol., 47:419–428, 1954.

166. ORTEGA Y GASSET, J. "Meditations on Quixote." Trans. by E. Rugg and D. Marin, with notes and introduction by J. Marias. New York: W. W. Norton, 1961.

167. ORTEGA Y GASSET, J. "History as a System." New York: W. W. Norton, 1961.

168. ORWELL, G. "1984." New York: Harcourt, Brace, 314 pp., 1949.

169. Oxford Universal Dictionary. London: Oxford Univ. Press, 2515 pp., 1955.

170. PASAMANICK, B. Research on the influence of sociocultural variables upon organic factors in mental retardation. Amer. J. ment. Defic., 64:316–320, 1959.

171. PAVLOV, I. P. "Experimental Psychology." New York: Philosophical Library, 653 pp., 1957.

172. PEIPER, A. Der Saugvorgang. Ergebn. inn. Med. Kinderheilk., 50:527–567, 1936.

173. PEIPER, A. Die neurologischen Grundlagen der psychischen

Entwicklung. Mschr. Kinderheilk., 87:179–203, 1941.

174. PENFIELD, W. and H. JASPER. "Epilepsy and the Functional Anatomy of the Human Brain." Boston: Little, Brown, 896 pp., 1954.

175. PETERSON, F. and L. H. RAINEY. The beginnings of mind in the newborn. Bull. Lying-in Hosp., N.Y., 7:99–122, 1910.

176. PFLÜGER, E. Die Lebensfähigkeit des menschlichen Foetus. Pflüg. Arch. ges. Physiol., 14:628–629, 1877.

177. PIAGET, J. "The Origins of Intelligence in Children." Trans. by Margaret Cook. New York: Int. Universities Press, 419 pp., 1952.

178. PIAGET, J. Psychology, interdisciplinary relations and the system of sciences. Moscow: XVIII Int. Congr. Psychol., 47 pp., 1966.

179. PLATT, J. R. "The Step to Man." New York: Wiley, 224 pp., 1966.

180. PRATT, K. C., A. K. NELSON, and K. H. SUN. The behavior of the newborn infant. Ohio State Univ. Stud., Contr. Psychol., No. 10, 1930.

181. RAINER, J. D. The concept of mind in the framework of genetics. Pp. 65–79 in: "Theories of the Mind," J. M. Scher, (ed.) New York: The Free Press of Glencoe, 748 pp., 1962.

182. RAMEY, E. R. and D. S. O'DOHERTY (eds.). "Electrical Studies on the Unanesthetized Brain." New York: Paul B. Hoeber, Inc., 423 pp., 1960.

183. RANK, O. "The Trauma of Birth." New York: Harcourt Brace, 224 pp., 1929.

184. RIESEN, A. H., K. L. CHOW, J. SEMMES, and H. W. NISSEN. Chimpanzee vision after four conditions of light deprivation. Amer. Psychologist, 6:282 (Abstract) 1951.

185. RIOCH, D. McK. Concluding remarks. Pp. 402–412 in: "Electrical Studies on the Unanesthetized Brain," E. R. Ramey and D. S. O'Doherty, (eds.). New York: Paul B. Hoeber, 423 pp., 1960.

186. ROBERTS, L. Activation and interference of cortical functions. Pp. 533–553 in: "Electrical Stimulation of the Brain," D. E. Sheer (ed.) Austin: Univ. Texas Press, 641 pp., 1961.

187. ROE, A. Man's forgotten weapon. Amer. Psychologist, 14:261–266, 1959.

188. ROGERS, C. R. and B. F. SKINNER. Some issues concerning the control of human behavior: A symposium. Science, 124:1057–1066, 1956.

189. ROSENTHAL, D. Changes in moral values following psychotherapy. J. consult. Psychol., 19:431–436, 1955.

190. ROSENZWEIG, M. R., D. KRECH, E. L. BENNET, and M. C. DIAMOND. Modifying brain chemistry and anatomy by enrichment or impoverishment of experience. Pp. 258–297 in: "Early Experience and Behavior," G. Newton and S. Levine, (eds.) Springfield, Ill.: C. C. Thomas, 785 pp., 1968.

191. ROSVOLD, H. E. and J. M. R. DELGADO. The effect on delayed-alternation test performance of stimulating or destroying electrically structures within the frontal lobes of the monkey's brain. J. comp. physiol. Psychol., 49:365–372, 1956.

192. RUSSELL, B. "A History of Western Philosophy, and its Connection with Political and Social Circumstances from the Earliest Times to the Present Day." New York: Simon and Schuster, 895 pp., 1945.

193. SADGER, J. Preliminary study of the psychic life of the fetus and the primary germ. Psychoanal. Rev., 28:327–358, 1941.

194. SARTRE, J. P. "L'etre et le néant; essai d'ontologie phénomenologique." Paris: Gallimard, 722 pp., 1943.

195. SCHER, J. M. (ed.). "Theories of the Mind." New York: The Free Press of Glencoe, 748 pp., 1962.

196. Science Editorial. Privacy and behavioral research. Preliminary summary of the report of the panel on privacy and behavioral research. Science, 155:535–538, 1967.

197. SCHULTZ, D. P. "Sensory Restriction, Effects on Behavior." New York: Academic Press, 216 pp., 1965.

198. SECHENOV, I. M. "Elements of Thought." In Russian (1878). Moscow: USSR Acad. Sci. Press, 1943.

199. SEGUNDO, J. P., E. GARCIA AUS JR., R. ARANA INIGUEZ and E. MIGLIARO. Respiratory, electrocortical and spinal responses to stimulation of fornix in man. EEG clin. Neurophysiol., 6:537–538, 1954.

200. SEM-JACOBSEN, C. W. Electrical stimulation-effects on speech in some areas around the third ventricle. EEG clin. Neurophysiol., 14:953–956, 1962.

201. SEM-JACOBSEN, C. W. "Depth-Electrographic Stimulation of the

Human Brain and Behavior: From Fourteen Years of Studies and Treatment of Parkinson's Disease and Mental Disorders with Implanted Electrodes." Springfield, Ill.: C. C. Thomas, 222 pp., 1968.

202. SENDEM, M. VON. Raum und Gestaltauffassung bei operierten Blindgeborenen vor und nach der Operation. Leipzig: Barth, 303 pp., 1932.

203. SHEER, D. E., (ed.). "Electrical Stimulation of the Brain." Austin: Univ. Texas Press, 641 pp., 1961.

204. SHERMAN, M. The differentiation of emotional responses in infants: I. Judgments of emotional response from motion-pictures views and from actual observation. J. comp. Psychol., 7:265–284, 1927.

205. SHERRINGTON, C. S. "The Integrative Action of the Nervous System." Cambridge: Cambridge Univ. Press, 2nd Ed. 433 pp., 1947.

206. SHERRINGTON, C. S. "Man on His Nature." Cambridge: Cambridge Univ. Press, 413 pp., 1941.

207. SIEGEL, A. I. Deprivation of usual form definition in the ring dove. I. Discriminatory learning. J. comp. physiol. Psychol., 46:115–119, 1953.

208. SIMMONS, F. B., J. M. EPLEY, R. C. LUMMIS, N. GUTTMAN, L. S. FRISHKOPF, L. D. HARMON, E. ZWICKER. Auditory nerve: electrical stimulation in man. Science, 148:104–106, 1965.

209. SKINNER, B. F. "Walden Two." New York: Macmillan, 1948.

210. SKINNER, B. F. Freedom and the control of men. Amer. Scholar, Special Issue, 25:47–65, Winter, 1955–56.

211. SKINNER, B. F. The design of cultures. Daedalus, pp. 534–546. Summer, 1961.

212. SOULAIRAC, A., J. CAHN, and J. CHARPENTIER. "Pain." New York: Academic Press, 562 pp., 1968.

213. SPELT, D. K. The conditioning of the human fetus "in utero." J. exp. Psychol., 38:338–346, 1948.

214. SPIEGEL, E. A. and H. T. WYCIS. Stimulation of the brain stem and basal ganglia in man. Pp. 487–497 in: "Electrical stimulation of the Brain," D. E. Sheer, (ed.) Austin: Univ. Texas Press, 641 pp., 1961.

215. SPIEGEL, E. A. and H. WYCIS. Stereoencephalotomy (thalamotomy and related procedures). Part I. Methods and stereotaxic

atlas of the human brain. New York: Grune & Stratton, Vol. I, 176 pp., 1952.

216. SPIEGEL, E. A. and H. T. WYCIS (eds.). Advances in stereo-encephalotomy. II. Pain, Convulsive Disorders, Behavioral and other effects of stereoencephalotomy. Second Int. Symposium on Stereoencephalotomy. Conf. neurol. (Basel), 27:456 pp., 1966.

217. SPRAGUE, J. M., W. W. CHAMBERS, and E. STELLAR. Attentive, affective, and adaptive behavior in the cat. Science, 133:165–173, 1961.

218. STEVENS, H. A. In: Int. Congr. Sci., Copenhagen, "Study of Mental Retardation," J. Oster, ed., Copenhagen: Berlingske Bogtrykkeri, Vol. 1, 1964.

219. STUBBS, E. M. The effect of the factors of duration, intensity, and pitch of sound stimuli on the responses of newborn infants. Univ. Iowa Stud. Child Welfare, 9:75–135, 1934.

220. SWEET, W. H. Pain. Pp. 459–506 in: "Handbook of Physiology," Section 1: Neurophysiology. Vol. 1. J. Field, H. W. Magoun, W. E. Hall (eds.) Washington, D.C.: Amer. Physiol. Soc., 779 pp., 1959.

221. SWEET, W. H. Participant in "Brain Stimulation in Behaving Subjects." Neurosciences Research Program Workshop. Dec., 1966.

222. TAYLOR, J. H. Innate emotional responses in infants. Ohio State Univ. Stud., Contrip. Psychol., No. 12:69–81, 1934.

223. TEILHARD DE CHARDIN, P. "The Phenomenon of Man." New York: Harper & Row, 318 pp., 1959.

224. TERZUOLO, C. A. and W. R. ADEY. Sensorimotor cortical activities. Pp. 797–835 in: "Handbook of Physiology," Section 1: Neurophysiology, Vol. II, J. Field, H. W. Magoun and V. E. Hall, (eds.) Baltimore, Md.: Waverly Press, pp. 781–1439, 1960.

225. THOMAS, A. and S. CHESS. An approach to the study of sources of individual differences in child behavior. J. Clin. exp. Psychopath., 18:347–357, 1957.

226. TILNEY, F. and L. CASAMAJOR. Myelinogeny as applied to the study of behavior. Arch. Neurol. Psychiat. (Chicago), 12:1–66, 1924.

227. TINBERGEN, N. Some aspects of instinct and learning in birds. Biol. hum. Affairs, 23:1–6, 1957.

228. TRACY, H. C. The development of motility and behavior reactions in the toadfish (Opsanus Tau). J. comp. Neurol., 40:253–369, 1926.

229. UMBACH, W. Tiefen-und Cortex-ableitungen während stereotaktischer Operationen am Menschen. Brussels: 1st int. Congr. Neurosurg., 1:161–170, 1957.

230. VAN BUREN, J. M. Sensory, motor and autonomic effects of mesial temporal stimulation in man. J. Neurosurg., 18:273–288, 1961.

231. VAN BUREN, J. M., C. L. LI, and G. A. OJEMANN. The fronto-striatal arrest response in man. EEG. clin. Neurophysiol., 21:114–130, 1966.

232. VOLTA, A. On the electricity excited by the mere contact of conducting substances of different kinds. Phil. Trans., 90:403–431, 1800.

233. WALTER, W. G. and H. J. CROW. Depth recording from the human brain. EEG clin. Neurophysiol., 16:68–72, 1964.

234. WALTER, W. G. Participant in "Brain Stimulation in Behaving Subjects." Neurosciences Research Program Workshop, Dec., 1966.

235. WARREN, H. C. "Dictionary of Psychology." Cambridge, Mass.: Houghton Mifflin, 372 pp., 1934.

236. WATSON, J. B. "Animal Education: An Experimental Study on the Psychical Development of the White Rat, Correlated with the Growth of its Nervous System." Chicago: Univ. Chicago Press, 122 pp., 1903.

237. WATSON, J. B. "Psychology from the Standpoint of a Behaviorist." Philadelphia: Lippincott, 429 pp., 1919.

238. Webster's Dictionary. "Webster's Third New International Dictionary." Springfield, Mass.: G. & C. Merriam, 2662 pp., 1961.

239. WEILL, G. and C. PFERSDORFF. Les functions visuelles de l'aveugle-né opéré. Ann. méd.-psychol., 93: Part 2, 367–382, 1935.

240. WEISS, A. P. The measurement of infant behavior. Psychol. Rev., 36:453–471, 1929.

241. WEISS, P. Self-differentiation of the basic patterns of coordination. Comp. Psychol. Monogr., 17:96 pp., 1941.

242. WEISS, P. The growth of science: its liberating force and limitation. Pp. 60–69 in: "The Knowledge Explosion. Liberation and Limitation." F. Sweeney, (ed.) New York: Farrar, Straus & Giroux, 1966.

243. WERTHEIMER, M. Hebb and Senden on the role of learning in perception. Amer. J. Psychol., 64:133–137, 1951.

244. WEST, L. J. Psychiatry, "brainwashing," and the American character. Amer. J. Psychiat., 120:842–850, 1964.

245. WOLFENSBERGER, W. Ethical issues in research with human subjects. Science, 155:47–51, 1967.

246. World Medical Association. Human experimentation code of ethics. Declaration of Helsinki. Brit. med. J., 2:177, 1964.

# World Perspectives

*What This Series Means*

It is the thesis of *World Perspectives* that man is in the process of developing a new consciousness which, in spite of his apparent spiritual and moral captivity, can eventually lift the human race above and beyond the fear, ignorance, and isolation which beset it today. It is to this nascent consciousness, to this concept of man born out of a universe perceived through a fresh vision of reality, that *World Perspectives* is dedicated.

Man has entered a new era of evolutionary history, one in which rapid change is a dominant consequence. He is contending with a fundamental change, since he has intervened in the evolutionary process. He must now better appreciate this fact and then develop the wisdom to direct the process toward his fulfillment rather than toward his destruction. As he learns to apply his understanding of the physical world for practical purposes, he is, in reality, extending his innate capacity and augmenting his ability and his need to communicate as well as his ability to think and to create. And as a result, he is substituting a goal-directed evolutionary process in his struggle against environmental hardship for the slow, but effective, biological evolution which produced modern man through mutation and natural selection. By intelligent intervention in the evolutionary process man has greatly accelerated and greatly expanded the range of his possibilities. But he has not changed the basic fact that it remains a trial and error process, with the danger of taking paths that lead to sterility of mind and heart, moral apathy and intellectual inertia; and even producing social dinosaurs unfit to live in an evolving world.

Only those spiritual and intellectual leaders of our epoch who have a paternity in this extension of man's horizons are invited to participate in this Series: those who are aware of the truth that beyond the divisiveness among men there exists a primordial unitive power since we are all bound together by a common humanity more fundamental than any unity of dogma; those who recognize that the centrifugal force which has scattered and atomized mankind must be replaced by an integrating structure and process capable of bestowing meaning and purpose on existence; those who realize that science itself, when not inhibited by the limitations of its own methodology, when chastened and humbled, commits man to an indeterminate range of yet undreamed consequences that may flow from it.

Virtually all of our disciplines have relied on conceptions which are now incompatible with the Cartesian axiom, and with the static world view we once derived from it. For underlying the new ideas, including those of modern physics, is a unifying order, but it is not causality; it is purpose, and not the purpose of the universe and of man but the purpose *in* the universe and *in* man. In other words, we seem to inhabit a world of dynamic process and structure. Therefore we need a calculus of potentiality rather than one of probability, a dialectic of polarity, one in which unity and diversity are defined as simultaneous and necessary poles of the same essence.

Our situation is new. No civilization has previously had to face the challenge of scientific specialization; and our response must be new. Thus this Series is committed to ensure that the spiritual and moral needs of man as a human being and the scientific and intellectual resources at his command for *life* may be brought into a productive, meaningful, and creative harmony.

This Series endeavors to point to a reality of which scientific theory has revealed only one aspect. It is the commitment to this reality that lends universal intent to a scientist's most original and solitary thought. By acknowledging this frankly we shall restore science to the great family of human aspirations by which men hope to fulfill themselves in the world community as thinking and sentient beings. For our problem is to discover a principle of differentiation and yet relationship lucid enough to justify and to purify scientific, philosophic and all other knowledge, both cognitive and intuitive, by accepting their interdependence. This is the crisis in consciousness made articulate through the crisis in science. This is the new awakening.

Each volume presents the thought and belief of its author and points to the way in which religion, philosophy, art, science, economics, politics and history may constitute that form of human activity which takes the fullest and most precise account of variousness, possibility, complexity and difficulty. Thus *World Perspectives* endeavors to define that ecumenical power of the mind and heart which enables man through his mysterious greatness to re-create his life.

This Series is committed to a re-examination of all those sides of human endeavor which the specialist was taught to believe he could safely leave aside. It attempts to show the structural kinship between subject and object; the indwelling of the one in the other. It interprets present and past events impinging on human life in our growing World Age and envisages what man may yet attain when summoned by an unbending inner necessity to the quest of what is most exalted in him. Its purpose is to offer new vistas in terms of world and human development while refusing to betray the intimate correlation between universality and individuality, dynamics and form, freedom and destiny. Each author deals with the increasing realization that spirit and nature are not separate and apart; that intuition and reason must regain their importance as the means of perceiving and fusing inner being with outer reality.

*World Perspectives* endeavors to show that the conception of wholeness, unity, organism is a higher and more concrete conception than that of matter and energy. Thus an enlarged meaning of life, of biology, not as it is revealed in the test tube of the laboratory but as it is experienced within the organism of life itself, is attempted in this Series. For the principle of life consists in the tension which connects spirit with the realm of matter, symbiotically joined. The element of life is dominant in the very texture of nature, thus rendering life, biology, a transempirical science. The laws of life have their origin beyond their mere physical manifestations and compel us to consider their spiritual source. In fact, the widening of the conceptual framework has not only served to restore order within the respective branches of knowledge, but has also disclosed analogies in man's position regarding the analysis and synthesis of experience in apparently separated domains of knowledge, suggesting the possibility of an ever more embracing objective description of the meaning of life.

Knowledge, it is shown in these books, no longer consists in a manipulation of man and nature as opposite forces, nor in the reduction of data to mere statistical order, but is a means of liberating mankind from the destructive power of fear, pointing the way toward the goal of the rehabilitation of the human will and the rebirth of faith and confidence in the human person. The works published also endeavor to reveal that the cry for patterns, systems and authorities is growing less insistent as the desire grows stronger in both East and West for the recovery of a dignity, integrity and self-realization which are the inalienable rights of man who may now guide change by means of conscious purpose in the light of rational experience.

The volumes in this Series endeavor to demonstrate that only in a society in which awareness of the problems of science exists can its discoveries start great waves of change in human culture, and in such a manner that these discoveries may deepen and not erode the sense of universal human community. The differences in the disciplines, their epistemological exclusiveness, the variety of historical experiences, the differences of traditions, of cultures, of languages, of the arts, should be protected and preserved. But the interrelationship and unity of the whole should at the same time be accepted.

The authors of *World Perspectives* are of course aware that the ultimate answers to the hopes and fears which pervade modern society rest on the moral fiber of man, and on the wisdom and responsibility of those who promote the course of its development. But moral decisions cannot dispense with an insight into the interplay of the objective elements which offer and limit the choices made. Therefore an understanding of what the issues are, though not a sufficient condition, is a necessary prerequisite for directing action toward constructive solutions.

Other vital questions explored relate to problems of international understanding as well as to problems dealing with prejudice and the resultant tensions and antagonisms. The growing perception and responsibility of our World Age point to the new reality that the individual person and the collective person supplement and integrate each other; that the thrall of totalitarianism of both left and right has been shaken in the universal desire to recapture the authority of truth and human totality. Mankind can finally place its trust not in a proletarian authoritarianism, not in a secularized humanism, both of which have betrayed the spiritual property right of history, but in a sacramental brotherhood and in the unity of knowledge. This new consciousness has created a widening of human horizons beyond every parochialism, and a revolution in human thought comparable to the basic assumption, among the ancient Greeks, of the sovereignty of reason; corresponding to the great effulgence of the moral conscience articulated by the Hebrew prophets; analogous to the fundamental assertions of Christianity; or to the beginning of the new scientific era, the era of the science of dynamics, the experimental foundations of which were laid by Galileo in the Renaissance.

An important effort of this Series is to re-examine the contradictory meanings and applications which are given today to such terms as democracy, freedom, justice, love, peace, brotherhood and God. The purpose of such inquiries is to clear the way for the foundation of a genuine *world* history not in terms of nation or race or culture but in terms of man in relation to God, to himself, his fellow man and the universe, that reach beyond immediate self-interest. For the meaning of the World Age consists in respecting man's hopes and dreams which lead to a deeper understanding of the basic values of all peoples.

*World Perspectives* is planned to gain insight into the meaning of man, who not only is determined by history but who also determines history. History is to be understood as concerned not only with the life of man on this planet but as including also such cosmic influences as interpenetrate our human world. This generation is discovering that history does not conform to the social optimism of modern civilization and that the organization of human communities and the establishment of freedom and peace are not only intellectual achievements but spiritual and moral achievements as well, demanding a cherishing of the wholeness of human personality, the "unmediated wholeness of feeling and thought," and constituting a never-ending challenge to man, emerging from the abyss of meaninglessness and suffering, to be renewed and replenished in the totality of his life.

Justice itself, which has been "in a state of pilgrimage and crucifixion" and now is being slowly liberated from the grip of social and political demonologies in the East as well as in the West, begins to question its own premises. The modern revolutionary movements which have challenged the sacred institutions of society by protecting social injustice in the name of social justice are here examined and re-evaluated.

In the light of this, we have no choice but to admit that the *un*freedom against which freedom is measured must be retained with it, namely, that the aspect of truth out of which the night view appears to emerge, the darkness of our time, is as little abandonable as is man's subjective advance. Thus the two sources of man's consciousness are inseparable, not as dead but as living and complementary, an aspect of that "principle of complementarity" through which Niels Bohr has sought to unite the quantum and the wave, both of which constitute the very fabric of life's radiant energy.

There is in mankind today a counterforce to the sterility and danger of a quantitative, anonymous mass culture; a new, if sometimes imperceptible, spiritual sense of convergence toward human and world unity on the basis of the sacredness of each human person and respect for the plurality of cultures. There is a growing awareness that equality may not be evaluated in mere numerical terms but is proportionate and analogical in its reality. For when equality is equated with interchangeability, individuality is negated and the human person extinguished.

We stand at the brink of an age of a world in which human life presses forward to actualize new forms. The false separation of man and nature, of time and space, of freedom and security, is acknowledged, and we are faced with a new vision of man in his organic unity and of history offering a richness and diversity of quality and majesty of scope hitherto unprecedented. In relating the accumulated wisdom of man's spirit to the new reality of the World Age, in articulating its thought and belief, *World Perspectives* seeks to encourage a renaissance of hope in society and of pride in man's decision as to what his destiny will be.

*World Perspectives* is committed to the recognition that all great changes are preceded by a vigorous intellectual re-evaluation and reorganization. Our authors are aware that the sin of *hubris* may be avoided by showing that the creative process itself is not a free activity if by free we mean arbitrary, or unrelated to cosmic law. For the creative process in the human mind, the developmental process in organic nature and the basic laws of the inorganic realm may be but varied expressions of a universal formative process. Thus *World Perspectives* hopes to show that although the present apocalyptic period is one of exceptional tensions, there is also at work an exceptional movement toward a compensating unity which refuses to violate the ultimate moral power at work in the universe, that very power upon which all human effort must at last depend. In this way we may come to understand that there exists an inherent independence of spiritual and mental growth which, though conditioned by circumstances, is never determined by circumstances. In this way the great plethora of human knowledge may be correlated with an insight into the nature of human nature by being attuned to the wide and deep range of human thought and human experience.

Incoherence is the result of the present disintegrative processes in education. Thus the need for *World Perspectives* expresses itself in the recognition that natural and man-made ecological systems require as much study as isolated particles and elementary reactions. For there is a basic correlation of elements in nature as in man which cannot be separated, which compose each other and alter each other mutually. Thus we hope to widen appropriately our conceptual framework of reference. For our epistemological problem consists in our finding the proper balance between our lack of an all-embracing principle relevant to our way of evaluating life and in our power to express ourselves in a logically consistent manner.

In spite of the infinite obligation of men and in spite of their finite power, in spite of the intransigence of nationalisms, and in spite of the homelessness of moral passions rendered ineffectual by the technological outlook, beneath the apparent turmoil and upheaval of the present, and out of the transformations of this dynamic period with the unfolding of a world-consciousness, the purpose of *World Perspectives* is to help quicken the "unshaken heart of well-rounded truth" and interpret the significant elements of the World Age now taking shape out of the core of that undimmed continuity of the creative process which restores man to mankind while deepening and enhancing his communion with the universe.

RUTH NANDA ANSHEN

# WORLD PERSPECTIVES

## Volumes already published

## About the Author

José M. R. Delgado was born in Ronda, Spain, and received his medical training at Madrid University, where he was Associate Professor of Physiology until 1950 when he came to Yale University to work with Dr. John Fulton. He is now Professor of Physiology at Yale, where he has developed techniques for electrical and chemical stimulation of the brain and has applied them to the study of primate and human behavior. He has published more than 200 scientific papers and is a well-known authority in neuro-behavioral research.

## About the Editor of this Series

Ruth Nanda Anshen, philosopher and editor, plans and edits *World Perspectives, Religious Perspectives, Credo Perspectives, Perspectives in Humanism* and *The Science of Culture Series.* She also writes and lectures on the relationship of knowledge to the nature and meaning of man and existence.

80 AG

546   8266 · 1